# HANDS ACROSS THE OCEAN

# Hands Across the Ocean

## MANAGING JOINT VENTURES

with a Spotlight on China and Japan

## Susan Goldenberg

HARVARD BUSINESS SCHOOL PRESS
BOSTON, MASSACHUSETTS

Library of Congress Cataloging-in-Publication Data

Goldenberg, Susan.
    Hands across the ocean : managing joint ventures with a spotlight
on China and Japan / Susan Goldenberg.
        p.    cm.

    Includes index.
    ISBN 0-87584-191-0
    1. Joint ventures—Management—Case studies. 2. Joint ventures—
Japan—Management—Case studies. 3. Joint ventures—China—
Management—Case studies. I. Title.
HD62.47.G65 1988    88-17756
658'.044—dc19    CIP

Printed in the United States of America.
92  91  90  89  88     5  4  3  2  1

*To My Parents*

## Also by Susan Goldenberg

The House of Steinway
Trading: Inside The World's Leading Stock Exchanges
The Thomson Empire
Canadian Pacific: A Portrait of Power
Men Of Property: The Canadian Developers Who Are Buying America

# CONTENTS

*Foreword*                              *xi*

## I Getting Involved

*1   The Decision*                          *1*
Cost-sharing, technological, and
marketing merits; Benefits versus li-
censing, distributors, and agents;
Government assistance; Outlook in
USSR for joint ventures.

*2   Planning the Venture*                  *29*
Importance of shared objectives and
outlook; Role in overall international
strategy; Examples of well-matched
and mismatched partners; Telecommunications ventures.

*3   Negotiations and Contracts*            *47*
Use of lawyers; negotiating strategy;
ownership split; The government as

partner; Component sourcing; Technology transfer; Trademark protection; Contract terms.

## II Joint Ventures with the Japanese and Chinese

*4   The Japanese as Partners*          73
Business similarities and differences; Role of unions; Case histories of troubled ventures that were saved or dissolved and the lessons they provide.

*5   The Chinese as Partners*          91
Chinese regulations; Approval procedures; Tax breaks; Description of locations for ventures; Foreign exchange problems; Sources of advance guidance.

*6   Some Case Histories of Joint*    113
*Ventures in China*
Finding a partner; The negotiating process; Dealing with the bureaucracy; Wages; Component sourcing; Solutions to the foreign exchange problem.

## III Running the Venture

*7   Living and Working*               139
*Conditions*
Residential and office accommodations; Infrastructure in China; Distribution and marketing problems in China, Japan, and India; Competing against a local monopoly.

8   *Management: Japanese*            *159*
*Partners*
Role of each parent company; Middle
management; Office layout; Staff recruitment; Role of women; Relationship to parent companies; Japanese
management of U.S.-based joint
ventures.

9   *Management: Chinese Joint*       *181*
*Ventures*
Wages and incentives; Shortage of
Chinese managers; Staff recruitment;
Role of expatriates; Conflicts over
venture's purpose; Introduction of
Western management methods and
organization; Quality control; Mer-
chandising.

10   *The Europeans*                  *201*
Examples of joint ventures established by prominent European firms
with U.S. and Asian partners in cars,
tires, agriculture, glass, telecommunications, high technology.

11   *Learning from Junior*           *225*
Lessons joint ventures teach their parents—how to be competitive internationally; Productivity and quality
control.

*Index*                               *235*

# *Foreword*

Joining hands across the ocean in international joint ventures is becoming essential to business strategy because of the growing tide of protectionism and the rapid development of new technologies.

Should our company consider a joint venture as part of its international thrust? If so, how do we go about establishing and running it? To help managers answer these questions, I interviewed executives at the parent companies of dozens of joint ventures as well as the ventures' on-site management. The interviews were conducted in the United States, Japan, China, the United Kingdom, Europe, and Canada. According to those engaged in joint ventures, this is the first book to approach the subject via practical case examples.

The executives discussed their experiences—good and bad—and provided illustrative anecdotes about how they reached their decisions, planned their ventures, and now run them. They spoke of the selection of a partner or partners, what happens when the government is the partner, negotiations, contracts, trademark protection, and foreign exchange problems. They also talked about daily operational matters such as management, recruitment, and training of local workers, wages and incentives, local sourcing of components, and the problems caused by poor infrastructure. Those that withdrew from a venture explained why. The cultural and philosophical differences that must be taken into account also were described. Finally, examples were given of the valuable lessons that successful joint ventures can provide their parents on how to be competitive internationally.

Because the emphasis of Western firms is—and will continue to be—on the Chinese and Japanese as joint venture partners, that is also the emphasis of this book. But reference is also made to joint ventures in South Korea, Taiwan, India, Mexico, and South America as well as to the outlook for joint ventures in the Soviet Union. A cross-section of industries is profiled: high technology, electronics, telecommunications, energy, automobile, tire, steel, glass, elevator, office and photographic equipment, food, beverages, pharmaceutical, personal care, and agricultural machinery.

I am exceedingly grateful to the many people who so generously took time to speak to me, and I thank them very much. As a Canadian, I also wish to express my appreciation to the Canadian Department of External Affairs and the Canadian embassies in Tokyo and Beijing. They assisted in setting up appointments in Japan and China for interviews I had secured through correspondence.

Toronto, Canada                              Susan Goldenberg
March 1988

# I

# Getting Involved

# 1   *The Decision*

During Japan's feudal period, the *daimyos* (feudal lords) sealed alliances through marriages of convenience. European royalty and American tycoons also have often married more for strategic reasons than for love.

Today's global business version of such alliances is the international joint venture, in which hands are joined across the ocean by associates from different countries. The partners can be companies or, in the case of state-controlled or mixed economies, private enterprise and government. The functions of a venture can be research, manufacturing, marketing, or a combination of the three.

The joint venture is the principal admission ticket of business into many of the world's most populous countries. China, India, the Soviet Union, South Korea, and much of Central and South America either bar foreign companies or severely limit their scope unless they have a local partner. "Until the last ten years, developing nations saw no way to acquire technology other than to purchase it, but as they increasingly realized the importance of the technology to their overall economic development, they raised more stipulations about local participation," says Lee Ting, business development and manufacturing director, intercontinental division, at Hewlett-Packard Company. "Our preference was complete ownership rather than joint ventures. But, we recognized we had to be open-minded and establish such ventures if we wanted access to make and sell our computers and measuring instruments in China, South Korea, and Mexico."

In the industrialized countries of the West as well as in Japan, joint ventures tend to be marriages of convenience between competitors. Not only can the foreign partner thereby leapfrog protectionist barriers but both sides benefit from sharing costs and technical and marketing expertise without having to resort to a merger or a takeover. In addition, since joint ventures provide the freedom for continued rivalry otherwise as well as for multiple associations, competition is fueled, not shrunk, as happens with mergers and takeovers. "Because A and B design and manufacture one component and A and C other parts, these alliances keep competition going," maintains Kristian Ehinger, general counsel, foreign holdings, at Volkswagen.

For example, Cable and Wireless, the large U.K. communications group, and Hutchison Whampoa, a Hong Kong-based conglomerate, are usually the fiercest of adversaries. But they joined forces in 1988 in a $150-million joint venture that will start in 1990 to provide satellite television services to China. The agreement is a coup—the venture will be the first by foreign companies to provide television service in China. The partners overcame their intense rivalry in this instance because each benefits from the other's strengths: C&W from Hutchison's contacts in China, and Hutchison from the C&W technology. Otherwise, their competition is as keen as ever. Indeed, at the very moment they formed their China partnership, they were bidding against one another for a contract to install cable television in Hong Kong.

Joint ventures also permit greater control than when local agents or distributors are appointed or a local firm is licensed to make a product. The risks of losing the investment made in a joint venture if it turns out to be a failure can be minimized by a small initial investment. In many cases, it has been under $1 million. Moreover, the damage can be kept slight through an escape clause that goes into effect when the venture runs into trouble. Should the venture succeed, however, the financial rewards are bigger than with licensing because the partners have a share in the profits.

By contrast, in licensing, a firm receives a set royalty, which may not be commensurate with the product's popularity. Also, with an ownership stake, each partner is fully committed to the success of the venture, unlike agents, distributors, and licensees, who represent a number of firms and cannot devote all their time to just one client.

The size of the market is another determining factor in weighing whether licensing or a joint venture is preferable. McDonald's Corporation deemed it sufficient to license three restaurants on the small Caribbean island of Aruba. But in Japan it has had a joint venture since 1971. The local partner helped McDonald's blanket the Japanese market to such an extent that there are now 580 outlets across the country, the largest number of McDonald's restaurants in the forty-four countries in which it operates outside the United States.

Another advantage of joint ventures over licensing is that they can provide greater protection for the company supplying the technology, especially as the partner usually demands the latest state-of-the-art information rather than several-years-old material that the supplier would be much happier to furnish so as to preserve its leadership. There are exceptions, of course. A notable one was Toshiba Corporation's decision to sell its most current semiconductor technology to Siemens, the West German electronics giant, instead of forming a joint venture. Toshiba saw the deal as a trade-off, because in return Siemens pledged that its computer division, a leader in sales to European governments and professionals, would begin purchasing computer components from Toshiba.

As a general rule, E. I. du Pont de Nemours avoids licensing technology unless it can sell the technology on a straight cash basis. As Paul Roessel, director of international planning, points out: "We stay clear of projects pegged to licensed technology, because once the other side has the technology, it is not uncommon to turn on the partner and force it to sell at a distressed price."

International joint ventures are not always formed between partners of equal strength. Sometimes a strong firm, eager either to enter or to broaden its penetration of a foreign market, joins in a venture with a weak local company in that market. The local firm, which may have vociferously objected to the trade tactics of its new partner's country of origin, swallows its protestations because the outsider is propping it up. The local community quiets any objections, too, pleased that it will not have to face the repercussions of a collapsing local company.

James Riley, senior vice president at Dataquest of San Jose, California, a research and consulting firm with many clients engaged in joint ventures, compares a successful venture to a well-constructed mathematical formula: "It adds the resources of both sides, subtracts from each participant's capital requirements, divides the time required to market, and multiplies the available technical talent. Joint ventures are dictated by today's fast pace and high costs. International telecommunications within industrialized countries are now taken for granted. As well, life cycles of products are shorter, capital investment requirements are much higher, and U.S. industry has lost its preeminence in some traditional markets. Ten to fifteen years ago, the number of fields in which the United States did not lead were exceptions; now, the strides of the Japanese, German, French, and others have reduced the United States to sharing leadership.

"Also, today, even the biggest companies lack the money, time, and talent for solo efforts. The ease of placing overseas calls and of air and ocean freight make Munich, Tokyo, or Seoul no farther away than Buffalo was from Corning, New York, twenty-five years ago. Finally, sometimes a joint venture can raise more money than its parents. Whereas a parent company in a prosaic, mature business arouses little excitement in investors, the spinoff of a small, interesting piece can readily attract funds."

The payoff of joint ventures can be enormous. In 1986, Olin Corporation of the United States and Asahi Glass Company of Japan together invested $800,000 to set up the joint production of parts for integrated circuits used in semiconductor devices. They predict sales will reach $30 million by 1990.

In 1956, the then tiny Xerox Corporation formed a joint venture in photocopiers with the Rank Organization of England (movies and cameras). Although Xerox had sales of just $7 million, it had the technology and so dictated the terms: the two would split annual profits up to £10 million equally, with Xerox to receive two-thirds of all profits above that amount. By the 1960s, profits surpassed the £10 million a year mark, and now that sum is made in the first quarter alone. In 1962, six-year-old Rank Xerox joined with Fuji Photo to form Fuji Xerox, which has become the third largest U.S.-associated company in Japan and the only one among the top five that is a joint venture.

"Xerox would not be a $10-billion-plus in revenue company today without joint ventures," vice chairman William Glavin states emphatically. "Back in 1956 the company lacked both the structure and money to go international. Yet it realized it had to, rather than wait to grow in the United States. Joint ventures enabled us to become international. Except for the United States, Canada, and India, where there is some public ownership of Xerox shares, all the company's facilities are joint ventures." Today, around 40 percent of Xerox's income comes from its international operations.

The Gillette Company credits joint ventures with more than tripling its reach. Founded in 1901, Gillette opened its first overseas plant in 1904. In 1970, it had twenty factories outside North America, located in Europe, Latin America, Australia, New Zealand, and Japan. Its markets, including North America, comprised 25 percent of the world's population at that time.

Between 1970 and 1986, Gillette added fifteen overseas factories at a rate of about one per year. Of these, all but two are joint ventures. The new plants are in developing countries, including China, India, Thailand, Egypt, Malaysia, the Philippines, Indonesia, Morocco, Kenya, Guatemala, and Jamaica. The populations of China and India alone constitute close to 40 percent of the world's total. "All told, Gillette now is in countries with 80 percent of the world's population," states Rodney Mills, executive vice president, Gillette International.

While most joint ventures start small on the premise that if they sour their failure will cause little damage to their parents, sometimes the parents are willing to invest much higher sums when the outlook is exceptionally promising. The foremost example is a joint venture in optical disks between the Dutch electronics giant N.V. Philips and Du Pont.[1] It was capitalized in 1986 at $150 million and entails the expenditure of an additional $400 million on facilities by 1990 plus $60 million annually on research and development. When they announced the joint venture, Du Pont and Philips predicted it would garner one-fourth of the world

---

1. Optical disk technology, based upon the recording and sending of information by light, makes possible the storage of audio and video data at a density thousands of times greater than that of standard magnetic disks.

market for optical disks, which is expected to reach $4 billion in the early 1990s. But within a year the forecast proved low; by then, the venture already had captured half the market.

National Steel, formed in 1983 in the United States by rival U.S. and Japanese steelmakers, demonstrates how a joint venture between a weak and a strong partner can work to the benefit of both. National Steel's parents are National Intergroup, which is also an oil distributor and pharmaceutical wholesaler, and Nippon Kokan, Japan's second largest steel producer and the fifth largest steelmaker in the world. The venture's name is derived from National Intergroup's original one when it was formed in 1929.

Richard Smith, vice chairman of National Steel at the outset, says each side saw benefits to the venture notwithstanding the global problems of the steel industry at the time of its establishment. "From a strategic view, National Intergroup had 100 percent of a steel company that was either breaking even or losing money and thus there was no source of income," he explains. "By selling part of it we could unlock some cash value as well as learn directly about Japanese technology. The advantage for Nippon Kokan is that the deal allows it to do business in the United States, the world's Number One market, despite government restrictions on Japanese steel imports."

In its first year National Steel made money. Then it disappointed its parents with heavy losses in 1985 and 1986. However, these losses were typical of the U.S. steel industry, which was being battered by soft prices and heavy imports. But when the joint venture bounced back in 1987 with strong profits, it justified its founders' confidence. The recovery was partly due to a stronger than expected demand from the automotive market, on which National Steel concentrates. But much of the success can be traced to productivity improvement measures and a healthier labor climate that both sides encouraged and nurtured.

Initially, U.S. firms were the principal suitors in international joint ventures, especially in Asia, where shared membership with a local partner was the price of admission. Today, it is the Japanese who are in the forefront of the joint venture search. Their reasons are interrelated. First, direct investment evades the protectionist barriers raised by countries concerned at the growing wave of Japanese imports. Second, *endaka* (rise of the yen) has made overseas investment cheaper for the Japanese. The yen has more than doubled in value against the U.S. dollar since February 1985, when one dollar bought 263 yen. Third, in Japan the emphasis is changing from "smokestack" industries to the service sector. "By the year 2000, Japan will have shifted from SCRAP—steel, chemicals, refining, aluminum, and pulp and paper, to NEOBASIC—new materials, electronics, optical, biochemical, aerospace, information services, and computer," predicts Yoshio Nakamura, senior assistant director, international economic affairs, at Keidanren (Japan Federation of Economic Organizations). The export of SCRAP industries in the form of joint ventures fits in with this national grand design.

North Americans and Europeans fret about the motives of the Japanese while rushing to form joint ventures with them. The thrust of the criticism is that joint ventures strengthen Japan's managerial and technological expertise at the expense of other industrialized countries. Western managers further warn that by creating factories and employment overseas, joint ventures "hollow out" the domestic economy and diminish the number of job opportunities at home.

The fears are not one-sided. Doomsayers in Japan maintain their country is the more threatened, since it relies on other nations for most of its natural resources. The hardliners on both sides find it difficult to conceive that both countries can be winners in joint ventures, as can local communities where jobs and tax revenues are generated.

On the other hand, some observers in Japan fault Japanese companies for not reacting sooner to the trade friction and *endaka* by investing earlier in overseas joint ventures. Shoji Oshima, general manager of the Tokyo office of British investment dealer Vickers da Costa, comments: "The ventures are small compared to the firms' overall size. In view of the worsening of trade relations between Japan and other industrialized nations, perhaps the companies should have done more earlier.

"There will be more joint ventures, especially as the higher yen lessens the outlay by Japanese firms and as a result their fears are allayed about the failure of overseas investments. The stronger yen also makes overseas factories more attractive, since wages on an hourly basis in Japan now exceed those in the United States and West Germany, its main industrial rivals."

The automobile industry, engaged in a frenzy of joint venture alliances, primarily between American or European firms and the Japanese, is a microcosm of the many strategic forces behind the creation of joint ventures by global competitors. On the one hand, new customers are urgently needed, because at home the blitz of first-time purchases has given way to the slower pace of replacement sales. Joint ventures in Third World countries are regarded as an answer since demand there is what it was domestically forty years ago. At the same time, car makers still see opportunities at home in special niche markets, but the limited demand for such cars would not justify spending the $1 billion it costs to develop a new car plant. Cost sharing in joint ventures makes pursuit of these customers possible. For the Japanese, joint ventures offer a solution to stagnant overseas sales resulting from import quotas and the inroads made by cheaper South Korean cars. Also, as the Japanese see it, the local content of joint ventures circumvents protectionist barriers.

The increase in joint ventures also reflects a fundamental shift in the nature of the automotive industry. Of the world's thirty-eight car manufacturers, only three are American now that Chrysler Corporation has acquired American Motors. By contrast, there are nine Japanese manufacturers. Worldwide, the U.S. share of automotive sales has fallen to under 40 percent. No longer does a strictly American car exist. Either it contains a mixture of U.S. and foreign parts or it is an import bearing the name of a U.S. manufacturer. Increasingly, U.S. car makers are establishing operations in cheap-labor countries such as Mexico and South Korea, where workers earn a fraction of the wages and benefits paid in the United States.

Auto analysts warn that by 1990 the United States will have to cope with a glut of 1.4 million cars, primarily because of the increasing number of Japanese auto firms building cars in the United States. Close to half the cars manufactured in the United States will be Japanese, a 100 percent increase over 1986. Forty percent, or about 640,000, will be hybrids made at U.S.-Japanese joint venture plants, of which the oldest—a partnership between General Motors Corporation and Toyota Motor Corporation—began as recently as 1983. General Motors, the world's biggest auto firm, sells 9 million cars and trucks per year worldwide; Ford Motor Company, 5.6 million; and Chrysler, 2.2 million. Toyota has sales of around 3.7 million vehicles.[2]

2. Chrysler also is outsold by the world's fourth largest car maker, Volkswagen, which has unit sales of 2.7 million per year.

The oversupply of cars is expected to escalate competition and hence shrink profits. Pessimists forecast that some firms will either go out of business or be acquired by stronger rivals. Thousands of jobs will vanish. By 1990, GM plans to close sixteen plants, affecting 30,000 workers. And, in Japan, 10,000 auto workers and 30,000 employees in auto-related industries are expected to lose their jobs.

The likely survivors in this fierce competition are joint ventures. "Transplant production, prompted by the high yen's depression of Japanese car makers' profits, is risky because it takes a long time to achieve high productivity and profits; thus, the firms are turning to joint ventures," says widely respected automobile analyst Professor Koichi Shimokawa of Tokyo's Hosei University.

A case in point is Toyota's proposed entry into the European market through a joint venture rather than on its own, as Nissan Motor Company, Japan's Number Two automobile manufacturer, has done. Nissan opened its own plant in the United Kingdom in 1986. Toyota needs a European manufacturing base in order to lessen its exports, which have declined in profitability because of the rise in the value of the yen against foreign currencies. Provided they can find a willing joint venture partner, Toyota executives have said they want to share the cost of a European facility because of concern about worldwide overcapacity in the car industry.

Also, joint ventures will breed more collaboration as their existence has exacerbated already tough world competition. "Market demand is very unstable," Shimokawa states. "In the old days, the industry was segmented by car size and price; today, there are many specialized categories in exterior and interior design, and even big companies cannot cover all concepts. To invest in all categories is precarious but, strategically, companies want to be in as many as possible. Hence, joint ventures, which draw on the partner's strengths, split the costs, and shorten lead times."

Cars need parts, and joint ventures in auto manufacturing are spawning others in components. "By 1992, about eight hundred companies in the United States will make Japanese auto parts compared to just fifty in 1986," predicts Joseph Phillippi, vice president and automotive analyst at Shearson Lehman Brothers Inc. The boom is due partly to a Japanese preference for buying Japanese auto parts of known quality, but a historic realignment by the Big Three U.S. automakers in their procurement policy is also responsible. "Traditionally, the Big Three made 70 percent of their parts in-house and only had short-term contracts with outside suppliers," Shimokawa says. "But with production facilities not readily adaptable to change and with quality erratic, the Big Three are moving to the Japanese system of long-range, single-sourcing contracts."

The scoreboard in joint ventures among car makers keeps lengthening. GM's list is the longest. It has three Japanese associates, one Korean, and one Swedish. The landmark association with Toyota is known as New United Motor Manufacturing, Inc. (NUMMI); it is located in a former GM plant in Fremont, California, south of San Francisco.

So satisfied are GM and Toyota with the collaboration that in 1987 they announced plans for a second joint venture to be located in Australia. Other cooperative ventures by them around the world are also likely. That such fierce rivals as the Number One U.S. and Japanese automakers are willing to form these links clearly indicates that they recognize their dominance does not make even them immune from the problems wracking the auto industry. Their Australian venture was triggered by an alarming collapse in that country's car and truck market, with 1986 sales at a fourteen-year low, including a drastic 24 percent decline from 1985. Moreover, the Australian government intends to shrink the number of car makers from five groups to three by 1992. GM and Toyota believe their speedy alliance will make them survivors.

GM also owns 38.6 percent of Isuzu Motors, making it Isuzu's largest shareholder. Isuzu supplies GM with components as well as with completed cars and trucks, while GM ships some parts to Isuzu. GM's participation was sought by Isuzu after the Japanese government lifted some of its restrictions against foreign investment in the late 1960s. Isuzu preferred selling some of its shares to a U.S. competitor rather than submit to a government directive that smaller car makers merge their operations into those of either Toyota or Nissan. Isuzu's action shattered the government's grand design and soon after Mitsubishi Motors Corporation linked up with Chrysler.

In August 1986, GM and Suzuki Motor Company announced plans for a $500-million small-car factory in the central Canadian province of Ontario. Scheduled to open in 1989, it is the only joint venture allowed under the proposed U.S.-Canada free trade agreement to take advantage of the U.S.-Canada auto pact signed in 1966. The pact gives foreign-owned companies operating in Canada duty-free access to the United States if the content of their cars is 60 percent Canadian. Although the free trade deal confines the pact's beneficiaries to GM, Ford, and Chrysler, the GM-Suzuki joint venture qualified as an exception because it preceded the new rules. The concern in Canada is that the free trade agreement could nullify the appeal to the Japanese of setting up other joint ventures in Canada rather than in the United States.

GM also owns 50 percent of Daewoo Motor Company of South Korea, which makes cars for GM from components supplied by Korean-based joint ventures formed by several GM parts divisions. In addition, GM and Sweden's AB Volvo started a U.S. venture in trucks in January 1988. Previously, Volvo, through its subsidiary Volvo White, produced more trucks in the United States than GM but had fewer dealerships. The partnership will substantially strengthen its representation.

General Motors' competitors jibe that its welter of collaborations has "inherent conflicts of interest." But Ronald Gilchrist, general director of overseas project development at GM, maintains that each serves a particular purpose. "Suzuki and Isuzu provide supportive technology; Daewoo, a low-cost manufacturing base; and Toyota, lessons in Japanese productivity and quality control techniques," he says.

Philip Fricke, automobile analyst at Goldman, Sachs, says NUMMI is a "real-life laboratory on the secret of the success of Japanese car makers—the integration of technology and people. Although NUMMI is in a plant built in 1963, it has suffered far fewer production problems than GM's Hamtramck plant in Detroit, opened in 1985 with the ultimate in high-tech equipment." Bearing out Fricke's observation, NUMMI spokesman Thomas Klipstine says the Nova, produced by NUMMI for GM's Chevrolet division, is ranked by GM "as its highest quality car."

The joint ventures of GM and Toyota are marriages of convenience spawned by today's vicissitudes in the car industry. By contrast, Diamond-Star Motors Corporation, the second U.S.-based automotive collaboration between Americans and Japanese, reflects the history of closeness between the partners, Chrysler and Mitsubishi Motors. Whereas GM and Toyota own nothing of each other, Chrysler owns 24 percent of Mitsubishi. Fifteen percent was acquired in 1971, when Mitsubishi approached Chrysler, and the rest one month after the creation of Diamond-Star was announced in 1985. Diamond-Star was preceded by a Chrysler-Mitsubishi joint venture in Australia.

The scope of Diamond-Star is more far-reaching than that of NUMMI, which now only makes cars based on existing Toyota models. Diamond-Star, which opened in 1988, will start by making a new sporty subcompact for which Mitsubishi designed the engine and transmission. The exterior trim and name of the car will differ for each partner.

As at NUMMI, which has the capacity to make 200,000 cars per year, the output at Diamond-Star will be relatively small. Only 240,000 cars will be produced annually, since the demand for such a model is expected to be limited. Still, says Michael Hammes, Chrysler vice president, international operations, Chrysler's $250-million investment is warranted because "the consumer must be satisfied in this age of choices of European, U.S., and Japanese cars. Often we can do it ourselves; sometimes, as in this case, it would not otherwise be economically justifiable."

The ongoing Chrysler-Mitsubishi connection has the added benefit for Chrysler of backdoor entry to South Korea, where Chrysler, unlike GM and Ford, has no local ownership. Mitsubishi, however, owns a piece of Hyundai, the leading South Korean car maker, and Hammes says this indirect link eventually could yield technology exchanges for Chrysler.

Arab American Vehicles, an Egyptian-based joint venture between Chrysler and an Arab investment group, is the world's first car plant to assemble vehicles for both the United States and the Soviet Union. For Chrysler, it had already made pickup trucks. Then in November 1987, the Soviets signed a two-year, renewable contract for the venture to make tractors because they could no longer export to Egypt since the Egyptian government had imposed strict limits on all automobile imports.

Ford is involved in cooperative efforts with two Japanese firms. Just as GM joined forces with Toyota, its peer in Japan, Ford chose its counterpart, Nissan. They plan a minivan joint venture in the United States and shared marketing in Australia.

Ford has also promised to buy half the output from a new Michigan plant of Mazda Motor Corporation, with which Ford has had a long association. The exterior of the Ford cars will differ. Ford executives are frank that the company's relationship with Mazda is rooted in self-interest. Ford bought 25 percent of Mazda in 1979, when Mazda, on which Ford relies for truck power-train components, suffered financial difficulties. While some associates might have severed their ties at such a troubled moment, Ford did not, because it "didn't want to lose a dependable supplier," explains L. M. Kazanowski, vice president, international business development.

The investment has paid off in other directions, too. Employing Mazda dealerships in Japan, Ford has become one of the largest-selling imports in that country. Before the Japanese government expelled it during World War II, Ford was Japan's Number One car maker. Anxious to foster Japan's youthful car companies, the Japanese government refused to let Ford resume production after the war.

Mazda, which automotive analysts praise for innovative product design and development, designed the layout and trained the workers at Ford's new plant in Hermosillo, Mexico. In New Zealand, costs were cut through pooling car production at Ford's plants and truck production at Mazda's. Marketing and distribution are separate. In South Korea, both Ford and Mazda have stakes in Kia, which is building a Mazda-designed minicar with Mazda components. Most of the cars are being sold by Ford in the United States; they are Kia's first exports to the United States.

Like the GM-Toyota and Ford-Nissan arrangements in Australia, Ford's collaboration with Volkswagen in Brazil and Argentina illustrates the use of joint ventures to save an enterprise. By pooling the facilities of Ford's two Brazilian and one Argentine plant and Volkswagen's three Brazilian and two Argentine plants, the two parent companies believe they can afford to stay in these countries. Before that, they were dubious about the Argentine market because of a 50 percent decline there in industrywide car sales between 1980 and 1985. VW especially wants to stay in Argentina, because it uses the factories there to make low-priced cars for sale in the United States.

North America does not have a monopoly on automotive joint ventures. Honda has one in England with the United Kingdom's Austin Rover Group. Toyota and Volkswagen will begin coproduction of small pickup trucks in 1989 at an underused VW factory in Germany.[3] American Motors (acquired in 1987 by

---

3. American car makers are not yet in joint ventures in Europe. However, each owns part or all of a luxury European sports car manufacturer: GM-Group Lotus of the United Kingdom; Ford Aston-Martin of the United Kingdom; and Chrysler Nuova-Automobili F. Lamborghini of Italy.

Chrysler), Volkswagen, Peugeot, and Renault of France, plus Daihatsu of Japan (an affiliate of Toyota), have joint ventures in China with state-controlled enterprises. Italy's Fiat plans one there. American Motors was the first foreign auto maker to go into China (in 1983). In addition to the AMC jeep manufacturing venture it inherited when it bought AMC, Chrysler has initiated its own joint venture in China. This project, for which construction is to begin at the end of 1988, will make automobiles for use as official cars and taxis.

For money-losing Austin Rover, the nearly ten-year-old collaboration with Honda in medium-size cars has played a major role in its survival because it can draw on Rover's engineering expertise. Thus, right after British Aerospace announced its intention in early 1988 to purchase Rover from the British government, it asked if Honda would continue the relationship. Honda agreed. (The government took over the auto maker, then known as British Leyland, in 1975 to prevent its collapse.)

The Honda-Rover association began in 1979 with Honda supplying existing technology for a Rover car. Honda prides itself on bucking current wisdom, and the license it granted Rover was the initial one by a Japanese car maker to an industrialized nation. Honda was also the first to build a U.S. plant, which opened in Ohio in 1982. Honda broadened the collaboration into a joint venture even as Rover lost money from 1983 until 1987 when, thanks to a substantial government grant, Rover made a profit. Director Taiichi Sakama says Honda proceeded because "by following a phased-in approach to equity participation, we could change direction, if necessary, based on lessons learned along the way." An agreement for the joint design and manufacture of a luxury car was signed in 1983, the year Rover's financial woes began, and production got underway two years later. When that project was a year old, Honda signed for joint design of a midprice car. The production agreement was finalized in 1987.

Both sides use existing factories to build cars for each other carrying the partner's name. The major equipment investment is by Honda, which is constructing an engine plant in England. Scheduled for completion in 1989, it will produce 70,000 engines annually for Honda cars to be built by Rover under their joint venture agreement as well as for some Rover models.

Rover is enthusiastic about the two deals, because through Honda's production in Japan of cars bearing Rover's signature,

Rover can establish a presence rapidly in Japan, where British cars are almost nonexistent. Honda is pleased, since its versions built by Rover are exempt from European import quotas. As a result, Honda is confident its European sales will triple. In addition, both companies regard the venture as an opportunity to break out from the production of small cars into larger, more expensive cars. At the moment, Honda's sales of the luxury model, which it calls the Acura and which Rover labels the Legend, surpass Rover's, but Honda had the advantage of a huge in-place sales network. Rover, absent from the United States for some time, had to start from the beginning.

To date, Honda is in no other automobile joint ventures. But anxiety over European quotas against Japanese imports caused the firm, which originated as a motorcycle manufacturer, to form a joint venture for mopeds with France's Cycles Peugeot. Initially, Honda made its mopeds with Honda engines in Belgium, which has no import restrictions. However, France has stiff quotas, Italy bans mopeds with Japanese engines, and Spain bars all Japanese motorcycles. Consequently, Peugeot engines will be used at Honda's Belgian factory for exports to European countries with quotas.

Trade friction between Japan and the West, a major factor in the Japanese decision to form overseas automotive joint ventures, also is prompting an increasing number of binational high-technology joint associations. The issue, for example, aided Hughes Communications to become the first outsider to gain entry to Japan's satellite communications market via a joint venture formed in 1985. Called Japan Communications Satellite Company (JCSat), the venture, of which Hughes owns 30 percent, forecasts annual sales of $250 million by the year 2000.

Japan was reluctant to admit Hughes because its technology surpassed that of Japan. As in the United States, broadcasting communications in Japan are government-regulated; furthermore, commercial satellites may transmit only to those areas in which they are located. The Japanese government, which until 1985 owned Nippon Telegraph & Telephone (NTT), was reluctant to admit Hughes because Hughes's system was superior to NTT's terrestrial one. NTT's system is subject to interference caused by the large number of islands that form Japan and by earthquakes in the region. Although the government opened Japan's telecommunications market in 1985 through privatization of NTT, the change was largely symbolic, since licensing and tariffs remained under considerable government control and the government wanted to protect NTT against a foreign invasion.

Fortunately for Hughes, it was able to capitalize on growing U.S. government irritation at the imbalance of trade between the United States and Japan. At 1983 and 1984 meetings with Japanese government officials, President Ronald Reagan and Vice President George Bush both cited Japan's stand on Hughes as a litmus test of its sincerity about welcoming U.S. imports. The pressure worked: Japan's laws preventing foreign firms from owning tele-communications firms were modified to allow up to a one-third interest. NTT was privatized in April 1985, and JCSat received its license from the government in June, "faster than it takes in the United States," says Hughes Communications president John Koehler.

The recent trade war over semiconductor chips between the United States and Japan has caused a marked deviation from the traditional avoidance of joint ventures by this industry, too. Normally, it prefers unpublicized "foundry agreements," in which a larger, usually Japanese, firm makes the parts designed by a small fledgling company, usually American. Four months after the July 1986 U.S.-Japan semiconductor agreement binding the Japanese to help U.S. producers gain increased access to the Japanese market[4] and to stop selling chips at excessively low prices, two of the world's leading chip manufacturers—Motorola of the United States and Toshiba of Japan—formed a $219-million joint manufacturing venture based in Japan. The plant will produce high-speed memory chips, in which Toshiba is a world leader, and microprocessors, in which Motorola leads.

The venture will raise Motorola's profile in Japan, where it ranks Number Three in semiconductor sales by U.S. companies. Texas Instruments, which since 1971 has had wholly owned operations in Japan staffed entirely by Japanese, ranks first, with sales nearly four times those of Motorola. On the surface, the joint venture appears to be a blow to Hitachi, previously the sole licensee of Motorola processors in Japan, but the reality is not that bad, explains semiconductor industry analyst Patricia Cox of Data-quest. "Hitachi has developed its own microprocessors based on

---

4. Semiconductor sales in Japan by U.S. companies constitute around 10 percent of the total market. By contrast, 60 percent of the high-speed chips known as 64K drams (dynamic random access memory) used by U.S. electronics firms are imported from Japan.

Motorola's and is stronger than Motorola in memory chip technology," she says.

Whereas avoidance of protectionist barriers has formed much of the rationale behind automotive and high-technology joint ventures, gaining market share is the main impetus for ventures in industrial equipment and consumer products. This motive, for example, fueled the recent rash of joint ventures between Japanese and Western manufacturers of hydraulic excavators used in construction and mining. Sales of these machines nearly doubled over the past six years, making the hydraulic excavator the biggest-selling construction machine. The joint ventures provide an opportunity to turn out enough excavators to meet demand, a goal that could not be accomplished single-handedly. Up to now, the joint manufacturing deals involve Mitsubishi Heavy Industries and Caterpillar and Hitachi in separate arrangements with Deere and Italy's Fiat.

Gaining market share was also the rationale behind a joint venture formed in 1981 for producing musical instruments, an area that might not readily spring to mind as a candidate for joint ventures. The partners are International Music Company (IMC) of Fort Worth, Texas, the world's largest guitar manufacturer, and Greeta Musical Instrument of India, that country's only guitar maker. In exchange for IMC's technology and manufacturing know-how, Greeta provides a low-cost manufacturing base. Also, because India is a leading source of ebony, rosewood, and specialty maple woods, the venture will enable IMC to make exotic-looking guitars at affordable prices.

An account of the joint venture experiences of General Foods Corporation, pharmaceuticals manufacturer SmithKline Beckman Corporation, and Eastman Kodak Company suggests some reasons why consumer products companies might decide on joint ventures instead of local distribution, licensing, or wholly owned subsidiaries.

General Foods prefers joint ventures to retreating from tough markets.[5] The company, which today derives one-fifth of its revenue internationally, was a late entrant into the global arena. Established in 1929 by a consortium of fifteen companies founded from 1885 onward, it waited until the end of World War II to

---

5. In November 1985, General Foods became a wholly owned subsidiary of Philip Morris Companies, Inc.

expand abroad. It began in Europe by opening subsidiaries and making acquisitions, but to its dismay found these methods of global growth unsuited to Japan.

There, a 100 percent owned subsidiary tried vainly for ten years to sell coffee, an item that produced 50 percent of General Foods' total sales in the United States. Because Nestlé enjoyed strong coffee sales, General Foods could not blame its troubles on a Japanese preference for tea. Instead, the company realized that it needed local knowledge of the market to do well, and rather than shut the plant it pragmatically overcame its reluctance about joint ventures. "Fifty percent of a potentially profitable joint venture was better than closure," says John Manfredi, director, international relations.

When this change in strategy worked, General Foods decided that joint ventures were best for Asia: a local partner would quickly steer it through the labyrinth of government approval agencies and plug it into a distribution system far more multilayered than that in the United States. General Foods found that what succeeded in Asia also rescued withering foreign enterprises elsewhere. In Spain, it again encountered Nestlé, which had 70 percent of that country's instant coffee sales. Since it could make no headway in the instant coffee market, General Foods opted for a joint venture in ground coffee with a local partner. It has done well. In Brazil, its wholly owned ice cream plant, the market leader, paid scant attention to confectionery and beverage sidelines. Consequently, they lost money, depressing overall performance. Rather than kill off these products, General Foods spun them off into what became a successful joint venture.

For its part, SmithKline viewed a marketing joint venture as the best route into Japan for Tagamet, an anti-ulcer drug that had set records in the United States since its introduction in 1976. SmithKline knew Tagamet would do well in Japan, because the Japanese suffer a high ulcer rate. Therefore, it did not want to follow its previous practice of licensing Fujisawa Pharmaceutical of Japan to make its products. Direct participation, it reasoned, would yield far greater financial returns than royalties from licensing. "We realized we must have broader access to all major world markets, especially Japan, the Number Two market after the United States, in order to generate sales to bankroll the heavy research and development investment pharmaceuticals firms must undertake," explains John Chappell, president of SmithKline &

French Laboratories-International, the division responsible for the joint venture decision. "Licensing was ruled out because the royalties would have been too modest to fund further research and development. Moreover, in a licensing arrangement, Tagamet would have been relegated to the status of just one more item in Fujisawa's sales list. By contrast, the joint venture company devotes 100 percent of its time to the sale of Tagamet."

SmithKline decided on a marketing joint venture in preference to one that also entailed manufacturing, as it did not want to go to the expense of building a plant in Japan. It persuaded Fujisawa to produce Tagamet in return for SmithKline's manufacturing a popular Fujisawa antibiotic in the United States. "There was no need for either of us to resort to a capital investment, since we each had the technology and capacity to make the other's product at a reasonable cost," Chappell says.

SmithKline invested "a couple of million dollars" in the joint venture. The hard part was getting Japanese government approval. SmithKline and Fujisawa reached their agreement in 1977, one year after Tagamet's U.S. introduction; it was not until 1981 that the Japanese government gave the go-ahead. SmithKline's patience paid off: Tagamet's annual sales in Japan exceed $100 million. Its success spurred the two firms to expand their venture into joint research and development. Any resulting new drugs will be sold by the venture.

SmithKline's joint venture arrangement in Japan was followed rapidly by another in South Korea, also with a former licensee. "South Korea is a little Japan: it is the thirteenth largest pharmaceuticals market in the world and one of the fastest growing," Chappell says. As with Japan, SmithKline had a product suited for South Korea—an antiworm drug. However, South Korea has even stiffer rules than Japan about foreign investment; it insists that joint ventures manufacture, not just market, so SmithKline had to contribute a factory on the basis of its 70 percent share. The investment was modest, though—$5 million.

To complete its Asian thrust, SmithKline has another joint venture in China. But in Taiwan and Thailand, which do not mandate local participation, it is the sole owner. "Total ownership is our preference, because life is easier when you're on your own, but commercial reasons in Japan and government regulations in Korea and China overcame our reluctance for joint ventures," Chappell concludes.

As part of Eastman Kodak's overhaul of its Japanese strategy from hands-off to hands-on to regain ground in Japan as well as internationally, the company switched from a distributorship arrangement to a joint venture with the same firm. The shift fits in with Kodak's game plan to increase its Japanese presence to the point where its chief rival, Fuji Photo Film, will have to divert funds earmarked for global expansion to the home front to combat Kodak in Japan. Kodak reasons that placing Fuji on the defensive at home will weaken Fuji's capacity to compete internationally against Kodak.

To understand what led to Kodak's decision, some history is necessary. Based on the length of its presence in Japan, Kodak should have been the leader, since it started selling there in 1889, just nine years after George Eastman founded the company. It was virtually unchallenged until 1934, when Fuji Photo was established. Subsequently, Fuji benefited from the Japanese government's shutting Kodak out of the Japanese market from 1937 until 1947, except for motion picture and aerial reconnaissance film. After World War II, Kodak's prewar presence did not save it from 40 percent duties on imports of color negative film, and in 1960, to keep better track of how much Kodak was sending to Japan, the Japanese government requested it to reduce its number of distributors from fifteen to two.

Kodak's choice for distributing its photographic products was Nagase & Company. A large trading house whose connection with Kodak dated back to 1922, when it started importing Kodak motion picture film, Nagase established an in-house division solely for Kodak products. Kodak's office-related equipment continued to be sold by Kusuda Business Machines, appointed a distributor in 1953.

The change by Kodak from hands-off to hands-on stretched from 1977 through 1986, when its joint venture with Nagase began. In 1984, Kodak realized that the small liaison office opened in Tokyo in 1977 was insufficient for it to contend with Fuji in what had become the world's Number Two photographic market. By then, Fuji had a 71 percent market share and Kodak a mere 13 percent. Also Kodak wanted a firsthand look at Japanese R&D in electronic image capture, the newest photographic technique.

Consequently, Kodak upgraded Japan from the company's "Triple A" group—Asia, Africa, Australia—to a separate region and revamped its strategy from a passive to an active role. It was determined to regain control over distribution of its products to have a direct impact on sales planning. Albert Sieg, Kodak Japan K.K. president, explains: "Manufacturers and distributors have different driving forces. Distributors want to maximize profits through minimization of the outlets where they distribute, so ours concentrated on big cities and ignored the rest of the country, with the result that in parts of Japan, Kodak had zero sales. Conversely, manufacturers regard promotion campaigns in smaller areas as worthwhile, because big city people travel there and their loyalty is lost if your product is unavailable. Manufacturers are more content than distributors to wait for long-term paybacks." Japan now places second after the United States in Kodak investment.

Achieving its plan was hard for Kodak. First, it had to prevent Nagase from feeling offended or losing face, a fate dreaded by the Japanese. Moreover, it had to overcome Nagase's argument that Kodak was committing a big mistake because it did not understand the Japanese market as Nagase did. These protests were assuaged by the absorption of all of Nagase's Kodak division employees into the joint venture and the appointment of the division's manager as president.

The venture quickly discovered that achievement of Kodak's goal of increased market penetration was difficult because of Japan's complex family-controlled distribution system, under which stores, by custom, purchase only from the current generation of family supplier. Kodak's solution: tie-in promotions, such as including a free roll of film in boxes of disposable Pampers diapers. Kodak reasoned that new parents would want to take many baby pictures. Sales justified the change in strategy. In 1986, according to Sieg, the sales of Kodak amateur film increased by 15 percent.

Initially, Kodak also broached a joint venture to Kusuda, but the small, weak Kusuda could not afford the investment; at Kusuda's suggestion, Kodak bought it out instead. Next, Kodak bought 10 percent, for the largest share, of Chinon Industries, which makes Kodak's 35 mm cameras, with an option for outright acquisition. Subsequently, Kodak went on to form a series of joint ventures with Japanese partners that have enabled it to speed up its diversification program. The program's aim is to lessen Kodak's dependence on photographic products.

In Japan, Kodak formed a joint venture in floppy disks with Mitsubishi Chemical Industries, Japan's largest chemical firm and a branch of the Mitsubishi trading group. It also built an R&D

facility to study commercial and industrial information gathering as well as image processing and compounds for semiconductors. These areas of research were chosen to avoid conflicts with R&D that Kodak conducts at its Rochester, New York, headquarters.

In the United States, Kodak plans to make alkaline batteries in a joint venture with Matsushita Electric Corporation of Japan. Scheduled to open in 1989, the venture is 70 percent owned by Matsushita and 30 percent by Kodak and is an outgrowth of Matsushita's previous production of batteries in Japan for Kodak. The joint venture will permit Kodak to start U.S. operations more quickly than it could have alone. The company also believes the association will enable it to produce batteries at a lower cost than its U.S. competitors.

Whereas Kodak, General Foods, and SmithKline view their Japanese-based joint ventures as marketing and distribution tools, Goodyear Tire & Rubber Company decreed that its joint venture in Japan, formed in 1985, would be for manufacturing only. It saw no need for a broader role, because it already had an extensive Far East and Australian sales and distribution network. But to make better use of that network, it decided it needed a plant in the region.

Its requirement balanced with that of Toyo Tire & Rubber, which wanted to get rid of one of its factories. Toyo also regarded a joint venture with Goodyear as a way to afford expansion into steel-reinforced radial tires, which have overtaken conventional rubber tires in popularity.

Toyo and Goodyear share the cost of manufacturing at their one jointly owned plant. Otherwise, there is no cooperation. "We are allies in terms of production and competitors in the marketplace, where tailored customer service is important," explains Philip Spanninger, director, technology and venture management, at Goodyear.

Gaining market share is the main impetus for consumer product joint ventures, but high-technology industries also regard them as a vital cost-saving measure. On average, it now costs $100 million to build a semiconductor plant, and this amount is likely to double by 1994. Consequently, high-tech executives are endorsing joint ventures between companies in different countries because of the economies of scale that result from production for two parents rather than one.

"The cost of technology is now such that the home market is not big enough to warrant the expense, thereby driving companies together," says G. H. Switzer, director, business planning and international strategic development, at AT&T Network Systems. While such costs could be recouped substantially through licensing technology, Switzer emphasizes that "licensing alone does not create an image of commitment. When an equity position is taken, the other side knows that its partner is making a long-term commitment and this confidence is critical for success."

Not going solo also reduces the risks of costly projects, which is why Westinghouse seeks partners in the construction of power plants. Its procedure is to produce the turbine generators and related equipment and to bring in the boiler supplier and construction firm. It prefers Japanese partners, because the Japanese government provides more generous export financing terms than the U.S. government does. The United States follows the Organization for Economic Cooperation and Development (OECD) guidelines on export finance, which state that the amount not covered by the government must be borrowed at regular rates from commercial banks. Japan, like the United Kingdom, France, and Italy, circumvents this requirement through loans at a fraction of the normal interest charge. "Joint ventures will continue as a way of life in our field for the next ten to fifteen years, because many developing countries want plants and they look to offshore export credit financing for such projects," says Gary Albrecht, manager, commercial programs, at Westinghouse.

International joint ventures are not the answer for every corporation. John Lewis, president of Amdahl Corporation, a computer and communications systems manufacturer, cites several shortcomings. "Success is not possible unless both parties have identical motivations," he cautions. "To me, a joint venture entails doing everything together, including marketing, and companies that normally compete may well want the other to stay out of its home market. Also, in joint ventures it sometimes is hard to know who is in charge—one or both of the parents or the venture itself. This makes decision making tough, and in our industry decisions must be made daily about prices, output, and financing."

He prefers Amdahl's relationship with Fujitsu, an association he describes as "unique cooperation by American and Japanese competitors without recourse to a joint venture." Established in

1970, Amdahl in less than two decades has reached $1 billion in annual sales. Fujitsu, formed in 1935, largely underwrote Amdahl's early development in a venture capital arrangement. Today it owns 49.5 percent of Amdahl, and the two cooperate on research and development and license technology to each other. In his memoirs, Taiyu Kobayashi, who was with the company since its inception and served for many years as chairman, writes, "It is no exaggeration to say that our encounter with Amdahl determined the route that led to today's Fujitsu." Fujitsu is now Japan's Number One computer manufacturer.

The Fujitsu-Amdahl arrangement originated because of complementary needs. Fujitsu could not break into international markets due to IBM's dominance. Amdahl, founded by an ex-IBM engineer, Gene Amdahl, knew how to design compatible equipment on which programs designed for IBM computers could run—the only way Fujitsu believed it could compete against IBM—but lacked development money. Amdahl literally had no funds in its Bank of America account when Fujitsu made its initial $5-million investment in 1970.

Harmony reigns now, but the early relationship was stormy over the issue of how much Fujitsu should be involved. With neither side impressed by the other's production skills, Fujitsu insisted on participation in the manufacturing, while Gene Amdahl wanted to do it alone. Also, Fujitsu believed Gene Amdahl was a far better engineer than manager. With his company once again on the brink of insolvency, Gene Amdahl was forced by Fujitsu to hand over the operations to a professional manager hired from General Electric. He remained for a while, though, as titular chairman.

Gene Amdahl was humiliated, but the toll was worse on Toshio Ikeda, manager of computer engineering at Fujitsu and in charge of negotiations. At the age of fifty-one, he suffered a fatal stroke shortly after the talks were completed. These talks ended in a compromise: the two firms' first computer was to be built primarily by Fujitsu and completed by Amdahl. The initial buyer was the U.S. National Aeronautics and Space Administration (NASA).

Fujitsu has three directors on Amdahl's board but leaves the daily operations to Amdahl. A prime benefit today is in research and development. Fujitsu, six times larger in terms of sales, has an R&D budget triple that of Amdahl, to which Amdahl has access. "We can pick what interests us and move into new areas we couldn't afford otherwise," Lewis says. One such choice, computer-related storage products, has become a $250-million-a-year business. "Our relationship is the closest thing to a joint venture without being one," Lewis adds.

At the same time, Amdahl regards Fujitsu as a buttress against a takeover. In 1984, Fujitsu forestalled a possible acquisition of Amdahl through its purchase of a large block of shares from an original investor in Amdahl that gave just three weeks' notice of its intention to sell out. But before the purchase, Fujitsu, concerned that Amdahl's prime asset, its high-tech engineers, might leave, asked Amdahl whether it objected. This provided Amdahl with the opportunity to request that Fujitsu limit its ownership to 49.5 percent until 1990, when the agreement will likely be renewed.

Even without the restriction, however, Fujitsu would not be interested in purchasing 100 percent of Amdahl. "What would be the advantage?" asks Rinzo Iwai, executive director, international operations, at Fujitsu. His comment stems from Fujitsu's shareholdings already exceeding the percentage required by law to get a piece of Amdahl's profits. In 1986, Amdahl's profits were $42 million.

Whereas Amdahl preferred to yield part of its ownership to Fujitsu to a joint venture arrangement, the 1988 acquisition of Firestone Tire & Rubber Company by Bridgestone Tire Company of Japan provides an example of how outside pressures can convert a joint venture into a takeover. Originally, Firestone had agreed to transfer its worldwide tire operations to a joint venture in which Bridgestone would have been the dominant partner with 75 percent. But then Pirelli S.p.A., a large Italian tire maker whose prior overtures to Firestone for a joint venture had been rejected, sought to purchase Firestone. That led to Bridgestone's revision of its joint venture proposal into a buyout. The merged company is the world's third largest tire maker after Goodyear of the United States and Michelin of France. Hitherto, Bridgestone already was in third place and Firestone in fifth. Pirelli's rank in terms of size is just behind Firestone.

The Bridgestone-Pirelli contest for Firestone arose from neither having much of a foothold in the United States, which accounts for 45 percent of the worldwide tire market. Moreover, both wanted a U.S. presence because the weak U.S. dollar caused the price of imported tires to increase to the detriment of their sales.

The degree of support at the government level for international joint ventures differs widely. The United States and Japan have no official programs to promote such cooperation. By contrast, the European Community is midway through a multimillion dollar shared effort to improve its members' competitiveness in information technology: office systems, microelectronics, and computer design and programming.[6] Called Esprit (European Strategic Program in Information Technologies), it was started in 1984 and is scheduled to operate until 1994. Half of its initial five-year budget of $1.7 billion was funded by the EC; the rest came from participating companies and academic institutions.

Information technologies were singled out because the EC considered its members "less prepared" in this "fastest growing major industry" than the United States and Japan. It also believed that trans-European collaboration would enable relatively small EC countries to afford a substantial investment on a par with those of the Americans and the Japanese.

So that the cooperation would not be classed as collusion, antitrust laws were revised to permit the shared research and resultant joint production and marketing agreements. To date, more than two thousand researchers are involved in projects. On the average, one out of every four proposals is approved. The EC is particularly pleased that ESPRIT has enabled small and medium-sized companies, with under five hundred employees, to engage in research. According to EC statistics, 53 percent of ESPRIT projects include firms in this category. The EC also boasts that more ambitious research is under way than otherwise would have been possible. In response to complaints about too much red tape, the EC plans legislation that will allow "European Economic Interest Groups" to skip registration throughout the entire community, provided they register in one member country.

Across the world, the government of Taiwan operates ITRI (Industrial Technology Research Institute) to attract high-technology joint ventures with the goal of transforming Taiwan from an assembler to an innovator. As an incentive, the government makes local professors available for research pertaining to joint venture programs. At the same time, it believes this will serve to stem the overseas brain drain of such experts. Taiwan's

---

6. The EC consists of Belgium, Denmark, France, Germany, Greece, Ireland, Italy, Luxembourg, the Netherlands, Portugal, Spain, and the United Kingdom.

approach is far different from the haphazard one of Spain, according to Samuel Felix of the international services division of Dataquest, which has both Taiwan and Spain as clients. "Taiwan's plan comes from the top and is specific; by contrast, Spain's stand is 'when I see it, I'll know it,' " he says.

The People's Republic of China has welcomed foreign investment in the form of joint ventures for almost a decade. The Soviet Union waited until January 1987 to enact legislation permitting Westerners to own up to 49 percent of a Soviet enterprise. Subsequently, the Soviets placed a nine-page advertising appeal in *The Wall Street Journal,* and Soviet leader Mikhail Gorbachev lobbied U.S. business executives during his December 1987 visit to Washington.

Some big U.S. companies like Ford, Occidental Petroleum, Monsanto, Singer, and Pizza Hut, a subsidiary of PepsiCo, are exploring the possibility of joint ventures with the Soviets.[7] But few quick deals are likely. The slow process has several causes. First, federal regulations bar U.S. corporations from providing the Soviets with technology that can be used for military purposes. U.S. officials pay particular attention to equipment which, although it may seem to have no connection with defense production, is capable of being transformed for this purpose. For example, the Soviets used a truck factory that Ford had built for them in the 1930s to produce combat tanks during World War II.

Other reasons for the wariness about joint ventures in the Soviet Union include that country's general ignorance of the private enterprise principles of profit and loss, cumbersome bureaucratic red tape, different accounting practices, and a scarcity of "hard" currency (U.S. dollars) available for repatriation of earnings to the United States. Many of these problems also have occurred in joint ventures in China. A further concern is what would happen if U.S.-Soviet relations were to sour, resulting in a U.S. trade boycott similar to the one imposed after the U.S.S.R. invasion of Afghanistan. Prospective Western partners will have to decide (as they did in the case of China) whether the advantages

7. Seven major U.S. companies have formed the American Trade Consortium to negotiate joint ventures with the Soviet Union. Six of the companies are in industry: Ford, Johnson & Johnson (pharmaceuticals), Eastman Kodak, RJR Nabisco, Chevron (oil), and Archer Daniels Midland (food processing). The seventh, Mercator Corporation of New York, is a merchant banker. The consortium's membership is open to other interested U.S. companies.

of tapping a large market outweigh the disadvantages of doing business in the Soviet Union.

Once managers conclude that a joint venture has more merits than licensing or the appointment of an agent or distributor, they must sell the decision to the company's senior management and board of directors and then hunt for a partner. For companies accustomed to instant expansion through mergers and acquisitions at home, this next stage in forming a joint venture can be a difficult challenge.

# 2   Planning the Venture

"And they lived happily ever after" is impossible in joint ventures unless the partners' objectives are compatible and unless the matchmaking is preceded by strong corporate global planning. Joint ventures will fail if they are viewed as rogue planets wandering separately from the rest of the corporate galaxy. It is essential that they fit into total strategy. Sometimes, they are just what is needed to force a company to reexamine its international operations.

"If a firm cannot find the right partner, it should delay its plans for a joint venture, because compatibility is the most important factor, analogous to 'location, location, location' in real estate," says Alan Bowbyes, vice president, corporate and government banking, at the Royal Bank of Canada. Compatibility is essential, because a 50:50 ownership split providing an equal balance of power is not always possible. Either the local government restricts foreign ownership to a minority position, or the partner supplying the technology insists on the majority interest on the grounds that it is "bringing the most to the party."

Compatibility can be readily measured, notes Richard Dulude, president, telecommunications, at Corning Glass Works. "Joint ventures work if one partner has the technology and the other, management and marketing expertise," he explains. "Also, the parents must have similar values and corporate cultures. Because Corning is technology-based, we look for a partner that shares our perception of the purpose of technology: to make something useful and worthwhile. The prospective partner's outlook is more important to us than whether it has the same technology, since the very concept of a joint venture implies a long-term relationship. We further believe good ventures are grounded in joint decision making, and we therefore want a partner that is comfortable with sharing authority."

Dulude knows whereof he speaks. Siecor Corporation, founded in 1973 in the United States by Corning and Siemens, the West German telecommunications giant, to make optical fiber, has grown to the point where it supplies 40 percent of the U.S. requirement. The primary reason Siemens was a good choice of partner, Dulude says, is that the two firms' technologies were complementary, not competitive. Corning had developed the fiber, and Siemens's specialty was the cable necessary to protect the fiber. Both firms share their R&D, protected by their respective patents.

The partnership has been beneficial for Corning. It has enabled the company to compete in the United States against AT&T and provided a wedge into Europe, where telephone systems are government-owned. For nationalistic reasons, European governments insist on domestic content. In Siemens's home base of West Germany, Siecor is a major supplier on a current government upgrading of the telecommunications network.

Dulude compares a successful joint venture with a happy family. "A good one is like a strong marriage in which the spouses talk a lot to each other. It takes more time to manage joint ventures than wholly owned foreign subsidiaries, first because a partner is involved and next because the goal is to make the venture self-sufficient, akin to a child growing up and standing on its own feet. Constant communication is essential about what direction the partners want the venture to take and to prevent flareups. Some of this dialogue occurs naturally; other times it must be initiated.

I compare it to the clock in my mind about how often I hear from my three sons. It's as if we have mutual extrasensory perception: when I'm dialing one from whom I haven't heard, he's calling me."

When joint ventures evolve from longstanding business relationships, the vital compatibility already exists. This was the case with Alcan Aluminium, the world's largest aluminum producer,[1] and Sumitomo Electric Industries, Japan's biggest manufacturer of electric wire and cable. Electricity is conducted by cable, and Sumitomo and Alcan became acquainted in the 1930s, when aluminum began to replace copper as the material for cable. The two firms cooperated on bids for cable projects around the world and exchanged technology.

Archie Black, executive vice president of Alcan and president of Alcan Pacific, regularly lunched with Sumitomo Electric's president on his twice-a-year visits to Japan. "He wanted to address the U.S. market in the newest cable material of optical fiber but was unsure how to proceed because it involves specialized marketing to electricity authorities," Black recalls. "Alcan is familiar with all this, so I proposed a joint venture." The result: a jointly owned optical fiber plant in North Carolina that opened in late 1987.

Starting from the beginning in a joint venture is far more difficult. John Manfredi of General Foods says, "Because it is such a critical step, it takes a lot of time. The process becomes even tougher when dealing with a foreign culture in a foreign language. To ensure mutual vision, shared short- and long-term goals, and credibility, General Foods insists that our prospective partner, as well as our side, repeat to each other their understanding of the agreement."

When companies talk about their joint venture partners, they usually refer to the "synergy" between them. The usual connotation of "synergy" is that each firm's technology and products complement the other's, but Carl De Martino, group vice president, international, at Du Pont, emphasizes that much more basic is the synergy of corporate ethics. "What are normal business practices in some countries, such as avoidance of taxes and discussion of prices and market share, are unacceptable to Du Pont,

---

1. Alcan is larger than the Aluminum Company of America (Alcoa), of which Alcan was a subsidiary until 1928.

as are what we judge to be inadequate safety and environmental precautions," he says. "Du Pont either backs out of projects in countries where its standards are not matched or makes plain what it wants and has its partner stick to the rules."

De Martino notes, though, that corporate ethics do not always involve a clear-cut decision between honesty and dishonesty; sometimes conflicts can arise from cultural differences. For example, Du Pont's policy forbids employees to accept presents worth more than fifty dollars. That places it in an awkward position with its Japanese joint venture partner, as the Japanese are frequent gift givers. The partner takes pleasure in giving Du Pont executives expensive souvenirs on anniversaries of the venture's formation. As these presentations usually take place in front of customers, a rejection by Du Pont would embarrass its partner. In order not to insult its partner, and at the same time not to violate its own rules, Du Pont asks its executives to accept the gifts and later to turn them in at the head office. Either a corporate property sticker is affixed and the items are placed in an office, so visiting Japanese will not wonder where they have disappeared, or the gifts are exchanged for cash and the money is donated to a local charity.

Du Pont has learned not to leap to conclusions about the behavior of the other side. Once, says Paul Roessel, director of international planning, Du Pont nearly withdrew from a joint venture with a partner in a developing country when the partner insisted that 2 percent of net income go to foundations. "We had visions of the money probably being destined for Monte Carlo, but it turned out to be a true commitment for the provision of education for young people to which our partner had already donated extensively. Since Du Pont also contributes to education, we had something in common and signed," he says.

Joint ventures have collapsed over lack of agreement on the color of the carpet at the venture—the red of one parent's carpet, the red of the other's, or a red shade unique to the venture. Such disputes appear trivial. But even when the synergy seems perfect, the partner may turn out to be the wrong choice, just as in an apparently ideal marriage that falls apart.

Usually the problem is that the partners disagree on the venture's purpose. For example, Gillette terminated a razor blade venture with a labor cooperative in Yugoslavia because of what Rodney Mills terms "an inability to agree on the direction and cost of growth." Gillette believed its partner was "far more interested in production than in marketing and selling." Particularly annoying was the partner's refusal to slow down output of a sideline in metal tape measures. "They would have kept making them until they spilled into the sea," Mills comments wryly. He points out that Gillette's low equity position of 21 percent placed it at a disadvantage, so that "every issue requiring negotiation was a lengthy hassle."

In another instance of conflicting goals leading to cancellation, Varian Associates, a large California electronics manufacturer, withdrew from a joint venture with Nippon Electric Company (NEC).[2] Varian maintained that NEC had honored only half their deal—the manufacture in Japan of semiconductor equipment using Varian technology—and not the part requiring it to sell Varian-made equipment in Japan. "We were transferring a lot of technology and getting very little out of the arrangement," says Larry Hansen, president of Varian's semiconductor group.

In other cases, unforeseen or uncontrollable circumstances are to blame. For example, Sharp Corporation, Japan's leading manufacturer of electric appliances and business machines, lost its joint venture partner, RCA Corporation, following RCA's acquisition in 1985 by General Electric. GE dissolved the agreement with Sharp because it makes the type of semiconductor chips that Sharp and RCA had planned to produce.

Economic factors can also precipitate cancellation, when the firms conclude that it is better for the preplanning money and time to go down the drain than to risk steep losses by proceeding. Such an instance occurred in 1987, when Bombardier, a Canadian manufacturer of rail, aerospace, and snowmobile products, withdrew from an automotive joint venture with Daihatsu Motor Company after two years of negotiations and several million dollars' worth of feasibility studies. Daihatsu and Bombardier were to make a minicar near Montreal, where Bombardier is headquartered. Bombardier said it reconsidered because it believed the minicar sector of the North American auto market to be overcrowded and that therefore the proposed joint venture had no future.

In still other cases, joint ventures are doomed because the negotiators lose their sense of perspective. "They become too deeply committed to the venture, since it relates to their own careers and success, or they get so friendly with the other side that they feel it impolite to raise questions," warns Andrew Zimmer-

---

2. *Nippon* is the Japanese word for "Japan".

man, director, information industry program, at the management consulting firm of Coopers & Lybrand. "Consequently, they are unwilling to listen to those who advise against the venture. For example, our firm is kicked out from time to time as the consulting firm because negotiators are disappointed when our market analysis criticizes their planned venture as a poor idea."

Joint ventures can also suffer from unrealistic expectations. "Instant success generally is rare, since most joint ventures start production a year or more behind schedule; yet during that time their administrative expenses still must be paid," Zimmerman says. "That sales will compensate for this outlay can be a false hope, because pricing of the product is often too high and has to be lowered. The expectation that the parent companies will handle the administrative functions, thereby saving the young venture from this expense, usually is not realized, because the systems of big companies are unsuited for small joint ventures."

When a venture encounters problems, its future largely depends on the commitment of the chief executive officers at the parent companies. International joint ventures suffer from the generally held conviction that distance and a foreign language place a firm that is accustomed to being in control at a disadvantage. Consequently, advocates of ventures must ensure that the enthusiasm of senior management and the board of directors does not flag.

"The importance of the opportunity must be demonstrated again and again, since many people at a company have not traveled outside the United States," says Tod Clare, vice president, international operations, at American Motors Corporation, at the time AMC became the partner in a joint venture Jeep plant in China.[3] "Some people are nervous just about going to Toronto, two hundred and fifty miles from the Detroit headquarters of the U.S. car makers. Most can't imagine what China is like; it seems so alien to them."

Serious delays in launching a venture can result from cumbersome head office decision making, a process bred by today's conglomerate form of business. One company willing to admit this—possibly because its joint venture went on to be successful—is Otis Elevator. Otis executives say that one reason its chief rival, Schindler Management of Switzerland, beat Otis into China, even

3. Clare resigned from AMC following Chrysler's acquisition of the company in 1987.

though Otis had longstanding ties there, was that United Technologies, the parent of Otis, had to integrate what Otis wanted into total company strategy. Three other divisions—Carrier (air conditioners), Pratt & Whitney (aircraft engines), and Essex (wire, cable, automotive components and systems)—were also interested in China. Aware of the difficulties regarding repatriation of dividends and shortage of foreign exchange, United Technologies was cautious about too great a commitment of company resources to China.

Those involved in joint ventures stress that the ventures do not occur in a vacuum but must be interlaced with total company planning, as United Technologies realized. Also, a venture should be structured so as to prevent power struggles with the parent's subsidiaries and other joint ventures. Jealousy between various wings of a company, whether subsidiaries or joint ventures, is all too common. Some companies even encourage such rivalry in the belief that it promotes greater creativity and output. Unfortunately, sometimes the participants become enemies, more intent on their internecine rivalries than on bigger and better results. Two popular solutions to this problem are to assign different products to each operation or to centralize international marketing at corporate headquarters.

Otis Elevator learned the hard way about the importance of internal harmony. According to William Mallett, general manager of China Tianjin Otis Elevator, the venture was cold-shouldered when it requested certain technology from a Japanese joint venture in which Otis also is involved. The Chinese project feared Otis's U.S. head office was placing the interests of Tianjin Otis second, since Otis only has a minority interest, whereas it is the majority partner in Nippon Otis Elevator.

As Mallett tells it, he and Wang Yun Qi, vice general manager at China Tianjin Otis Elevator, devised a plan to get their way based on Otis's anxiety not to offend the Chinese. During Mallett's vacation at home in Australia, Wang sent a blistering telegram of protest to Otis's president at world headquarters in Farmington, Connecticut. The telegram reminded the president that he had promised a transfer of the technology. Mallett says the maneuver worked and the information arrived post-haste.

Nippon Otis executives recount a different version. President Yukio Saishoji recollects he was dispatched by Otis to China Tianjin Otis in its first two years to supervise production, double output, train workers, and inaugurate inventory tracking and quality control programs. Saishoji says that while he was there production rose from six hundred to one thousand units and that he trained seventeen university graduates to carry on when he left.

Some companies have a formula regarding how much of their global budget will be allocated to international joint ventures. At Gillette, for example, where they are crucial to the company's global drive, ventures do not receive more than 10 percent of the company's annual budget. Often, the amount is much less. The proportion is low because the ventures usually are smaller projects located in Third World countries.

Although these nations contain 75 percent of the world's population, Rodney Mills says, Gillette's investment in them will never equal 75 percent of the company's expenditures. However, he adds, the size of these markets could lead "in the fairly far-distant future" to Gillette devoting as much as 30 percent of its capital to expansion in them.

Gillette's international joint ventures fit into its overall strategy to increase its international market share. Consequently, the company does not push for overnight growth in profits. "Our first concern is about the number of units sold rather than price and profit margins," Mills says.

Similarly, U.S. food companies view overseas joint ventures as opportunities to broaden their sales. But instead of trying to sell their entire array of products, the food firms prefer to begin with basic items. For example, General Foods stresses brands that are the top sellers in markets where it is already active. The emphasis works: 75 percent of its sales are derived from such products, up from 60 percent in 1980. The firm's targets are populous countries where the drinking of coffee is uncommon: for instance, it figures that if only 5 percent of the Chinese switched to drinking coffee, that would create a new target market of fifty million potential coffee buyers. Consequently, General Foods now has joint ventures to make its Maxwell House coffee in China, India, Japan, South Korea, and Taiwan—all formerly tea-drinking nations. Each of General Foods' Asian-Pacific operations is a joint venture. It has three in China, one in Japan with two plants, one in South Korea with three plants, and one in Taiwan.

In the H.J. Heinz Company's joint venture in China, which began in 1986, Heinz elected to begin with infant cereals, for which it was certain of constant demand. Most Chinese women work outside the home, and many leave their children at government-run day care centers. Heinz convinced its partners, the General Corporation of Agriculture, Industry, and Commerce and United Food Enterprises of Guangzhou (Canton) to persuade government nurseries to serve Heinz-made cereals.[4] Heinz regards China's large population as a way to rapidly expand its consumer universe. Before its entry into China, Heinz claimed it reached 15 percent of the world's consumers. China alone has another 20 percent, so that through this joint venture, Heinz's potential consumer base has more than doubled.

Nabisco Brands also considers China an important part of its global portfolio.[5] Its concern was how to fit China into that portfolio. Nabisco makes four dozen kinds of cookies; close to three dozen kinds of crackers; ten beverages; two dozen confectionery and snack products; canned vegetables, fruits, and puddings; and margarine, cereals, and pet food. Its dilemma was which products would be most compatible both with Chinese tastes and with the limited production experience of its partner, Yili Food Corporation.

The winnowing process began with a decision to concentrate on biscuits and crackers. Cheese flavors were ruled out, since the Chinese dislike cheese. Nabisco was reluctant to start with fancy filled cookies because of its partner's relative lack of production experience. Nabisco was also worried about the availability of quality ingredients. Eventually it settled on five items: Ritz and Escort crackers, Premium soda biscuits, and two plain cookies—Marias and Social Teas. Ritz accounts for 40 percent of production, with the remainder evenly divided. Marias were chosen over Lorna Doones because they are easier to make. Also, the Chinese have less of a sweet tooth than Westerners do, and Marias are not as sugary.

For some companies, the involvement in international joint ventures triggers a rethinking of total corporate strategy. This was the case at Polysar Limited of Sarnia, Canada, the world's largest

4. The Wade-Giles system of transliterating Chinese into English, named after the two nineteenth-century Englishmen who devised it, has been replaced by the *pinyin* ("spelling sounds") system since the 1950s and officially since January 1, 1979. Thus, for example, Canton is Guangzhou and Peking is Beijing.
5. Like General Foods, Nabisco became part of a tobacco company in 1985, when it merged with R.J. Reynolds.

producer of synthetic rubber. Polysar derives 72 percent of its sales from outside Canada. "Until 1983 strategic planning was handled by a twelve-person corporate planning department whose hundred-page reports largely were ignored," says William Pursell, director, corporate strategy. "Little basic strategic thinking was done; Polysar tended to react rather than act." In 1983, having suffered a record loss, Polysar decided it should spell out its strategies, so that management would have specific goals to reach. A line manager, knowledgeable about operations, was assigned to spearhead the planning.

When Pursell, with fourteen years of international experience, became director of corporate strategy, he encouraged Polysar executives to think conceptually by asking them to imagine they were writing Polysar's 1995 annual report and to describe what had happened between 1983 and 1995. Their remarks were consolidated into a "Vision for the Year 2000." That vision calls for Polysar to be one of twenty petrochemical companies expected to be active internationally at that time.

Included in the projections was in which geographical areas Polysar should concentrate its investment. The consensus was that Polysar's "vision" could not be realized if it were to stay in its "traditional, comfortable markets" of Canada, the United States, and Europe. Polysar's choice for growth, like that of many companies, was the Asia-Pacific region, from which it was deriving only 6 percent of its revenue in the early 1980s. That proportion should soon jump dramatically thanks to three joint ventures in China as well as others under consideration in Taiwan, Korea, and Thailand. In early 1987, Polysar began to probe the Chinese market by becoming the first Western company to supply a Chinese firm with modern latex technology. The information was provided to a small plant near Shanghai in return for a 50 percent interest. The latex is destined for carpet backings and paper coatings, both of which China was still making with forty-year-old production methods.

"Demand was so pent-up that trucks were lined up outside the factory the day it reopened its gates," Pursell says. "Consequently, the remodeled plant was profitable from its first day." With that undertaking a runaway success, Polysar quickly became a 50 percent partner in the construction of another latex plant, also near Shanghai. Scheduled to start operation in 1990, the factory's output will be four times greater than that of the pilot project.

Polysar's third joint venture in China, a $25-million polystyrene plant near Guangzhou, also plans a starting date in early 1990. This venture shows how the market outlook can change during the lengthy preparation time of a joint undertaking. Fortunately for Polysar, the change is for the better. When it first considered the venture, the demand for polystyrene was low. Polysar decided to proceed, however, because it wanted a presence in China. To reduce its risk, it kept its investment to 25 percent and agreed to the request for inclusion by Alberta Natural Gas Company, Canada's fourth largest gas pipeline company. The Chinese own the rest. Now that the project is under way, polystyrene has regained its popularity. Nonetheless, Polysar is restricted by an unwritten agreement from buying out the interest of Alberta Natural Gas.

Like many companies, Polysar divides its global operations into North and South America, Asia-Pacific, Europe, and the rest of the world. By contrast, Du Pont divides responsibility on the basis of product lines. The group vice president of each department runs it as a separate profit center, with authority over its worldwide planning and investments. As a supplement, Du Pont's international department assists the product divisions with their planning; handles daily administrative matters; ensures uniformity in approaches so that no department uses conflicting sales methods, for example, in the same country; and integrates any joint ventures into Du Pont's entire global planning.

"We do not regard our international joint ventures as isolated endeavors," states international group vice president Carl De Martino. In practice, this means that employees throughout Du Pont, whether at the head office in Delaware or across the world, are encouraged to suggest how the company can expand overseas sales in existing and new markets for Du Pont products. Du Pont's board of directors' executive committee must approve projects exceeding $10 million. At any one time the committee may consider as many as five projects. "Its yardstick is which countries are pivotal to Du Pont's future, since the company naturally will not spend money on a plant where there will be no market for its products," international planning director Paul Roessel says.

Du Pont believes Philips-Du Pont Optical Company, its joint venture with N. V. Philips to make optical disks, meets its criterion perfectly. When the venture was formed in 1986, the market for optical disks was on the verge of an explosion in sales, so that the venture was market-driven. Also, the partners were content that their operating styles, engineering, and marketing skills were complementary. Lastly, the two had, as Du Pont put it, the "gumption to work together."

Certainly, both parents had the money and talent for solo efforts. Du Pont's 1985 revenue was $29.5 billion, of which electronic sales exceeded $1 billion.[6] Philips's 1985 sales totaled $22 billion, of which its consumer and professional electronics products divisions each accounted for more than $6 billion. There was no obvious need for Philips, which had developed optical disk technology in the late 1960s, to become a partner with Du Pont, which was not a leader in this business. Indeed, 80 percent of Du Pont's growth in electronics was due to acquisitions or extensions of existing technologies rather than to pioneer development. Instead of forming a joint venture, each company could merely have obtained a license for the other's product and advanced its own sales independently.

But both decided that competition would be exorbitantly costly and that they had more to gain as partners. "It had the one plus one equals three arithmetic that makes any business attractive," said Michael Hartnagel, director of storage products at Du Pont and a member of the joint venture task force. For Du Pont, it was an opportunity to become a leader in an industry of the future. For Philips, it meant cooperation with one of the world's leading electronics materials suppliers. Moreover, Du Pont has many U.S. data-processing and photo-imaging customers, to which Philips wanted access.

Both could benefit from the coordination of work at Du Pont's U.S. facilities with that at Philips's European ones. Furthermore, the two firms were not strangers, having worked together before. As Hartnagel said: "Was it feasible for one company to go it alone? Yes. But did it make sense? No. It required a tremendous amount of financial and managerial resources. We were smart enough to realize we could not do everything ourselves."

Philips and Du Pont also realized they had to get together quickly if they were to be in the forefront of the market by 1990, when optical disk sales are expected to top $4 billion. Based upon the recording and reading of information by light, the optical disk

---

6. Since the venture was formed in 1986, the partners predicated their agreement on 1985 results.

system stores thousands of times more information than the previous technology, magnetic tape. It is claimed that one disk alone can hold the unabridged dictionaries of every language in the world and that its accompanying laser reader can locate any word in less than a second. Businesses, libraries, publishers, government agencies, and record companies are all expected to embrace the process.

Besides having complementary technologies, Philips and Du Pont each brought different customers to the venture. Philips has a worldwide web of alliances through acquisitions and joint ventures. Foremost is Polygram, the U.K.-based record producer that is the leading distributor of prerecorded compact disks. Since it is 90 percent owned by Philips, it is a readymade large "captive customer." Polygram's director of international record operations moved over to the joint venture as its consumer products marketing director.

Philips's network also embraces Japan, where it is in a joint venture to produce two-way systems linking compact disk players and personal computers, and Taiwan, where it is in a joint venture to produce assembly kits for compact disk players. In addition, the Dutch giant is a partner with Control Data Corporation of the United States in Optical Storage International, which produces storage systems. Optical Storage's Netherlands plant and Philips-Du Pont Optical Company plan to supply disks to Optical Storage's U.S. facility, which specializes in hardware rather than in programming. Du Pont has valuable connections, too. In 1985, it sold $1 billion in electronic products to U.S. computer, data-processing, and telecommunications firms, all of which are a target audience for optical disk technology.

Du Pont and Philips already knew their management styles harmonized from a joint venture they had established in 1981. The outfit, Philips-Du Pont Magnetics Company, was formed to produce magnetic tape for video, audio, and disk purposes. From this experience the companies learned they were alike in their dedication to new technology, international expansion, and aggressive marketing. Both were prepared to back their pledges of mutual interest with substantial infusions of facilities, cash, and research and development knowledge.

Together they contributed $150 million toward initial capitalization plus *all* their previous activities in optical storage technology. Philips also handed over its compact disk technology, its product development center at its headquarters in Eindhoven, the

Netherlands, an audio compact disk plant in Hanover, West Germany, and a small video and data disk plant in Blackburn, England. The Hanover factory is the largest of its type in the world. Du Pont provided its optical disk technologies, expertise in the use of plastics and electronics for data-related transmission, and the research and development center at its Wilmington, Delaware, headquarters.

Philips-Du Pont Optical has a hefty budget of its own. By 1990, just four years after its creation, it will have spent $400 million on new facilities, notably plants in the United States and France. The $60 million it has earmarked annually for research is to be divided between the Netherlands, West Germany, and the U.S. facilities. The marketing director flies regularly between the United States, where he is based, and Europe to ensure that the R&D efforts complement rather than duplicate or compete with one another. Although its headquarters are near Amsterdam, Philips-Du Pont Optical's worldwide marketing is handled from the United States. The venture is run by a five-person management team whose unanimous consent is required for any operational changes.

Even when joint ventures have undergone extensive preparation, they can develop in unexpected ways. This is well demonstrated by the vicissitudes in telecommunications joint ventures. AT&T has partnerships with N.V. Philips, three organizations in Taiwan, and Gold Star Semiconductor Limited of South Korea. In 1987, ITT Corporation transferred its sixty-year-old telecommunications equipment manufacturing business to a joint venture in which France's Cie Générale d'Electricité (CGE) is the majority owner. Just through its formation, the venture—called Alcatel—instantly became the world's second largest telecommunications supplier after AT&T.

The principal reason for the alliances is to share today's staggering costs of research and development. Although the sales of these giants are in the billions of dollars, they blanch at the average of $1 billion and several years it takes to develop modern computerized telephone exchanges. Moreover, the schedule of the outlay has changed radically. With previous generations of equipment, expenditures occurred at the outset and were amortized through the product's lifetime. But today's much more sophisticated devices entail both higher initial development costs and continued R&D over their entire life span.

A broader customer base, immediately provided by the combination in the ventures, spreads the expenses. "These partnerships were motivated by a need to reduce risk through being in several markets simultaneously," says Francis McInerney, telecommunications analyst at Northern Business Information. "This compensates for today's shorter product life cycles and ensures long-term profitability."

AT&T's joint ventures have had mixed results. In South Korea, it believes, it has achieved its goal of controlling, through cooperation, Gold Star's ambitions. "Korea's 'national charter' is to knock Japan out of businesses in which both are engaged and to improve its balance of trade," explains David Poticny, manager, international operations, AT&T Network Systems. "For example, it bought or borrowed automobile technology and now is intent on selling cars worldwide. The goal of the Koreans is to supply *your* market. They would like AT&T to sell them technology and then buy the product from them. We can prevent this only by controlling the flow of technology to our partner. We do that by supplying technology that, while advanced, is five years old."

The AT&T-Philips deal, reached in 1984, involved a relative newcomer to joint ventures—AT&T—with a firm that, until a series of setbacks in 1987–1988, had been enthusiastic about such alliances. Besides the one with Du Pont, it has five in China, covering optical fiber, video recorders, car radios, color TV tubes, and video disk players.

Philips believed the alliance with AT&T would revive its struggling telephone exchange business. For its part, AT&T hoped Philips's European roots would overcome protectionist sentiment in Europe against a U.S. telecommunications company, especially one on the mammoth scale of AT&T. "Most European governments control their country's telephone system and regard telecommunications as a strategic preserve," points out McInerney of Northern Business Information. Unfortunately for the venture, known as APT, its parent companies miscalculated that its European content would make it acceptable.

AT&T realized it had misread the mood in Europe in April 1987, when the French government awarded the contract to build a second public exchange for the French network to Ericsson of Sweden rather than to APT. Ericsson previously had beaten APT in a bid to acquire CGCT (Compagnie Générale de Constructions Téléphoniques), France's second biggest public exchange manufacturer after Alcatel. The rebuff was not a complete surprise, however, because French President François Mitterrand had publicly criticized Philips when APT was formed for betraying European solidarity by joining forces with an American company.

The rejection caused AT&T and Philips to restructure APT in early 1988. AT&T decided to supply the venture with a greater range of products on the premise that since its technology is regarded as a world leader, APT's access to more products would enhance its ability to sell in Europe. The wisdom of this decision was quickly proved when Spain shortly afterward placed a substantial order with APT.

In return for its injection of more of its technology, AT&T requested that the venture be changed from 50:50 ownership to one in which it now has 60 percent. Philips agreed to sell 10 percent of its stake to AT&T because it wanted to concentrate on its much more successful electronics business. It is probable that Philips may further dilute its ownership so that APT can increase its number of European owners and expand its appeal on the Continent. Despite APT's difficulties, there should be no shortage of suitors for a stake in the venture because of the access that would be gained to AT&T's technology. One of the first interested parties likely will be Italtel, Italy's largest telecommunications manufacturer, which wants to upgrade Italy's telephone system, now widely regarded as inefficient.

The reduction of its shareholding in APT was one of a number of joint venture disappointments that Philips underwent within a matter of months. It was preceded by the collapse of talks with Whirlpool Corporation of the United States for a joint venture in household appliances. Next, Agfa-Gevaert, part of the West German Bayer group, declined to join in the Philips-Du Pont arrangement. Then, after retreating from an equal to a minority interest in APT, Philips's joint venture in medical diagnostic equipment with General Electric Company (GEC) of the United Kingdom fell through. The proposed company would have been the world's second largest in its field. GEC (no relation to the U.S. General Electric) owns Picker International of Cleveland, a major U.S. medical equipment manufacturer.

Why the GEC-Philips deal fell through is a sobering commentary on the impact of the falling U.S. dollar—a lesson on the detrimental effect currency fluctuations can have on international ventures. Under the terms of the deal, GEC was to inject about

$200 million as compensation for its smaller size, so that it could have equal ownership in the venture. But, subsequently, the fall in the dollar undermined Philips's profits to the level of GEC's. The U.K. company then argued that its contribution should be decreased. Philips refused to renegotiate, maintaining that its currency exchange problems were temporary. With neither side willing to budge, the venture was aborted. But the concept of an international partnership was not. Both Philips and GEC immediately began hunting for new associates.

GTE Corporation of the United States and Siemens of West Germany planned a U.S. joint venture in public telephone-exchange equipment. Instead, Siemens wound up absorbing GTE's U.S. and international transmission systems business, plus its public switching and business operations in Italy, Belgium, and Taiwan. This resulted from a basic conflict of interests the two firms had at the outset.

Although the stated purpose of their negotiations was to amalgamate their U.S. public telephone-exchange equipment operations, what each really wanted was for the other to abandon its products. When neither would yield, the talks collapsed. Francis McInerney says it would have been far more to their mutual benefit for Siemens, a newcomer to the fiercely competitive U.S. telecommunications market, to have bought GTE's North American telecommunications operations. "That would have juxtaposed with GTE's desire to get out of manufacturing and concentrate on sales and service," he says. "The problem was that Siemens was too proud to admit its product had few U.S. customers."

Hans Decker, the New York-based president of Siemens Capital Corporation, which oversees Siemens's telecommunications activities, maintains that surface similarities between the two firms initially hid underlying incompatibilities. "It sounded very easy because we had lots in common businesswise and in management styles, but in practice there turned out to be many overlaps," he reflected shortly after the negotiations fell apart. He added that Siemens was reluctant to forsake its technology because of costly adaptation necessary for the U.S. market. Siemens had hoped to recover this money through economies of scale achieved by manufacturing for its and GTE's customers.

For ITT, the transfer of its telecommunications business to the Alcatel joint venture did work out as planned. ITT had been seeking a way to improve its balance sheet, which had been depressed by its difficulties with new equipment and lagging sales. ITT's telecommunications revenue had shrunk from 30 percent of the conglomerate's total in 1981 (its other activities include insurance, finance, and Sheraton hotels) to 23 percent in 1985, the year preceding Alcatel's formation. "ITT is a classic example of a company that had positioned itself well but was vulnerable because of high development costs," McInerney says. "It was unique as an American company with transnational European business, but its newest technology, the System 12 digital telephone switch, cost billions of dollars and didn't work. The company had huge orders it could not fill. Therefore, the time had come for it to cut cleanly and get CGE to take over the risk."

For CGE, then state-owned, the deal provided an opportunity to become a world leader overnight. Previously, France had accounted for 90 percent of its customers. It also fit in with the government's privatization strategy. Not only did CGE's growth make it more attractive to investors when the government subsequently sold back its shares but also it enhanced interest in the entire denationalization program, since CGE is the largest of the sixty-five state companies involved.

At first, skeptics wondered whether CGE had bought a white elephant. Although CGE's interest was in ITT's order book, not its technology, speculation was that CGE's older products would cause customers to buy from rival firms instead. However, events seem to be proving the doubters wrong. Alcatel's birth luckily coincided with the conclusion of major improvements to the System 12 that led to a surge in orders.

Thus, the bedrock of joint ventures is compatibility and a welcome place in overall corporate planning. The next step is to hammer out a contract in which both sides are winners, the hallmark of successful negotiations. It is easier said than done.

# 3  Negotiations and Contracts

Managers of successful joint ventures maintain that if associates have to refer to their contract, a partnership is in deep trouble. They also point out that firms which are normally competitors will continue to be.

"You are partners in one thing and at war in others," states George Crossett, vice president, primary glass, glass group, at PPG Industries. He should know. Although Pittsburgh-based PPG, one of the world's leading manufacturers of glass, paint, automotive and industrial coatings, and organic chemicals, and Asahi Glass Company of Japan were in a joint venture, they battled each other for projects in China.

Good contracts take into account the percentage each side will own, trademark protection, technology transfer, staffing, and in the event of dissatisfaction, termination procedures. The permutations differ, of course, depending on whether the marriage is between private-sector corporations or between free enterprise and the government in state-controlled or mixed economies. Drawing up contracts that satisfy both sides can stretch out for months, sometimes years, of tedious negotiations.

Most joint ventures are equity projects in which each side invests money. But some take the form of contractual ventures—cooperative efforts in development, manufacturing, and/or services. China, for example, prefers contractual agreements in energy projects so as to retain control over its natural resources. It took its stand when energy prices were at record highs and foreign firms were pressing for equity participation in order to make large profits. However, with prices now lower, contractual agreements are to the benefit of the outsiders, because they provide greater assurance of payment.

The outlook for business also influences which form is best. Xerox, for instance, has an equity joint venture in Shanghai in copiers and a contractual one in Beijing that supplies Xerox electronic printers to Chinese computer users. James Shapiro, in charge of Xerox operations in China, Hong Kong, Singapore, Australia, and New Zealand, says projected sales dictated the natures of the two joint venture agreements.

Whereas insufficient volume was forecast for the printers to justify an equity investment, Shapiro states, there is a big potential market for copiers from the 400,000 plants in China and the massive government bureaucracy. "Although the production equipment at factories is no more advanced than U.S. machinery of thirty to forty years ago, all the administrative functions are the same in both places," he says. "Most important, lots of reports are written in China, and copiers make possible their speedy distribution throughout the system." He forecasts startup production of ten thousand copiers. Worldwide industry output is 500,000 machines.

To succeed at the bargaining table, negotiators must first agree among themselves so they will present a united front to the other side. Nabisco, for example, confined its team to three persons so as not to "overwhelm" the Chinese counterparts in negotiations for a joint venture biscuit factory in Beijing. The three close friends met constantly to map out their strategy and thereby prevent any divisiveness in front of the Chinese.

One of the Nabisco men was its in-house attorney, William Seidler. Nabisco sent him along even though Asians—Chinese and Japanese—interpret the presence of a lawyer as a sign of distrust on the part of its prospective partner. "Mutual trust" is of paramount importance to the Asians. They prefer to establish a sound relationship and then work out the legal details, whereas North Americans are accustomed to having a lawyer sit in from the start.

Nevertheless, Seidler says, he was readily accepted "because I have gray hair and the Asians respect age." Also, Seidler's manner is low-keyed rather than abrasive. He elected to play the role of middleman, saying "my directors won't accept this." Gerardo Rodriguez, vice president, international operations, an affable man, assumed the part of the "meanie," and his assistant was the "diplomat."

Otis Elevator, by contrast, readily admits that internal dissension contributed to delays in negotiations for its now thriving joint venture in China. The Chinese logically sent their invitation to enter into negotiations to the head of Otis Asia–Pacific, who began the discussions. Subsequently, head office decided it should be in charge. This midstream switch "confused" the Chinese, says an Otis participant. Ultimately, the two sides grew close, hugging one another in affectionate greetings. The Chinese representatives referred to Eino Latvala, now retired from Otis but its vice president of strategic planning during the negotiations, as a "respected older brother."

For Americans, negotiations abroad are often unlike any to which they are accustomed. Whereas bargaining sessions between U.S. companies can be compared to the back and forth of arm wrestling, international negotiations often have the flavor of a boxing match with the technical knockout awarded to the side that haggles longest.

Europeans and Far Easterners grow up in a bazaar atmosphere in which everything from the purchase of food to telecommunications equipment is subject to bargaining followed by more bargaining. "Whether the other side is German, Swiss, Dutch, Japanese, Korean, or Chinese, they are astute traders who are in no rush and keep working on a deal to their advantage," remarks AT&T's David Poticny. "American corporations are not accustomed to haggling or dramatics, but with Europeans and Far Easterners, the bargaining never stops. For example, when we negotiated with N.V. Philips of the Netherlands, they were at us mercilessly to get 'two,' and then when we agreed, they asked for 'three.' This would continue even between toasts at dinner."

To further illustrate his point, Poticny recounts an anecdote: "When the Dutch negotiators came to the United States, they tried to get the hotel to give a special rate because it was their first visit. The hotel refused, but did offer a free breakfast; this pleased the Philips' people, since they felt they had at least won a bargain of some sort."

Poticny developed a successful counterstrategy. Aware of Dutch preferences for lots of coffee, offices with windows, and a later start and end of the work day, he insisted on 7:30 a.m. meetings in windowless rooms and no coffee. "By 10:00 a.m., I had an agreement," he laughs. Subsequently, he found "just the threat of such meetings could produce the desired results." The psychological warfare was supplemented with double-edged words. "I grant you're twice as smart but you think you're four times as smart and you're not," Poticny would say in what he terms "both a compliment and a kick in the teeth."

Joint venture veterans disagree on the importance that should be attached to the split of ownership. Some are adamant that at least 51 percent is essential for management control. Chase Manhattan Bank, for example, sold its 49 percent stake in Chase National Bank Egypt, one of the more successful joint ventures in Egypt, in 1987 in line with its policy of reducing minority holdings worldwide. Its partner, the National Bank of Egypt, Egypt's largest commercial bank, purchased the Chase's shares. By contrast, others insist on a minority interest to avoid the necessity for financial consolidation of a yet-to-prove-itself endeavor.

For most companies, management control counts far more than majority ownership. Archie Black of Alcan Pacific is a proponent of this approach. He is at ease with joint ventures after many years of experience. "It is crucial that joint ventures make the distinction between ownership and management," he says. "It is the ownership that is shared, not the management. An organization can have only one chief executive officer; if not, the result can be disastrous. If there is a hassle between the owners, it should be in the boardroom and not involve the local chief executive officer.

"Some companies insist on veto power but if the stage is reached where it has to be exercised, the venture has failed," Black continues. "Joint venture agreements should be filed, not used; the only time they should be referred to is in a dispute, and if there is a dispute, it's too late to look at the contract. If the partners have shared objectives, they can file their agreement."

In any event, percentage splits can be renegotiated, and are, when one side wants to wrest management control from the other.

This is why even a slight change, from 50 percent to 51 percent, was so important to Xerox in its relationship with the Rank Organization. The change, made in 1969, thirteen years after Rank Xerox was established, came about because of Xerox's belief that "Rank was not growing Fuji Xerox, jointly owned by Rank Xerox and Fuji Photo, quickly enough," says Xerox vice chairman William Glavin. "Xerox wanted direct management control in order to proceed with expansion of Fuji Xerox from a distributor to a manufacturing and research and development facility."

Today, Rank Xerox is only a "residue" of the original setup, with Rank's role reduced to that of an investor, says Robert Reiser, group vice president, international operations, at Xerox. Xerox has toyed with the idea of buying out Rank, but Reiser says, "the price would be very high for the gains we would achieve. We already have management control, so why bother?"

In other cases, reversals suffered by one partner can be used by the other to gain ownership control. A notable example is provided by Wheeling-Nisshin, a joint venture formed in 1985 in the United States by Wheeling-Pittsburgh of the United States and Nisshin Steel Company, Japan's sixth largest steel producer, to make galvanizing steel for automobiles. The initial arrangement called for a 50:50 ownership split and equal board representation of two persons from each side. Also, the venture was given the authority to guarantee its loans, and Wheeling-Pittsburgh was to handle administrative functions. But Wheeling-Pittsburgh's bargaining position was critically weakened because, like all U.S. steelmakers, it suffered losses from the softened demand for steel. When it declared bankruptcy in 1985 after the joint venture contract was signed, Nisshin insisted on revision of the terms in its favor.

As a result, Wheeling-Pittsburgh's ownership was shaved to one-third and Nisshin's increased to two-thirds. Nisshin dominates the venture's board, with four directors to its partner's two. Nisshin, rather than the venture, is guaranteeing the loans, and the venture takes care of its administrative functions, rather than Wheeling-Pittsburgh as originally planned. Wheeling-Pittsburgh does have an option to increase its ownership to 50 percent by 1991, but as this depends on its guaranteeing half of Wheeling-Nisshin's debt, the chances are slim that it will take up the option.

The venture's president John E. Wright III says that Nisshin remained interested in the project, despite Wheeling-Pittsburgh's difficulties, because it wanted access to the U.S. market in galvanized steel. This type of steel is the only one for which demand has increased in the United States in recent years. Wheeling-Pittsburgh agreed to a lesser role because it believed Nisshin, as the Japanese steel producer with the most modern facilities, could help make Wheeling-Nisshin's facility the most automated of its kind in the world.

In another instance, Island Creek Corporation, a subsidiary of Occidental Petroleum, turned adverse circumstances to its advantage. Midway through negotiations for the $650-million An Tai Bao surface coal mine in China, the world's largest, coal prices tumbled. The slump caused the departure of Oxy's U.S. partner, Peter Kiewit Sons' of Nebraska, which had held 25 percent. The temptation for Oxy was to follow suit, but it realized that if it pulled out from the venture, the largest to date in China, its negotiations for cooperative drilling of China's offshore properties would be endangered.

Thus, instead of withdrawing, Oxy took the offensive in the negotiations, and its boldness gained it significant concessions. First, China agreed to acquire Kiewit's stake. That upped China's holding in the mine to 75 percent, 50 percent through the initial participation of the China National Coal Development Corporation and the rest by the newcomer, Bank of China Trust and Consultancy Company. Second, Oxy used the depressed outlook for coal to force the Chinese to back down from the exorbitant wage rates they had originally demanded. China charges foreigners steep premiums for workers reassigned from their regular work units to joint ventures. The government retains the surcharge, which is equivalent to ten times or more what the workers take home. The levy causes many firms to decide against investing in China, because it eliminates the original advantage of relatively cheap labor rates.

Before the coal price decline, Oxy had agreed to pay twelve dollars an hour, on a par with top salaries in the United States. After the slump, it successfully insisted on wages being tied to how much a miner produces. Foreign partners in joint ventures in China, concerned about what they regard as lax work habits, demand such incentive systems to encourage productivity.

Satisfactory terms aside, Oxy also weighed the long-term outlook for coal and concluded it was promising. "The agreement is for thirty years, and both we and the Chinese believed when we signed in July 1985 that the collapse in coal prices was short-term," says Richard Chen, vice president, Asian affairs, at Oxy. The optimism was not justified by the time the mine opened in September 1987, but the problem of how to sell the coal rests solely with the Chinese coal agency, which is responsible for all marketing.

Joint venture partnerships between private enterprise companies require much cultivation to flourish, but if irreconcilable differences cause a divorce, at least it occurs out of the limelight. The situation is much more ticklish when the partner is a government. There is always the possibility of nationalization, although that shadow also hangs over wholly owned foreign subsidiaries. What follows are the success stories of Alcan and Northern Telecom in ventures with a foreign government, and the unhappy experience of Polysar.

In 1987, Northern Telecom (Nortel), Number Two in North America in telecommunications equipment sales (after AT&T), and the Turkish Post, Telephone & Telegraph (PTT) agency celebrated their joint venture's twentieth anniversary of manufacturing systems for the PTT. For Nortel, which is controlled by Bell Canada Enterprises, a publicly traded company, the joint venture made possible a transition from Canadian to multinational without immediately competing with European and U.S. telecommunications giants. Subsequently, the confidence it gained convinced Nortel it could succeed even in the fiercely competitive U.S. market. Sixty percent of its sales are now in the United States. The Turkish venture remains an exception in Nortel's global strategy. In countries where the economy is not government-controlled, it prefers to be solo through wholly owned subsidiaries, exports, or licensing. That way it does not have to share profits.

The joint venture provided the Turkish PTT with instant access to the modern technology for which it was desperate because of a twelve-year backlog of subscriber orders. Although Nortel was relatively unknown internationally, Turkey unhesitatingly accepted it as a partner because of Nortel's superior equipment and because Nortel's parent, Bell Canada, was—and is—one of the world's richest telephone companies.

Although Turkey owned the majority—51 percent, which later went to 69 percent—Nortel supplied all the management and technical workers, who then trained the Turks. Today, only two of the two thousand employees are from Nortel. When the venture decided to install more sophisticated equipment in the early 1980s, it turned to Nortel, not because Nortel was one of its parents but because it had what the venture wanted. Nortel was the pioneer in computer-activated digital switches, which provide greater clarity and accuracy and which handle more calls than the earlier analog system that converts sound waves into electrical signals. Nonetheless, in order to decrease its dependence on Nortel, the Turkish PTT recently began to buy also from Nortel's competitors.

For Alcan Aluminium, which has plants in twenty-six countries and sells to one hundred more, intervention by the Brazilian government in a massive $400-million project in the Amazon jungle spelled the difference between staying or leaving when the market turned soft. The venture has an intriguing history. Alcan's chief geologist at the end of World War II acquired U.S. government wartime aerial surveys, from which he deduced there was a rich deposit of bauxite, the principal ore of aluminum, on a tributary of the Amazon. He sailed up the river, then walked twenty miles through the jungle to verify his theory.

Alcan built a small site, but when the 1973 oil shortage triggered an aluminum industry slump, Alcan withdrew. The Brazilian government, anxious for development of the Amazon region, beseeched Alcan to stay, promising the risk would be shared by local partners, including itself. It also pledged that the project would be its chosen vehicle for bauxite exploration.

Alcan agreed, and three years later Archie Black joined the president of Brazil at a signing ceremony at the mouth of the Amazon. The next three years were devoted not only to opening the mine but also to constructing a town with schools and a hospital for eight thousand people (twelve hundred mine workers and their families), roads, and an airport. Almost thirty years elapsed between the discovery of the bauxite deposit and the first shipment. Although Alcan, experienced in bauxite mine projects, supervised the work, it requested only a 24 percent share, limiting its proportion of the output to that amount. "We didn't need more," Black explains.

The troubles that can arise in ventures between government and private enterprise are represented by Polysar's experience in Mexico, where foreign ownership was restricted to 40 percent. It shows that disagreements with a government, exacerbated by clashes with local managers, can erode all the provisions of a contract that "guaranteed" the foreign partner management control.

Polysar's story begins in 1964, when Petroleos Mexicanos (Pemex), Mexico's government-owned oil company, invited Polysar to be a part owner in a synthetic rubber plant. Pemex selected Polysar both because the company is the world's largest synthetic rubber producer and because, with all tire firms as the target audience, Pemex did not want to single out one as a partner. Polysar invested only $6.6 million. The joint venture, Hules Mexicanos S.A. (Humex), became Mexico's largest rubber producer, with a 40 percent return on equity despite the peso's devaluation.

Because Mexico "desperately" needed Polysar's technology, "it agreed to terms that could not be obtained today," says William Pursell, who was sales director for North America from 1973 to 1983, with responsibility for Humex. Polysar was permitted to nominate in perpetuity the plant's director-general, who was to have the deciding vote over all key items, including investment, management, and changes to the articles of incorporation. Thus, Polysar had veto power even though it was the minority shareholder.

For the first fifteen years the partners got along beautifully because success masked inherent conflicts about where the rubber would be sold. At most, Polysar favored modest exports to prevent shipments into Polysar sales territories; on the other hand, the Mexican government wanted the country to grow through exports. For years the domestic demand for rubber was so strong that nothing was left for export, forestalling an early clash between the two sides. But as Humex, then headed by the third director-general appointed by Polysar, undercut Polysar's prices in its chief markets of the United States and Italy, the enthusiasm of Polysar executives waned. "They felt Humex was attacking Polysar at its heart," Pursell says. For his part, the local manager also had grounds for annoyance: Polysar, which had had a Mexican distributor before Humex was formed, refused to make Humex its new distributor. Also, Polysar's technical office in Mexico was reluctant to share its expertise with Humex.

Polysar, which had prided itself on having the upper hand, discovered that in reality the agreement carried no weight, since the director-general, according to Pursell, "began to run the company as if it were his own. His decision to attack Polysar's markets infuriated Polysar; hence, when the situation subsequently became tough in Mexico, nobody at Polysar cared to help him." At the same time the director-general was alienating Polysar, he lost his chief Mexican ally when the representative from Pemex, with whom he had played tennis, was fired for accepting bribes. The bribes were unrelated to the Humex venture. The new man appointed by Pemex to Humex wanted a stronger role than his predecessor.

The situation worsened when the government, in an effort to reduce Mexico's debts, ordered government companies to restrict their raw material imports. The government designated Humex a state company; Polysar regarded it as independent. This time, the director-general sided with Polysar and continued to import because he wanted Humex to remain profitable. His stand led to a showdown in 1985 between Polysar and Pemex when Pemex insisted he be fired and that it choose his replacement.

Two weeks later, the situation deteriorated further. A Pemex official tipped off the director-general that he was about to be arrested for alleged "irregularities" about his personal finances. The charges pertained partly to his ownership of an expensive home. "As the police came up one elevator, he went down another," Pursell says. He fled across the U.S. border. Polysar said they had no vacant positions for someone of his status, and Mexico barred him from reentry. He wound up starting a business in Houston.

As early as 1984, when the management crisis erupted at Humex, concurrently with Mexico's economic slump, Polysar decided to withdraw from Humex because of its "minimal strategic value." Polysar had similar plants in Canada and Belgium. Moreover, well before the director-general was fired, Polysar realized Pemex was discontented with Polysar's unilateral authority. Concerned that the loss of its most long-standing foreign partner would deter other prospective foreign associates, Pemex urged Polysar to stay but would not yield the point that might have persuaded Polysar to do so: relinquishment of ownership control.

Polysar delayed its pullout out of concern that as the minority owner it would not be offered full value for its shares. But the situation shifted in its favor when the government directed that Pemex sell its shares, too, as part of a privatization program of companies no longer deemed strategically important to the country's commercial development. Because the government wanted to sell Humex as a complete package, Polysar, despite the devaluation of the peso, could insist on a price for its shares commensurate with their value of more than $20 million. That amount was between five and six times Polysar's initial investment. The sale was completed in 1988.

To avert problems like Polysar encountered, joint venture veterans suggest spreading local shareholding in countries where the government is a direct participant in the venture or lays down restrictions as to the extent of outside ownership. This strategy, accomplished by including a second concern or selling shares to the public, dilutes the power of the major local shareholder. It works particularly well if the second domestic participant is the chief rival of the first, such as Hughes Communications' partners in JCSat—Mitsui and C. Itoh. In India, where foreign ownership cannot exceed 40 percent, General Foods insists that at least one-third of a project be sold to the public to ensure widespread support.

Before negotiating a contract in a developing country, companies would also be well advised to determine whether suitable components or ingredients are available. For example, because the quality of India's drinking water does not meet the standards of industrialized nations, General Foods chose in its joint venture there to make carbonated beverages, which require processed water, instead of powdered drinks.

The other problem with developing nations is that for reasons of national pride they demand the most advanced technology, even though they are ill equipped to use it. To concede to their ultimatums can be to their detriment, since the venture can become saddled with costly equipment. Warns G. H. Switzer of AT&T: "When transferring technology, care is essential to prevent the creation of too large a cost base. If AT&T were to duplicate its big U.S. systems in countries where the volume of lines is far less, it would create a noncompetitive capital base. We try to hit on an equilibrium between a country's desires and our cost management criteria."

Negotiations over technology are further complicated by the concomitant issue of component sourcing. When companies operate alone, the regular procedure is to shop around for the best quality and price. In joint ventures, however, this priority must give way to the aspiration of the host country to build its own technical infrastructure. A delicate balance must be struck between the domestic partner's opposition to imports and the more technically advanced partner's desire to import if local components do not meet international standards. AT&T, for example, "educates" local producers by providing specifications and testing some components.

How prickly the local sourcing issue can become is illustrated by the automotive joint ventures of the Japanese. For their cars to be accepted as American or European, rather than feared as Trojan horses assembled from Japanese-sourced components, the Japanese agreed to buy parts locally. The manner in which they have done this has angered the Americans and Europeans, who charge that although the Japanese are purchasing locally, they are doing so from suppliers they encouraged to follow them to the West. The Japanese retort that lack of a written formula on how much local content is required makes for ambiguity. For example, some European countries are closed to Japanese imports or coproduction; others call for "substantial" local sourcing. Only Belgium is explicit—60 percent domestic content. However, the European Parliament is considering specific guidelines.

The situation in China epitomizes the conflict between the yearning of developing countries for the most advanced technology and their equally strong desire to promote their own equipment. "We try to tell China, 'Please slow down. The first step cannot be an advanced project,' " says Kazuya Hanazuka, public relations officer at Hitachi. Hitachi has a joint venture in China in television sets. "But they insist on receiving the newest technology, which they often just shelve." Stories in the official Chinese press bear this out. They have charged that millions of dollars worth of foreign and Chinese equipment is rusting, unused, or unwrapped at many plants, "covered in dust like a giant animal in a deep sleep for four to five years."

China is not totally bereft of technology, but most of it is for defense rather than for commercial purposes. China makes high-speed military jets and is bidding to launch satellites for the United States as well as to supply it with radar equipment. However, because little attention has been paid to civilian products, most are forty years behind U.S. versions. Thus, foreigners insist that joint ventures begin by assembling parts imported from their home bases.

One firm managing to solve this dilemma is Xerox. Its recently launched joint venture in copiers in Shanghai began the traditional way—assembling imported parts. Ultimately, Xerox's method of making copiers, in which 80 percent of the parts are purchased from outside suppliers, will lend itself to local sourcing, which is why Xerox chose Shanghai as the site. James Shapiro explains: "Shanghai is an industrial center, and the venture will call on the factories in the area to make motors and other important parts. For local sourcing to work, factories must be nearby because of the close relationship that is necessary between designers and production people."

China, like much of the world, uses metric measurements like grams, meters, and liters, whereas U.S. consumer products are made in pounds, feet, and quarts. But Xerox designs products intended for worldwide use in metric, as do most U.S. multinationals.

Shapiro says that the commitments by Xerox to transfer state-of-the-art technology and to use local parts give it a competitive advantage over the many Japanese rivals also seeking to sell copiers to China. "Because Japan has fewer natural resources, it is essentially an exporter of technology; therefore Japanese companies are reluctant to transfer their latest technology to a country they view as a long-term competitor," he comments. "Xerox, by contrast, has a philosophy of engaging in joint ventures in the international market, because it at least gets half the pie."

The overriding concern in technology transfers is if a company hands over all its data a competitor might use it to overpower the company. Wary Westerners remember that in the past Far Easterners shaved the top off integrated circuits and peeled away the circuitry layers to discover how they worked and then made similar ones. To prevent further "borrowing," those who own the technology do not agree in negotiations to pass on their knowledge of the next generation of equipment. They also keep watch through management and financial control and board representation, stipulating that expenditures above a stated level for designated equipment must have their approval.

Equally hard to negotiate are arrangements for transferring technology. The process entails far more than the mere exchange of blueprints and casual conversations between engineers. How complex it can be is demonstrated by the procedures involved in the formation of APT, the AT&T-Philips joint venture begun in 1984. The planning was geared to when the venture had to make its first deliveries, with schedules devised for each step, ranging from training one hundred Philips engineers at AT&T to documentation for the fifteen thousand components shipped to the venture's Holland site. Decision after decision was necessary. Should air transport, cheaper for small items, or sea shipment, cheaper for bulk freight, be used? Should AT&T send component kits for assembly, or should the venture buy directly from European and Japanese suppliers? What would be the best way to make future "mini" transfers of new technology?

Because the schedule of the technology transfer was geared to delivery dates, David Poticny of AT&T realized two months before the deadline that the partners were behind schedule. To AT&T, Philips was the culprit, and its behavior was traceable to the European mode of never-ending negotiations. "When AT&T sets a shipment date, it works round-the-clock to meet it; in Europe, if they don't meet the target, the attitude is 'so be it,' " Poticny remarks. "In Europe, if customers make requests, they are often told their inquiries caused a delay when there would have been one anyway," he adds. Of course, American firms are not always punctual either, but Poticny regards AT&T as a paragon. "I wish Philips had taken as much care in the daily management of the business as it did about negotiations," he comments ruefully. "When I asked about the timetable, they replied they thought they would meet it. So I said to remove 'think' from their statement and develop a plan. At first, they tried to figure out why I personally wanted the deadline met. Now, having agreed with my arguments, the first group repeats my speech to the next group." Despite these conflicts, AT&T and Philips were equals in their material management systems. Both employ sophisticated computer tracking.

In other cases, where labor is cheap, checking is done manually and there is no concern about the cost and time devoted to even the cheapest items. AT&T encountered this with Gold Star, its Korean partner. "Our shipments of screws are sent in ten-pound lots with one thousand screws per pound," Poticny explains. "The Koreans count each screw and will send a telex complaining a shipment is ten screws short even though such screws cost one one-hundredth of a cent in Korea and their telex costs far more than the bag of screws. Still, to Gold Star, hiring screw counters is not a waste of money. It creates jobs, and the hourly salary is only fifteen cents."

Joint venture negotiations can also bog down over trademark protection. The lack of such laws in developing countries frequently scares off U.S. companies. In Mexico, non-Spanish trademarks are in the public domain. Broadly speaking, India prohibits foreign trademarks. It bends the rule, though, if the name is supplemented with Indianized prefixes or suffixes.

China's trademark laws were not passed until 1983, four years after the country opened its doors to foreign investment. Despite the rules, unauthorized use of Western trademarks continues. The Chinese have two excuses for these violations: either their isolation blocked any possible knowledge of the trademarks, or if they did know of their existence, they were unaware of their registration. When China introduced patent protection laws in 1984, it charged eighty dollars for the government briefing but gave a free memento—a quartz watch inscribed, "In commemoration of the promulgation of the patent law of China."

The trademark dilemma especially bedevils consumer goods manufacturers whose success is contingent on recognition of their labels. Those intent on joint ventures have devised varying solutions. General Foods, which has no global trademark, is not wedded to worldwide use of its Maxwell House, Tang, and Kool-Aid names. Thus, in India, Tang is sold as Ju-C. Prevented by India's rules from employing its usual Atra razor blade trademark, Gillette resurrected its 7 O'clock brand name, familiar to Indians from past use by the company. For Indianization, the suffix EJTEK was added.

William Seidler of Nabisco emphasizes that outright title to a trademark should never be granted a joint venture because grave problems can ensue if the deal sours. In addition, he says, the venture should pay a royalty for use of trademarks. Determination of how much the Chinese will pay can result in stiff haggling. American companies, accustomed to widespread recognition of their labels, believe compensation should be high; the Chinese argue the sum should be low because few, if any, people in China would recognize the trademarks. To get Nabisco's partner to agree, Seidler offered to register the partner's name, at Nabisco's expense, in neighboring countries to which it might want to export.

Besides specifying a royalty fee, Nabisco's contract contains a series of protective clauses for its trademarks:

- Advertising using the trademarks must indicate they are owned by Nabisco.

- Nabisco has the right to check the venture's products to make certain they meet Nabisco's standards.

- The joint venture cannot sublicense trademarks or register similar ones in China or elsewhere.

- At least ninety days' notice must be given of plans to export goods using the trademarks, so Nabisco can take whatever steps it deems necessary to protect its rights in export territories.

China still lacks a copyright law, which is why its quest for high-technology joint ventures is often rebuffed. Potential investors also complain that the country has inconsistent policies on the protection of software, patents, and other intellectual property. Thus, when foreign investors enter the Chinese market with a brand name product, they frequently discover the item is already being produced on a generic basis

SmithKline Beckman is among the firms that have encountered this unforeseen complication. Nonetheless, it is proceeding with plans to make its Tagamet anti-ulcer remedy under its brand name. Its persistence fits in with SmithKline's strategy: to produce Tagamet in China that is suitable for export under the name by which it is known worldwide. Still, John Chappell, president of SmithKline's international division, concedes that generic competitors will drive down prices in China so that return on investment will have to come from volume rather than from the usual high margins.

It can take up to two years for China to grant patent protection. But far more unsatisfactory than the slowness of the patenting process is that it excludes any invention patented abroad before 1985. This means that the many Chinese enterprises that have copied pre-1985 technology are exempt from paying royalties. Joint ventures avoid this problem because the Western partner controls the flow of technology to the Chinese side.

Another thorny issue in negotiations concerns export commitments by the venture. Understandably, the host country favors maximum exports to earn foreign exchange, of which most Third World nations have a dire shortage. On the other hand, the incoming partner is wary of exports because the products might not be of international quality or might cut into its own global sales.

"Never agree to export a percentage of the output, because if the venture becomes a giant, the proportion of the product eligible for export also increases vastly," Nabisco's Seidler advises. "Instead, always specify a quantity." Nabisco, for example, insisted on a ceiling of nine hundred tons per year from its joint venture biscuit factory in Beijing. Initially, the project will produce six thousand tons per year of five lines of biscuits, with one or two more types to be added in the first five years. "Nine hundred tons—15 percent of output—could even be dumped in a river and the project would still make money," Seidler says.

Otis Elevator readily acquiesced to the export of 25 percent of the output from its China joint venture. But it was really as restrictive as Nabisco, because it added a protective proviso: no exports until the sixth year and then only if "international market conditions and prices as well as quality and delivery schedules" are satisfactory. This is a popular clause with Western partners because, in effect, it postpones exports indefinitely, which is why the Chinese strongly object to it. They maintain that it is one-sided and connotes "mistrust among friends."

A number of firms permitted me to read their contracts. Their common strategy is the imposition of Western management principles in the Far East, or when the Japanese go overseas, a Japanese team structure. The wording is simple, in stark contrast to Western legalese. This is obvious at the outset in the preamble. In the Far East, trust is more important than contractual terms; thus, the opening sentence often reads, "Through friendship based on the principles of equality and mutual benefit."

What follows is a summary of common elements in the joint venture contracts of several companies:

1. *Amount each side is investing in cash, technology, equipment, land, or a combination.* The type of currency—that of the Western or local partner—should be stipulated. China veterans warn that the Chinese tend to overvalue their land, equipment, and buildings, which are substandard compared to what is available in industrialized nations.

2. *Duration of the agreement.* Some contracts are in perpetuity. Others cite a precise termination date. In the case of NUMMI, the U.S. Federal Trade Commission stipulated a twelve-year life span to preclude the antitrust issues that otherwise could arise from this collaboration between the world's Number One (GM) and

Number Three (Toyota) car makers. As part of its ruling, the FTC also declared that NUMMI could only manufacture. Sales must be handled separately by each partner, and NUMMI is prohibited from asking about the respective plans of the partners. It also cannot act as a conduit for supplier information or be included in orders placed by GM and Toyota. When the twelve years terminate in 1995, either parent company can buy out the other or NUMMI can become independent.

After the NUMMI pact was approved by the FTC in April 1985, Chrysler sued GM and Toyota on grounds of antitrust violations in an attempt to block the venture. Chrysler charged the alliance would have a "devastating effect" on competitors because GM and Toyota were price leaders in their respective markets One week before the trial was to begin, Chrysler dropped the lawsuit. The main provisions in the settlement stated that GM and Toyota would reduce their "active cooperation" after eight years and that GM would buy no more than 250,000 cars annually from NUMMI. Neither stipulation was of significance because GM has only sixteen management people at NUMMI and had never planned to purchase more than 250,000 autos per year from NUMMI. Moreover, output at NUMMI has yet to exceed 170,000 cars per year. Chrysler's withdrawal from the lawsuit was viewed as a prelude to establishing its own joint venture and, sure enough, it did so six months later. The agreement for Diamond Star, its coproduction effort with Mitsubishi, is for ten years (1988–1998) with provisions for an extension. Like GM and Toyota, Chrysler and Mitsubishi will market separately.

Chinese laws limit joint venture contracts to a specific life span subject to renewal. While the maximum length is thirty years, the usual duration is ten. Foreign partners maintain it often takes ten years for a manufacturing venture to reach full speed and therefore, as protection, they insist on the inclusion of termination rights in the contract. The Chinese oppose such a clause, arguing that divorce should not be discussed before marriage.

3. *Which decisions require the outside partner's concurrence.* Normally, these decisions comprise everything of importance ranging from the venture's articles of association to its business plan, operating policies, and capital spending over a stated amount. Some contracts have a $50,000 ceiling, others a $100,000 limit.

4. *Which side will provide specifications for the design of a new plant or redesign of an existing one, and which will arrange for the architect, budget, and schedule.* Usually, the Westerners and Japanese insist on supplying the guidelines, and the other side supervises the work.

In Tokyo, land prices are very high. In the twelve months ending June 30, 1987, they rose an average of 86 percent on top of a 34 percent hike in 1986. Prices are quoted per *tsubo,* the area of two standard-sized *tatami* (straw mats), which is 3.3 square meters. In the Ginza, Tokyo's fashionable shopping district where land rates are the highest in Japan, the cost reached a high of $20,370 per square foot ($220,000 per square meter). Under pressure from the foreign diplomatic community, which cut back on its operations to save on rent, the Japanese government cracked down on speculative land trading. By early 1988, there were signs of improvement, with prices down by as much as 50 percent in some areas of Tokyo.

In China, the government owns virtually all the land and charges a site-use fee, the equivalent of the Western property tax. As in the West, the assessment rate varies from place to place, depending on how developed a community is. Until 1986, China's levy ranged from 5 RMB (renminbi) to 100 RMB per square meter.[1] At the then prevailing rate of exchange of 2.79 RMB to the U.S. dollar, the minimum levy was $1.79 per square meter, 17 cents per square foot, and $7,200 per acre. The maximum was $35.80 per square meter, $3.40 per square foot, and $145,000 per acre.

---

1. China officially changed the name of its currency from *yuan* to *renminbi* in 1969, but *yuan* still is used informally. 1 yuan = 1 renminbi (RMB).

Because the land is often substandard and poorly serviced, foreigners grumbled that China's levy was grossly unfair. They contended that they could buy high-grade industrial property at home for what they were paying for low-grade land in China. In industrialized countries, factories are close to major highways and rail lines. Even in major Chinese cities, plants are frequently along bumpy dirt roads or on narrow lanes in the midst of small grocery stores and dilapidated houses.

In response to foreigners' complaints, the Chinese government in October 1986 narrowed the range of the site-use fee. It is now 5 RMB to 20 RMB per square meter. At the 1986–1988 rate of 3.7 RMB to the U.S. dollar, the minimum levy is $1.35 per square meter, 12 cents per square foot, and $5,500 per acre. The maximum is $5.40 per square meter, 50 cents per square foot, and $22,000 per acre.

Also, in March 1988, China began to sell land rights to foreigners who want to buy long-term leases to develop sites. Although the land continues to belong to the state, lease-buyers can sell their land rights, if they wish, or use them as collateral for loans. This permission by the government is a historic reversal of a forty-year-old policy: when the Communists gained control of China in 1949 they declared an end to foreign ownership of Chinese property. However, not many foreigners are expected to become purchasers because the site-use fees are so low they see no need to lay out the money for land rights, especially as the prices are expected to be extremely high.

5. *Board representation.* The following observations apply particularly to ventures in China, where the foreign partner insists on equality even though it is the minority owner, because it wishes to be truly in control of the venture. The Chinese agree because of their need for up-to-date technology.

In joint ventures in China, each partner has an equal number of members on the board, with the chairman from one side and the vice (or deputy) chairman, who doubles as president, from the other. Usually, the foreign side supplies the first deputy chairman and the Chinese, the chairman, with rotation every three or four years sometimes spelled out. Some boards meet quarterly, others semiannually.

The board is assigned ultimate authority over the hiring and firing of workers. Some ventures do not specify the number of employees, so as to allow maneuvering room against attempts to overload the project with surplus staff. Other contracts deliberately specify the maximum; these workers are then spread over two or three shifts.

The provision that the venture can fire workers is a new concession for China, which hitherto operated on the "iron rice bowl" principle—lifetime employment for industrial and commercial workers whether they worked hard, played cards, or slept on company time. Most ventures also offer an incentive plan that rewards total staff rather than individual performance. In an effort to boost productivity, year-end bonuses are scaled to the percentage that profit exceeds projections. There also are penalties such as warnings and fines for substandard behavior. For example, serious warnings apply to lateness and sleeping on the job; fines are imposed for improper use of equipment, violation of safety rules, creation of scrap, damage to blueprints, and smoking in restricted areas.

6. *Labor allowances.* In China, joint venture contracts must include labor allowances. The following is a sample program with per-person levies in Chinese currency: soft drinks, 12 RMB per year; birth control pills, 2.5 RMB per month; family visitation, 0.5 RMB per month; hazardous or unpleasant work, 1.6 RMB per month; clothing allowance, 25 RMB per year; hygiene (baths and haircuts), 3 RMB per month; food, 5 RMB per month. Middle managers get a bicycle allowance of 18 RMB per year (a bike costs 200 RMB). Joint venture agreements should try to avoid providing subsidies toward housing for Chinese employees, a responsibility that the Chinese authorities seek to share with foreign partners.

Items that seem strange at first glance, such as birth control pills and hygiene allowances, reflect conditions in China. The pills are in line with China's population control program. The hygiene provisions are essential, since the dwellings of most workers lack plumbing, and toilets and showers are in communal bathhouses.

Annual vacation after one year is three days, with a bonus day if the venture's monthly targets are exceeded. A leave of absence for a honeymoon is five days, for maternity one hundred days, and for paternity one week. Some contracts agree to provide up to 200 RMB toward the higher education of an employee's child and an 80 percent study allowance for workers. At Gillette's razor blade joint venture, there is one more clause—two free disposable razors and ten free blades per quarter.

7. *Who pays expatriates' expenses.* Usually, the venture is responsible for their air fare, accommodation, and salaries. Sometimes the venture pays for food; in other cases, the parent company does. The expatriates' parent company pays for laundry and weekly telephone calls home plus extra ones for employees whose families live in danger zones. Gillette, for example, allowed one expatriate from Manila to make several calls to check on his family's safety during the turmoil after Philippine President Ferdinand Marcos was ousted. Head office also provides a video recorder and stacks of movie cassettes for evening relaxation.

Expatriates in China, where there is little entertainment on which to spend their salaries, have their paychecks sent to their families in the currencies of their native countries. Because they work in "hardship" zones, they receive two weeks' rest-and-recreation leave every two months, with air fare paid.

8. *Accounts.* These are kept both in English and in the partner's language. They include a profit-and-loss statement, inventory of assets, summary of the previous year's activities, and a proposal for the allocation of reserve funds and distribution of profit. Related cor-

respondence includes a translation in the partner's language.

9. *Dividends.* These are usually remitted in U.S. dollars even if the foreign partner is not from the United States because the U.S. dollar is the prevalent foreign currency. U.S. dollars rather than the local currency should be specified in places like China, where the government, concerned about low foreign exchange reserves, is reluctant for foreign currency to leave the country. Similarly, it should be stipulated that any repayment of loans plus interest should be in U.S. dollars, as should the buyout of the foreign partner in the event the venture terminates.

10. *Technical know-how.* The partner with the technical know-how pledges to supply blueprints, manuals, and factory management techniques in return for an annual royalty. In populous nations, such as China and India, where the initial mandate of the venture is to obtain market share rather than good profit margins, the royalty is often slightly below the standard charge.

    A key phrase is "latest technology," on which developing nations insist. This is where diplomacy comes into play—to balance this request against the equally urgent desire of the supplier not to lose its technological supremacy.

11. *Trademark protection.* This includes the reversion to the original owner of all trademark rights from the venture if the partnership dissolves.

12. *Sales force.* Whether a partner's sales force will be used or whether the venture will have its own should be stated in the contract. There is no consensus as to which approach is better. Usually, the venture is appointed the sole distributor for imports from the outside partner; in turn, that partner is the venture's international distributor.

13. *Export intentions.* The Chinese prohibit profit repatriation unless a venture has a foreign exchange balance.

Foreign exchange can only be earned through exports but if output is below international quality, ventures are thwarted in their export efforts. One solution is to include a clause in the contract permitting the venture to generate foreign exchange by acting as an export agent for other projects or for Chinese enterprises.

14. *Disputes and arbitration.* Disputes are first referred to the relevant body where the venture is located. The next recourse is the International Chamber of Commerce in Stockholm, which serves as a global arbitrator.

15. *Termination.* Should the partners choose to dissolve their arrangement, one side buys out the other. The purchaser must pay a preagreed proportion (30 percent is common) of the book value of the seller's initial investment plus an amount, to be negotiated, for good will.

Now that the preliminary considerations of starting joint ventures have been outlined, those with the Japanese and the Chinese—in which there is, and will continue to be, keen interest—are examined in detail.

# II

# Joint Ventures with the Japanese and Chinese

# 4  The Japanese as Partners

The United States and Japan—possessors of the world's most powerful economies and its fiercest commercial combatants—are the foremost partners in international joint ventures. Since 1985, more than six hundred joint ventures have been established between Japanese and U.S. companies.

A Japanese corporation has much to offer a Western partner. It brings a shared belief in the principles of capitalism as well as advanced technology and skills in quality control and productivity improvement. Japanese companies are familiar with such Western management techniques as management by objectives. Moreover, there are no foreign exchange problems because the yen is easily convertible.

However, common economic principles do not guarantee the success of a joint venture between Japanese and Western partners. Edwin Merner, director of the British-owned Schroders Investment Management (Japan) and a long-time resident of the country, observes: "The ventures often fail because their partners' purposes clash, with each side trying to get something out of the other and give as little as possible in return.

"The Japanese judge foreign companies only by their performance in Japan, not by their success at home. By contrast, the typical foreign company believes its domestic record means it will do well anywhere. But it doesn't always turn out like that, because what works in New York does not necessarily apply to Tokyo. Also, the venture often is doomed from the outset owing to poor management. Japanese firms tend to contribute second- or third-class staff, and foreign companies either do not send qualified people who understand Japan's cultural differences or, if such managers are sent, they stay for just a few years. All these factors contributed to the rapid collapse of many joint ventures in the 1970s between British and Japanese merchant banks."

Merner adds that the difficulties of comanaging a venture have prompted some U.S. corporations to steer clear of the arduous process of finding a joint venture partner in Japan. Southland Corporation, for instance, prefers to license the concept of its 7-11 convenience stores in return for a fat royalty.

On the other hand, McDonald's is so pleased with its Japanese partner that it assigned the partner management control of McDonald's restaurants in Japan.

Merner says it is a wise decision. "Other foreign fast-food chains failed because they did not adapt to the Japanese market. In the United States, most outlets are franchised and are in residential, drive-in, and business locations. By contrast, in Japan they are company-owned and are mostly in shopping and business districts. Also, as space is so expensive, they are smaller."

Although Westerners and the Japanese both believe in the profit motive, their thinking is not identical, a factor which must be taken into account in joint ventures to prevent their failure. "Joint ventures between Western and Eastern cultures are like interracial marriages," warns Yoshio Terasawa, executive vice president of Nomura Securities, with experience both in Japan and the United States. "Marriages even between members of the same race are not constantly peaceful and harmonious and interracial ones face even more difficulties. Unless the partners understand each other very well, tragedy can ensue."

The Japanese generally find Europeans have more empathy than Americans, says Terasawa. "Europeans tend to be more international-minded than Americans, who can be very provincial, feeling that everything in the United States is Number One," he says. "Europeans are more sophisticated. Their reaction is to think about why Japan does something, whereas the immediate response of Americans is that it is bad."

The principal philosophical difference between Japanese and American corporations is that the Japanese are not as concerned about short-term financial performance. "They will put up with losing propositions for five years because their bankers have deeper pockets than those in the United States," comments Thomas Yamakawa, a senior partner at Price, Waterhouse's New York office. "Japanese banks provide bigger loans to keep clients from turning to competitors. Also, companies do not worry as much as in the United States about quarterly performance, because there is less pressure from shareholders."

The conduct of Hughes Communications in the formation of Japan Communications Satellite Company (JCSat), its joint venture with Mitsui and Itoh, is a useful case study of the many ramifications that must be considered in putting together a joint venture with the Japanese. The process began with background research. "Before we started our talks with Mitsui and Itoh, I scavenged libraries for books on how to deal with the Japanese, as well as about their architecture and literature. I also spoke to friends who had worked in Japan," John Koehler, president of Hughes Communications, recalls. His main "tutor" was an executive at Hughes Aircraft International Services who had the unusual background of serving in both the Japanese Imperial Navy and the U.S. Army during World War II.

From his studies, Koehler learned such "superficial" things as how to be persistent in a low-keyed rather than a highly emotional way. He also mastered "the ceremonial stuff," such as who sits where. "The Japanese executive in charge sits farthest from the door, and the senior American next to him, with their staffs aligned alongside like sparrows on a telephone line. I usually sat beside the senior Japanese representative because I did most of the negotiating, but when somebody over me at Hughes joined us, I moved down a spot."

Proper comportment helps, but the attitude conveyed is crucial. "Most important," stresses Koehler, "is not to take negotiating positions, but rather to get across that you are working as a partner for the long term." Still, Koehler encountered some amusing and surprising deviations from textbook advice. While the Hughes team, anxious to be polite, was prepared to bow in Japanese style when greeting the Japanese negotiators, the Japanese, most of whom had spent time overseas, were just as eager to practice American customs and shake hands. Also, Koehler found, textbook statements that Japan does not use lawyers was not actually standard policy. "We started without a lawyer, and it was our Japanese partners who suggested that attorneys be called in early to make drafting of the contract easier."

JCSat marks the first time that rival Japanese trading companies have joined forces in a joint venture. The connection is also a coup because Japan's trading houses, conglomerates with vast arrays of holdings in nearly every industry, dominate the country's economy. Hughes and Itoh have had dealings since the 1950s. Mitsui, seeking to expand its telecommunications business, knocked on their door.

Akira Mizukami, executive managing director of Mitsui's information business and electronics group, says the alliance with Hughes and Itoh embodies Mitsui's liking for joint ventures and its desire to expand its telecommunications business. Mitsui is in fifty telecommunications-related joint ventures, mostly with other Japanese firms. The venture with Hughes and Itoh is by far the largest. "In 1984 [one year before Japan's telecommunications system was privatized], we realized the satellite age would come to Japan. So did the Americans. RCA, Ford, and Honeywell as well as Hughes were searching for Japanese partners," Mizukami says. "After careful study, we chose Hughes, because it was already the most active in Japan." Both Mitsui and Itoh regard JCSat as essential to their long-term strategies of shifting from reliance on iron, steel, machinery, and chemicals, all of which are stagnating, to information industries.

On the surface, it would seem that Hughes would be at a greater disadvantage with two partners rather than one. Two could gang up, or each of them could want its own way, thereby protracting discussions. But Hughes realized that a triumvirate was the only way to achieve equal power in view of the Japanese curtailment of foreign ownership of domestic telecommunications firms to a maximum of 33 percent. With one Japanese partner, Hughes would have been in the minority, with little say over how its technology was to be used. With the three-way split, Hughes owns 30 percent, Mitsui 30 percent, and Itoh 40 percent. As the largest shareholder, Itoh supplies the chairman, a titular position.

The president comes from Mitsui; he takes an active role, but the power is vested primarily in the managing director, who is from Hughes.

The obvious first choice for Hughes as a partner would have been Nippon Electric Company (NEC), Japan's leading telecommunications manufacturer. NEC and Hughes had done business together for thirty years. But, in this instance, Hughes considered NEC to be a threat, because it has the capability to be a competitor in satellite production. Mitsui and Itoh complement Hughes's technology expertise with their financing and marketing skills. Moreover, the combination "makes it clear JCSat is not wedded to just one trading company," explains Fred Judge, JCSat's managing director. "This distinction is vital, because to succeed we must have as customers the affiliates of all Japan's trading companies."

According to Mizukami, it was easy to put together the three-way venture, even though Mitsui and Itoh are in rival Japanese consortia to develop a new international telecommunications link for Japan. As he recalls, "Mitsui had no objection to the tie-up with Itoh." John Koehler of Hughes has a far different recollection. He grimaces as he reviews the delicate transactions conducted over sushi and sake to reduce the tension: "Itoh felt its longer association with us qualified it as the lead company; Mitsui, which is almost two centuries older, proudly regards itself as senior."

What helped ease the adversarial atmosphere was that JCSat evolved gradually rather than springing up overnight. The process began with a "trial marriage"—an initial agreement signed in September 1984 for a planning task force—which was followed by the establishment of a planning company in February 1985. The actual venture could not commence until the government had approved its license. The partners had everything in place "by 9:00 a.m., April 1, 1985," when approval was expected, but there was a two-month delay. Koehler says the existence of the schedule was the glue that held the venture together. "It generated a spirit of cooperation among all of us," he comments.

Joint venture negotiations with the Japanese must take into account what unions, as well as management, want, because approval of the unions is vital. In Japan, the workers are regarded as the true owners of a company rather than the shareholders, a view different from that in the United States. The Japanese consider shareholders of secondary importance, since they do none of the physical work and are fickle, selling their shares when they please.

"In the United States, companies are bought and sold with no real feeling for the workers, whereas in Japan an enormous amount of time is devoted to what will happen to the work force," says Albert Sieg, president of Kodak Japan. "There is great concern that if a foreign subsidiary or joint venture fails, the Americans will sell to someone else or withdraw. Only when agreement is reached about the workers is the Japanese side comfortable." He speaks from experience. Kodak's negotiations for the outright purchase of Kusuda took just one month, but its joint venture talks with Nagase stretched over seven months, three of which were devoted to ensuring the security of workers, whom Nagase was transferring to the new company.

Sieg dryly adds that the unions deliberately drag out the negotiations as "a courtesy" to the boss they are leaving: "In Japan harmony is more important than honesty, and the employees who are to be transferred do what is expected—they display shock and horror. After all, if they were to jump instantly to the joint venture, they would signal that they disliked their original employer." In the case of Kodak Nagase, once these formalities were over, the transfer was easy. Nagase had devoted a department to Kodak business, which merely had to be lifted out to become the joint venture. Sieg continues, "Employees in the long run really have no alternative but to move over, so their concern becomes negotiation of the best possible deal." Typically, workers are paid bonuses for joining the venture and guaranteed that their wages and benefits will be the same as at their former company.

When the Japanese go overseas, they are less enthusiastic about unions. In Japan, unions are organized on a company basis and therefore are docile. But in the United States, unions are organized by crafts or industries, with membership from many corporations, and they frequently engage in violent strikes. Moreover, the contracts of the many groups that make up the labor force at one company expire at different times, so that there is always the possibility of a series of walkouts. This diffuse organization is a difficult one on which to impose the Japanese team approach, in which there are few job categories, so that one worker can perform many kinds of tasks. Because they wish to transpose their system, the Japanese try to engage in joint ventures where unions are excluded. To avoid obstructionism over their methods, they frequently hire people without experience.

Just as American companies often find the process of tracking down the perfect mate in Japan daunting, the Japanese encounter similar problems when they are the suitors in America. Toshiba's efforts to locate a U.S. partner to make color picture tubes for television sets and color display tubes for computer terminals and office automation equipment serves as a good example. Toshiba regards joint development as the latest step in its evolution since World War II from being a purchaser of U.S. and other foreign technology to being a supplier.

"Immediately after the war, when a poor Japan required help from the United States and other developed countries, the grade of information required and sent was very raw," explains Kinichi Kadono, executive vice president of Toshiba's electronic components division. "As Japan grew richer and as technology progressed, two-way cooperation developed. Now Japan is in its third stage of postwar recovery—global expansion that necessitates many worldwide factory sites."

The United States was pinpointed as the best spot to make parts for television sets and computers because it is the world's largest market for these products. Kadono says that Toshiba ruled out 100 percent ownership of a U.S. plant because "it would not be welcome" in light of the fractious U.S.-Japan trade environment. Toshiba feared that since it already owned a color television facility in Tennessee, an additional foray into the U.S. market would arouse its principal U.S. rivals, RCA and North American Philips, to pressure Congress to impose protectionist measures against Toshiba.[1]

Kadono's hunt for a partner began at General Electric, but GE's insistence on a higher return on investment than Toshiba thought necessary caused the talks to collapse after eight months. Next, Kadono approached RCA Canada (now owned by Mitsubishi) on the premise that a Canadian base would be as good as one in the United States, especially since Toshiba wanted to sell in all of North America. "Because the United States and Canada are friendly neighbors, I mistakenly thought that there were no trade barriers between them," Kadono remarked. "Instead, I discovered that they are separated by steep customs duties and that color picture tube components would have to come anyway from a U.S. supplier."

1. In 1987, N.V. Philips upped its stake in North American Philips from 58 percent to 100 percent.

His last solicitation was at Westinghouse Electric. Westinghouse wanted to reenter the color tube business after closing its own facility eleven years earlier. But it was handicapped by a need to catch up on a decade of new technology in the field. Therefore, Kadono's overture was welcome. Because Westinghouse was in a weaker bargaining position, unlike GE it readily concurred with Toshiba's projection of a lower return on investment at the outset, since the initial emphasis would be on gaining market share. Their joint venture had a further significance: it emphasized their break with previous partners. General Electric had owned 10 percent of Toshiba for thirty years, and Westinghouse had been a large shareholder in Mitsubishi. Both these relationships had terminated some years earlier.

Located in New York State, in a former Westinghouse factory, the $100-million joint venture now ranks third in sales in the United States after RCA and Philips. Its name—Toshiba Westinghouse Electronics Corporation  stems from a compromise on the division of ownership. Toshiba wanted 51 percent, but Westinghouse insisted on 50 percent in return for the use of its name. The Solomonic solution: Toshiba has 50.1 percent, Westinghouse has 49.9 percent, and they share the billing.

The joint venture between Westerners and Japanese that is cited most frequently by other partnerships as a model is Yokogawa-Hewlett-Packard (YHP). Formed in 1963 by Hewlett-Packard and Yokogawa Electric Works (YEW), a major Japanese manufacturer of meters and other instrument control equipment, YHP, located in a Tokyo suburb, makes electronic measuring instruments. It has grown at a faster pace than all of HP, no small accomplishment considering HP's huge expansion in the past quarter century. In addition, it is one of only three joint ventures in Japan to have won the prestigious Deming Award. The Deming prize, established in 1951, is the most authoritative prize in Japan for quality control. It is named after W. Edwards Deming, an American who was invited in 1950 by the Union of Japanese Scientists and Engineers to teach them about his revolutionary concept of quality control, an idea that had received scant attention in the United States. Deming's theory is that better quality improves productivity and hence lowers prices, increases market share, and creates more jobs. YHP won the award in 1982.

It is impossible to guess from YHP's strength today that at one time its very survival was at stake because both partners, despite agreement on paper, were poles apart in their actual intentions. HP initially decided that it needed a direct presence in Japan to compete properly as Japan's economy became increasingly strong. HP also hoped that an on-site facility would curtail the copying activities of its Japanese competitors.

Although HP's preference was a wholly owned subsidiary similar to those it had in England and West Germany, Japanese limitations on foreign ownership precluded this approach. Instead of forming a joint venture, HP could have licensed a Japanese company to make HP products. This alternative was rejected because licensing only reaps modest royalties, whereas in joint ventures the profits are shared.

Despite the fact that Yokogawa Electric Works' electronic measuring instruments were a sideline, HP believed it would make an ideal partner: First, HP reasoned, despite its majority 51 percent ownership Yokogawa would not be an overbearing partner because it lacked technological superiority in this field. Second, HP assumed, YEW would not be reluctant to reassign its electronic instrument employees to the joint venture, since these workers formed but a small portion of the YEW labor force. Unfortunately, HP came to regret both assumptions: it became convinced that YEW took too much of a hands-off attitude and that it assigned far too many employees to the venture as a chance to get rid of surplus staff.

At the outset, though, these seeds of discontent were not apparent and the negotiations proceeded smoothly. Both sides agreed that HP's transfer of technology was of paramount importance. YEW was amenable to equal board representation for HP despite its smaller ownership. Furthermore, they concurred regarding which side would contribute what. Yokogawa's responsibilities were to be providing management and production personnel as well as instruments complementary to those HP was assigning to the venture. HP's obligations were to be primarily concentrated in technology, but in addition it was to hand over blueprints for existing products, train design engineers in the United States, and assist in the development of new equipment.

But beneath the surface amiability lay deep misinterpretations, or what Yokogawa's chairman termed "the cloud and arrow syndrome." As HP's chief negotiator later described the problem, "When HP thought Yokogawa-Hewlett-Packard management was agreeing with HP, in reality they were saying that HP did not fully understand Japanese business philosophy." In hindsight, HP realized its mistake had been to distance itself from YHP save for assigning one person, a production coordinator, whose role was purely advisory and who had no authority to speak for HP.

The first indication of problems arose when HP reviewed architectual plans for YHP's factory. HP felt it was far too big, based on productivity rates per square foot at HP plants. The building was scaled down in size, but what was glossed over at the time was that HP alone had protested. Its Japanese partner believed bigness was a sign of faith in YHP's success, but instead of saying so, expressed its opposition by taking a passive role during the dispute—"the cloud and arrow" syndrome. HP's pleasure at its victory also blinded it to the fact there was insufficient verification of sales forecasts. Had these been more thorough, it would have been obvious that the plant was still too large.

Because management responsibility had been assigned to Yokogawa personnel, HP "chose to ignore" the relatively large number of people transferred by Yokogawa, the purchase of far too many vehicles and expensive new tools, and time-consuming, costly duplication of paperwork by the use of both YEW and HP forms. Precise quantities for all these items were not specified in the contract, nor were they fully discussed before or after the agreement. The failure to pay attention to these vital details resulted in first-year losses, although HP had expected YHP would break even. Since acceptable reasons for the losses were cited, such as inexperience of personnel, one-time startup expenses, and sales below projections, HP was not unduly upset, especially as Yokogawa did not appear to be, and "after all, it had a management philosophy similar to HP's."

This deliberate disregard of the facts continued, and YHP's financial condition worsened. In 1965, it was so badly off that it had to apply for a $1-million bank loan. The bank's response caused HP to remove its blinkers. The bank stated that to survive YHP would require another loan within two years, and that it would not grant the $1-million loan unless both HP and Yokogawa signed guarantees. High debt ratios were common at that time, so Yokogawa was prepared to sign. But HP finally became as tough as if YHP were totally under its control and subject to its regular financial guidelines. It refused to sign unless action was first taken to ensure YHP's turnaround. It backed up its ultimatum by sending over a team of production, marketing, and accounting experts, who reported that YHP's overhead could kill it.

At that point, two years into the venture, HP calculated its four alternatives: to guarantee the loan and trust everything would work out; not to guarantee the loan, stop the flow of technology, and thereby squeeze the life out of YHP; to sell out; or to take over management control from Yokogawa. It settled on the last option because if YHP could be rescued, HP would achieve the objectives that had prompted it to seek the joint venture in the first place. Confronted with an HP decree that rather than sign the guarantee HP "would take whatever marbles were left and go home," Yokogawa acquiesced.

HP assigned manufacturing, marketing, and accounting "comanagers" to work with their Japanese counterparts. An American and a Japanese were appointed copresidents. Sales targets and employees were reduced to more realistic levels, with the surplus workers reluctantly reemployed by Yokogawa. Twenty percent of the equipment was sold and inventory controls implemented. Later, a training program was started at HP's Palo Alto, California, headquarters. The participants included YHP's Japanese copresident. Within a year the crackdown paid off as YHP posted its first profit. It now has one of the best productivity records of HP wholly owned or affiliated companies, and management has reverted to the Japanese.

In retrospect, HP and Yokogawa realized that the terms of their contract were based on the false assumption that their management philosophies were "basically alike." An analysis by HP concluded that there had been "no meeting of minds on the purpose, goals, and framework of the joint venture, without which it was impossible to set mutually acceptable limits. Joint ventures require compromise, but it is also essential that policies and limits be established *before* the questions arise. It took a full year of operation and some losses until these lessons were brought home."

The other problem, according to the analysis, was that "HP thought it had entered into a full-scale, two-way partnership with Yokogawa and counted on it to take an active interest in the venture, provide technology on a continuing basis, and above all, assist in its management. This did not occur." Indeed, Yokogawa came to regard YHP as an investment as well as a supplier and thus was willing to let HP increase its stake to 75 percent in 1983 on the joint venture's twentieth anniversary.

HP's experience is an object lesson about the limitations of joint venture contracts. Its report concludes: "In any joint venture the management philosophy, aims, and goals of the partners are of overwhelming importance. With parallel interests and clearly defined objectives and responsibilities existing between the partners, practically any joint venture agreement will be adequate. Without these, even the most detailed, carefully worked out, and elaborately phrased agreement is likely to fail."

Yokogawa-Hewlett-Packard illustrates how Western and Japanese partners can overcome seemingly irreconcilable differences even after the ink is dry on the contract. Another possibility is that a partner unsuitable for one firm can turn out to be an ideal match for another. For example, there are the differing reactions of two high-tech California firms—LAM Research Corporation and the much larger Varian Associates—to their separate joint ventures with Tokyo Electron Ltd. (TEL), a large independent Japanese electronics and semiconductor manufacturer. Varian is happy with TEL; LAM dissolved its partnership after three years.

Tokyo Electron is a pioneer among Japan's present generation of entrepreneurs. Because the chances for young Japanese managers vaulting to promotions over their age group are slight at large Japanese firms, where employees tend to advance in clusters, more and more young Japanese are now starting their own businesses rather than adhering to the tradition of lifetime commitment to an employer. But, in 1963, when TEL was launched by two former executives of Nissho Iwai Corporation, a large trading house, their boldness stood out. Cofounder and current chairman Thomas Kubo modeled TEL on the small venture companies created in the early 1960s by ex-employees of big computer manufacturers in the United States. Kubo witnessed this when he was on assignment to Nissho Iwai's New York office.

TEL started as a distributor of semiconductor components, then quickly branched into manufacturing, since, as Kubo explains, "market share cannot be gained through distribution alone." Joint ventures were designated as its vehicle for quick growth, with the game plan calling for the foreign partner to supply the technology, the venture to manufacture, and TEL to distribute. For U.S. partners, TEL sought firms that, like itself, had started small. Besides Varian, TEL has two other U.S. partners. Thermco Systems, now a division of Allegheny International, and TEL have coproduced furnaces for semiconductor production for more than twenty years. GenRad Corporation is a more recent associate, linking up for the manufacture of chip testers.

The three ventures account for one-fourth of TEL's revenue; nonetheless, it does not contemplate any further ones in the near future. The chief obstacle is the scarcity of competent managers. All three joint ventures are independently managed. "Good managers are 50 percent of why joint ventures succeed; unfortunately, there are few people around with a technical background and managerial experience who also speak English," Kubo declares.

TEL and its biggest partner, Varian, have much in common. Varian, whose high-tech products range from defense systems to wafer fabrication equipment for semiconductors, is a small company that grew. It began on a shoestring budget of $22,000. Today, its assets exceed $790 million. Varian, like many other U.S. electronics firms, rushed to form an alliance with a Japanese competitor as an alternative to being overrun as the Japanese seize an increasingly larger market share and leap ahead in certain technologies.

Large sums of money are at stake. By 1990, the electronics business is expected to be the world's fourth largest industry, up from ninth place in 1982. That is the good news for U.S. manufacturers. The bad news is that their share of high-technology trade has fallen to under 25 percent over the past twenty-five years. Some of the slippage was inevitable, since the United States was alone at first in the then infant industry. But much of the erosion is attributable to Japanese determination to overtake the United States as world leader in this field. While the U.S. proportion has declined, the Japanese share has tripled, and much of that increase has come from sales in the United States.

The normal response when an industry is under attack is for the government to impose protectionist barriers, which is what the Reagan administration did in 1987 against Japan's semiconductor manufacturers. But collaboration also makes for survival, and Japanese as well as U.S. firms have a powerful incentive to form joint ventures; together they can more readily afford the exorbitant cost of facilities. Over the last decade, the price for a 60,000-square-foot integrated circuit factory has soared from $6 million to $100 million. By 1994, this cost could be as high as $200 million.

It was in this environment that Varian and TEL joined forces in the mid-1970s. Varian executives had learned a painful lesson from Varian's unhappy joint venture with NEC. Varian believed that all NEC had wanted to do was to suck out Varian's technology, not sell Varian's equipment. "Our chief mistake was not

to have had control over what was done and how it was done,"
says Larry Hansen, executive vice president at Varian and president
of its semiconductor division.

Consequently, Varian moved slowly into the joint venture
with TEL, with which Varian's Japanese customers had acquainted
it. At first, Varian merely designated TEL as its distributor in
Japan instead of immediately transferring its technology as it had
with NEC. Three years later, in 1978, Varian, pleased with TEL's
performance and also under pressure from Japanese customers to
manufacture in Japan products tailored to Japanese needs, augmented its arrangement with TEL to a manufacturing joint venture. This time, though, Varian insisted on providing the chairman
(Hansen) and on his having the sole authority to decide what would
be done and how. He chose to give TEL-Varian a dual personality:
it makes some products from scratch and assembles others from
kits supplied by Varian. In both cases, TEL pays Varian a royalty.
Hansen runs TEL-Varian from Varian's Palo Alto headquarters,
although there is a constant flow of people and information between the two countries. The president of the venture, recruited
by TEL from a local firm that buys from TEL, is Japanese. Hansen
rejected on-site Varian management because of the high cost of
living in Japan, made higher by the strengthening of the yen against
the U.S. dollar. Hansen estimates that posting just one expatriate
in Tokyo would cost $400,000 per year.

By 1985, the seven-year-old TEL-Varian venture was a $50-
million business. But accompanying pride in this achievement
were regrets about the rapid growth, because it brought overex-
pansion and overhiring. When 1986 revenues, reflecting a worldwide slump in semiconductor sales, plunged to one-fifth of 1985's,
the boom was over. Suddenly, how to save TEL-Varian was the
pressing issue.

In the United States, the automatic response to a downturn
is layoffs. This custom is spreading to Japan, but there the preference is to retain people through bad times. TEL took back many
surplus employees, but the venture had to come up with a response
of its own. Its ingenious solution was the creation of a research
and development program in Japan to absorb engineers, thereby
ensuring they would still be around when an upturn occurred.
TEL-Varian's effort was not an expensive device to preserve jobs,
since engineering wages are lower in Japan than in the United
States. Also, new product development will offset the investment.

TEL-Varian also owes its survival to Varian's deep pockets. With close to $1 billion in sales, Varian could withstand the semiconductor industry's downturn. The much younger and smaller LAM Research Corporation could not.

When TEL and LAM first met in 1980 it looked like a mating between an elephant—TEL—and a flea—the newly born LAM. The two were introduced shortly after LAM's establishment by TEL's representative in the United States, Samuel Kano, who was impressed by David Lam's method of etching designs on semiconductor wafers. Kano suggested that TEL distribute LAM's products, but TEL hesitated for a year because Lam had yet to complete his work. Shortly after it began distribution for LAM, TEL suggested stepping up to a joint venture, maintaining that this would place LAM closer to its Japanese purchasers. LAM agreed, believing the connection would provide credibility and customer relationships that otherwise would take years to nurture. The venture flourished in its first years, 1983 and 1984. Unfortunately, the semiconductor industry then collapsed.

"When a venture makes money, everybody is happy; when it loses, the conflicts begin," Kano reflects. He became president of LAM's LRC Asia division in 1986 after leaving TEL and working briefly for a Japanese securities firm with which LAM dealt. "For a large company like TEL, with sales of $465 million in 1984, quarterly losses of $500,000 are nothing, but for a small, young company like LAM they are an enormous problem," Kano continues. After six months of red ink, LAM recommended employee layoffs, but its suggestion was regarded as "almost immoral" by the Japanese.

At the same time, LAM was angered by an alleged conflict of interest on TEL's part through its sales representation for companies making products similar to LAM's and by TEL's development of an etching process modified, Kano says, from LAM's system. TEL retorted that although the equipment bore a resemblance it was not identical. LAM then charged that TEL was splitting hairs.

The financial losses and the conflict over product lines compounded LAM's disenchantment with an on-site joint venture factory as the best way into Japan's market. "In our business, direct contact with customers is much more important because feedback from them is necessary for progress," Kano states. "We felt the information received from TEL was filtered, not because of deliberate concealment but because of the difficulty of expressing it in English."

The joint venture contract contained a clause permitting either side to withdraw, with sixty days' notice, should sales fall to a certain point. "A very low minimum was chosen, since it was assumed this would never happen—but it did," comments Kano. Termination was also possible if TEL were to sell identical equipment by a competitor or a similar line of its own; whether TEL was infringing in this respect depended on each partner's interpretation.

After its divorce from TEL, LAM was free to do what it deemed best for itself. What it wanted, now that it was familiar with the Japanese market, was to license its technology. Also, it only wished to grant TEL a short-term, five-year license for existing equipment and to reserve for itself arrangements about new machinery. Kano concedes that licensing is less lucrative than joint ventures, but, he says, LAM favors licensing because the problems of cross-arrangements do not exist. "Joint ventures must be managed carefully when the partners are from different cultural backgrounds," he notes.

Because it handles sales for its joint ventures, TEL was under fire from them as well as from their American parents. Its task was made more onerous because it also had to cope with internal problems arising from an incorrect reading of the severity of the semiconductor industry's problems. TEL's reliance on chips for 50 to 70 percent of its revenue backfired when the market plummeted in 1985 and 1986. Unfortunately for TEL, it had changed executives just before this critical time.

Kubo took early retirement in 1984, when semiconductor sales were setting records. Six months later the slump occurred. Kubo's successor chose to dismiss the decline as temporary and proceeded to expand output. His confidence was unfounded, and the impact on TEL was crushing. In just twelve months, its net income dropped from $30 million to $4 million. Finally, Kubo felt he had no alternative but to fire the man after twenty months in the position. Kubo's decision was not an easy one because senior executives in Japan are rarely fired.

Kubo returned to the presidency and he was able to take advantage of TEL's role as the sales arm for all its joint ventures in his turnaround strategy. For example, prior to the crisis, each salesperson had a car. Now there is a carpool, reducing TEL's fleet by one hundred vehicles. The upward spiral of the yen has helped, too, because it has inspired the joint venture partners to assign more research and development responsibilities to the joint ventures.

It is natural to prefer discussing successes rather than failures. One Japanese firm willing to be forthright about a joint venture failure is Mitsubishi Motors Corporation. Its unhappy experience involved a joint venture in Australia with Chrysler Corporation. After years of roller-coaster performance by the venture, Chrysler departed, leaving Mitsubishi with a lemon. Its predicament is an object lesson as to what can happen when a firm's visions of grandeur cloud its judgment.

At the outset, Mitsubishi tiptoed carefully into the relationship with Chrysler. Its initial involvement was supplying knock-down car and truck components, which Chrysler assembled and sold under its name. The arrangement began after Chrysler bought 15 percent of Mitsubishi Motors in September 1971. All went well until 1978, when Chrysler, awash in red ink, including $19 million in losses in Australia, beseeched Mitsubishi to purchase one-third of its Australian operations. Mitsubishi elected to overlook the losses and become a partner because it had stars in its eyes about Australia.

"The company wanted to be in Australia and was confident of a turnaround," says Kazuya Miki, who was assigned responsibility for the project at Mitsubishi Corporation, Mitsubishi Motors' parent company, after being its on-site manager. Mitsubishi's confidence was warranted: strong profits were made from 1979 until 1982. Thus, when Chrysler, desperate for funds as it struggled to survive, offered to sell its two-thirds share in 1980, Mitsubishi grabbed it.

Shortly afterward, Mitsubishi began to wonder if Chrysler was the real winner as losses, offset by occasional years of profit, multiplied. Mitsubishi reacted like a typical American company: it almost halved its labor force. Miki feels that layoffs are acceptable "under extraordinary circumstances" like those in Australia. However, the Australian Labor Government supported the opposition of the seven unions at the plant to the Japanese team approach and prevented Mitsubishi from implementing this cost-saving procedure.

Another recourse, importing cheap parts, was out of the question as the yen skyrocketed to twice the value of the Australian dollar. The Australian dollar is worth seventy cents U.S. Consequently, Australia's 15 percent ceiling on imported components was reached twice as fast. "The local content rules perhaps overprotect local suppliers inasmuch as they were making profits when all car manufacturers, buffeted by an overall industry downturn, had losses," Miki comments.

Fortunately for Mitsubishi, not all its deals Down Under worked out so badly. In New Zealand, it bought out a family-owned firm to which it had exported, secure in the knowledge that New Zealand has no local content regulations.

Despite the disintegration of some joint ventures between Japanese and foreign partners, and the hot rhetoric on both sides in various trade disputes, more joint ventures are inevitable because each side needs the other. "It's logical for them to get together as they complement one another," Price Waterhouse's Yamakawa remarks. "The outlook is bright for many more."

# 5 *The Chinese as Partners*

With one-fifth of the world's population and a pressing need for hotels, cars, hydroelectric power, telephones, elevators, computers, coal mines, food-processing plants, and so forth, China is a magnet for today's corporate Marco Polos. However, in their enthusiasm over tapping a market of 1 billion people, many among the first group of outsiders allowed high expectations to distort realistic appraisals. Their experiences provide valuable lessons for those planning to invest in China.

China is just starting to accept the concepts of private enterprise and profit on an extremely limited basis. Generally, Chinese companies are not advanced in technology, quality control, or productivity and are unfamiliar with Western management techniques. Moreover, the renminbi is not traded on the foreign exchange market. On the other hand, China has the attractions of a larger population to whom to sell, cheap labor, and generous government tax breaks to joint ventures.

As of November 1987, according to the China State Economic Commission, there were four thousand joint ventures in China. The commission reported that one-third of the ventures were making foreign exchange profits, one-third were profitable in terms of nonconvertible Chinese currency, and the remainder were losing money.

This chapter deals with the Chinese government's tax breaks and regulations, approval procedures regarding joint ventures, the lack of hard currency (U.S. dollars), the chief locales for ventures, and where to get advance guidance. Chapter 6 describes the joint venture experiences of a cross-section of companies representing all industrial sectors.

Perhaps the best advice for those hesitating to invest in China because of the horror stories about foreign exchange shortages, lackadaisical workers, and inadequate infrastructure comes from Tod Clare, who was in charge of American Motors' international operations when its China joint venture became a symbol of foreigners' discontent. In 1986, it shut down for seven weeks because of a lack of foreign exchange. The closure, and the international attention it attracted, prodded China to relax many of its rules applying to joint ventures.

Clare says that business conditions in China reflect the Chinese philosophical concept of yin—darkness and death—and yang—heat and life. He comments: "Which is the real China— the vast market ripe for the taking, or the morass? The answer is neither and both—yin and yang. China has tremendous potential for companies willing to make a long-term commitment, but it also is a country whose culture and bureaucracy guarantee frustration for any business person who hopes to set up shop quickly and start raking in revenues and profits as in the United States, Latin America, Europe, or even Japan."

The bad publicity, and a dramatic 47 percent drop in foreign investment in China in 1986, mask the fact that the yang is beginning to outweigh the yin. According to the National Council for U.S.-China Trade, 1986 looked terrible because 1985's results were skewed out of proportion by three $100-million-plus undertakings by U.S. firms—Occidental Petroleum's coal project; a natural gas pipeline by Atlantic Richfield Company; and a real estate complex in Shanghai by Atlanta developer Portman Properties. Normally, investments are under $10 million. Indeed, the council points out that, despite the detrimental press coverage,

U.S. equity joint venture investment in China almost doubled between 1985 and 1986, rising from $140 million to $263 million. According to the council, U.S. companies were involved in 190 joint ventures in China by the end of 1987.

Although it is the world's most populous country, China participates in just 2 percent of world trade. For China, joint ventures are a means to increase exports or to provide substitutes for imports. At first it welcomed foreign investment in the form of hotels and assembly plants, but now it also wants high-technology, energy, transportation, and communications projects that will contribute to its modernization and industrialization. To date, about 40 percent of joint venture investment is in hotel development and only 15 percent in heavy industry.

Chinese officials have made their position very clear, yet many foreign investors have chosen to ignore their statements. The foreigners' goal is to sell within China. They proceed with joint ventures, convinced that once in China they will be able to achieve their purpose by maintaining that the products manufactured are not good enough for the international market. The divergent aims of the Chinese and foreigners have engendered some of the bad press about joint ventures in China. So have protests over "bourgeois liberalism"—a catchall phrase for the adaptation of anything Western—despite Chinese government statements that they were isolated pockets of opposition.

China hopes its image will improve as the twenty-two incentives for foreign investment that it established in October 1986 settle into place and become better known abroad. The measures provide what initial outside investors said was essential for them to stay and for China to attract more foreigners: major tax breaks, management and foreign exchange concessions, and a reduction in red tape.

A specific timetable of three months now is in force for government approval of joint ventures; previously, the process consumed a year or more. Site-use fees cannot exceed 20 RMB per square meter; earlier there were no controls, and gouging of up to 500 RMB often occurred. Export and technologically advanced enterprises have been given priority in obtaining water, electricity, transportation, and communication facilities. The rates payable are to be on a par with those charged local state enterprises. Businesses exporting 70 percent or more of the value of their products are eligible for a 50 percent reduction in income taxes. For most joint ventures, this means they pay a 10 percent tax compared with the former 15 percent.

To assist joint ventures that are short of foreign exchange, the government allows swaps between the haves—hotels—and the have-nots. In their capacity as "bankers," the hotels charge a service fee. Their assessments are 4.65 RMB to 5 RMB to the U.S. dollar versus the regular rate of 3.72 RMB. In addition, the government exchanges currency when the need arises; it charges 3.72 RMB per U.S. dollar.

The management concessions grant joint ventures autonomy over wage levels, incentives, hiring, and firing, as in the West. Local work units, which used to drag their feet over transferring personnel whom joint ventures wished to hire, have been instructed to cooperate.

The October 1986 policies would not have been formulated without persistent grumbling on the part of many foreign investors. But much of the credit goes to American Motors Corporation, which deliberately threw a public temper tantrum to accomplish what months of quiet meetings and memoranda had not. When AMC roared, the Chinese government listened, because Beijing Jeep, the joint venture in which AMC became a partner in 1983 after four years of negotiations, had a high profile as the country's first automotive coproduction and one of its biggest joint venture projects. Whereas joint ventures normally are launched on $10 million or less, Beijing Jeep was capitalized at $51 million. AMC took a 31 percent stake with an option for 18 percent more. It invested $8 million in cash and another $8 million in technology. Its partner, Beijing Automotive Works, put in $35 million in capital, plant, and equipment.

AMC gambled on China because its four-wheel-drive Jeep is well suited for the country's poor roads. Eighty-five percent of the country's roads are ungraded and cannot handle all-weather traffic. AMC also was confident that China is poised on the threshold of a car-buying boom, and its optimism is backed by Chinese government forecasts. The China Automotive Industry Corporation has set a national goal of increasing annual car and truck production to 13 million by the year 2000, compared with the 250,000 the thirty-nine automotive factories now produce annually (equivalent to the annual output at one U.S. plant). AMC believed the surge in demand in China would compensate for a decline in the rate of growth in developed countries.

"Today there are fewer than three people for every automobile in the United States, Canada, Japan, and Western Europe," Tod Clare explains. "That means most future sales in these markets will be replacements for the current vehicle pool. It's a different story in the developing countries, however. These countries are the real growth markets of the future—the places where there will be the kind of growth we enjoyed in the industrialized countries during the 1950s and '60s. In India, there are more than four hundred people for every car; Indonesia, more than one hundred; Egypt, forty-eight; and Mexico, fifteen. These countries are all dwarfed by China, where there are more than eleven hundred. So, of course, we viewed China as an enormous market opportunity."

AMC's second strategic reason for wanting to be in China was to establish a major low-cost manufacturing base in the Far East, which would place AMC on a competitive footing in the region against Japan, South Korea, and Taiwan. Says Clare: "You can't hope to compete against them if you rely exclusively on U.S.-manufactured products, but you can if you manufacture and export from China, where labor and shipping costs are lower than Japan's. Notwithstanding fine quality and design, the Japanese have lost their competitive edge because their low-ball currency days are over. Now that it appears the yen:U.S. dollar rate of exchange will not backtrack much from the post-World War II record set in 1987, their day in the sun is over."

China's cost advantage permits Beijing Jeep to compete against the Japanese in the production of right-hand-drive vehicles, an area in which the Japanese, whose domestic cars have right-hand drive, normally would have the advantage over the Chinese, who usually manufacture left-hand-drive autos as U.S. car makers do. Because labor costs at Beijing Jeep are a modest thirty cents per hour, it can afford the extra tooling necessary to make right-hand-drive Cherokees for sale in southeast Asia as well as left-hand-drive ones for sale elsewhere.

The venture makes two Jeep models. From the beginning it manufactured the BJ 212, based on 1950s technology and using 100 percent Chinese parts. In September 1985, twenty-one months after the venture began, production was started on the Cherokee, similar in design to a vehicle of that name introduced in the United States in 1983 by AMC. Unfortunately, this vehicle, intended to enhance good will between the Chinese and U.S. partners, wound up instead as the cause of dissension and eventually precipitated the venture's shutdown.

In September 1985, each side believed the Cherokee was a further manifestation of their commitment to each other. AMC thought it was carrying out its pledge to provide state-of-the-art technology. It was the first time the Cherokee was to be produced outside the United States, even though AMC also had joint ventures in Venezuela and Egypt and coproduced Jeeps in Mexico with its then majority shareholder, Régie Nationale des Usines Renault. In addition to transferring the technology, AMC also contributed $6 million toward an assembly line for the Cherokee.

Beijing International Trust and Investment Corporation, an arm of the Beijing municipal government, confident that the Cherokee would bring in foreign exchange through sales within China in U.S. dollars, provided a loan of $8.5 million for the new equipment. The Chinese conception of the Cherokee's role was the root of the problem: whereas the BJ 212 was, and is, priced in Chinese renminbi, the Cherokee was cast in the role of foreign exchange earner and was priced only in U.S. dollars.

Unfortunately, the Cherokee's debut was ill timed. At the beginning of 1986, the Chinese government slashed its foreign exchange allocations to joint ventures because it was alarmed over a $4-billion drop in its foreign exchange reserves in 1985. China still had $11 billion in reserves, far more than most developing countries, but it wanted to stave off further erosion.

The curtailment stranded joint venture projects, such as the Cherokee, that depended on foreign exchange ("forex" or "FX" in local parlance) to pay for imported parts. Moreover, the alternative of obtaining forex from foreign residents in China did not materialize because they preferred to conserve their funds for other purposes. Most foreigners based in China travel in a company car or use the reasonably priced taxis. They saw no need to buy the Cherokee, especially since a 60 percent duty on imported parts is a major factor in the U.S. Beijing Jeep's Cherokee costing considerably more than its U.S. cousin. The Cherokee retails for about $11,000 in the United States; in China, it costs $19,000.[1]

By spring 1986, Beijing Jeep faced a dilemma. On the one hand, thanks to strong sales of the BJ 212, it was making healthy

---

1. Foreign cars generally fetch high prices in China. Signs posted by expatriates on the bulletin board in the supermarket at the Holiday Inn in Beijing advertise four-year-old Toyotas with 15,000 miles for $7,000.

profits. But this money was in renminbi and Chinese regulations prohibit profit repatriation by the foreign partner unless the joint venture has a positive forex balance. Beijing Jeep did not have excess forex because of the Cherokee's problems. Indeed, its foreign exchange reserves had run out, forcing president Donald St. Pierre, an AMC expatriate, to close down the venture. "I did it to save the venture," he explains. "I had no foreign exchange and was just about out of business."

The closure was accompanied by a battle in the media between AMC and the Chinese. In a well-orchestrated campaign, AMC was supported by press coverage of problems of other joint ventures as well as by harsh words from the U.S. Embassy in Beijing. AMC charged that most of the decline in China's foreign exchange reserves was due to the Chinese importing the very kind of consumer goods—television sets, refrigerators, and cars—they said they wanted to make internally through joint ventures. What particularly irritated AMC was that at the very time it was helping China develop its automobile industry, China bought 35,000 passenger cars from Japan.

The Chinese countercharged that three Japanese autos could be purchased for the price of one Cherokee. They also maintained that AMC was partly the architect of its own miseries and that its mistakes were representative of those made by many joint venture partners in China. Although its initial investment of $8 million substantially exceeded what most foreign partners contribute, the amount, according to the Chinese, was insufficient to justify AMC's forecast of 20,000 vehicles per year, half for export, by 1990.

As of mid-1987, Beijing Jeep produced nine cars per day, up from seven two years earlier. In late 1987, output doubled to eighteen per day. Since Chinese businesses operate nine hours per day, that amounts to two cars per hour. By contrast, a U.S. auto factory makes thirty to forty cars per hour.

Beijing Jeep typified the clashes between foreign and Chinese partners over the purpose of joint ventures. The Chinese felt AMC had reneged on the terms in their contract calling for joint design and production of a new Jeep. AMC did cooperate on the design of a prototype but suggested postponement of further work when the exhaust system, noise controls, and speed failed to meet international standards. Its conclusion is one drawn by many outsiders, dissatisfied with the quality of Chinese parts and

workmanship. While understandable, AMC's stand aroused sus-
picion among the Chinese as to AMC's sincerity. The resentment
on the part of the Chinese colored their reaction when the forex
crisis erupted.

Yet many foreigners, some of whom were on the brink of
pulling out because of forex shortages, were astonished that it was
St. Pierre who spoke out. Born in Canada, he has substantial Far
East experience, having been posted in Japan and Indonesia. Colleagues describe him as "quiet-spoken and non-bombastic." After
he shut down Beijing Jeep and made his concerns widely known
through interviews with influential U.S. and European newspapers, St. Pierre was congratulated by grateful joint venture managers at the hotel restaurants in Beijing where expatriates gather
for meals.

Beijing Jeep was back in business after AMC officials traveled
to Beijing for a showdown with Chinese officials. Together, they
thrashed out a compromise. For their part, the Chinese now allow
Beijing Jeep to swap renminbi for U.S. dollars with joint venture
hotels. The government and the venture also trade currency directly. In addition, a new payment system was implemented for
Chinese Cherokee buyers, most of whom are government agencies. Formerly, they paid entirely in renminbi. Now, they pay 60
percent of the price in U.S. dollars. Sales to the foreign community
are in U.S. dollars only, but St. Pierre says, these purchases account for only 7 percent of total Cherokee business. As a result,
the Cherokee is earning forex, making it possible for the American
parent—Chrysler since its takeover of AMC—to repatriate dividends averaging $150,000 per month.

In addition, the venture has launched an extensive program
to localize production of the Cherokee. However, while Tod Clare
at the outset predicted 80 percent Chinese content by 1990,
St. Pierre estimates 50–60 percent as being more realistic considering the slow development of a Chinese automotive parts industry
and the scarcity of joint ventures in this field.

Westerners and Japanese often are at odds on trade issues, but
regarding China they speak as one in voicing their frustrations
about the difficulty of doing business there. "The Chinese have
the short-term outlook of commercial merchants," reflects Yoshiaki Fujiwara, general manager, business promotion, corporation
planning division, at Mitsui. In 1985, Mitsui established a joint
venture company in Beijing for the leasing of textile, plastic, and

other industrial machinery. "When their forex reserves are up a bit they throw open their door, and when they are down they shut it," Fujiwara continues. Like many joint ventures, Mitsui's had a difficult time disciplining workers in the days before the October 1986 regulations allowing the dismissal of insubordinate employees. Fujiwara adds, "Titles did not carry power, and Chinese who were made managers were not accustomed to giving or enforcing orders."

The worst infraction that Fujiwara recalls as a result of worker insubordination involved a very important client who had traveled two thousand miles by train for an appointment at the venture. Train travel in China is arduous, and when the visitor arrived in Beijing he was exhausted. Fujiwara recalls: "The venture's driver had been told to pick up the client and take him to his hotel, but instead he went to a movie. Under the regulations existing then in China, we couldn't fire him but only cut his salary. We could have asked the local authorities for a replacement; however, there was a good chance he would have been worse."

Despite a strong campaign by the Chinese government to spread joint ventures along its coastline through preferential treatment, most foreign investors prefer to locate in the south, near the money markets of Hong Kong. About 45 percent of foreign projects are in the southern province of Guandong, the closest province to Hong Kong, and 15 percent are in Fujian Province, immediately to the north. The cities of Beijing, Shanghai, and Tianjin each have about 5 percent.

In China, the world's third largest country after the Soviet Union and Canada, much of the topography and climate is so harsh it discourages settlement. There are mountains in the west, semiarid steppes and barren deserts in the northwest, and rain forests in the tropical south, part of which are subject to monsoons. Northern China, including Beijing, is often swept by dust storms from the Gobi Desert and other dry northern terrain. Winter temperatures drop to zero Fahrenheit, and summer temperatures reach the nineties. In southern China, the temperature ranges from a moderate fifty to sixty-five degrees Fahrenheit in the winter to eighty to ninety in the summer. Outside of hotels, few places in China have air conditioning.

Each Chinese city offers a different deal to attract joint ventures. The general practice is to provide whole or partial tax exemptions for five years, and sometimes longer, for low-profit projects. About two dozen places along China's coast have even better arrangements. They are known as Special Economic Zones, the open cities, and the open coastal areas. In all cases, the preferential treatment is not automatic but must be requested.

In 1980, as part of its "opening to the outside world," China established four small Special Economic Zones (SEZs): in Shenzhen between Hong Kong and Guangzhou; Zhuhai near Macao; Shantou in the northeast of Guangdong Province; and Xiamen in the south of Fujian Province. Some are designated entirely as SEZs; only a portion of others is set aside. They seek to attract joint ventures through faster approvals and tax breaks. Whereas elsewhere in China local tax ceilings rarely exceed $5 million, in the SEZs the figure is $15–18 million for heavy industry, $10 million for light industry, and $30 million for nonindustrial enterprises such as hotels. Corporate taxation rates are 18 percent lower than the national levy. For projects capitalized at $5 million or more, there are tax holidays of up to five years. High-technology ventures are eligible for the maximum exemption; the service sector is exempt for the first profit-making year and receives a 50 percent reduction in the next two years.

The city of Shenzhen, situated northeast of Hong Kong's Kowloon Peninsula and southeast of Guangzhou, used to be the entry point into China for visitors coming from Hong Kong and heading for Guangzhou. Since 1978, direct train and plane routes have eliminated the stopover, but Shenzhen's proximity to Hong Kong made it an obvious candidate for SEZ status. One-sixth of the city, more than one hundred square miles, was declared a SEZ early in 1979. Since then, Shenzhen's population has swelled more than tenfold, to 300,000. Projects in the area include hotels, knitting mills, a glove factory, and expanded vegetable, fruit, livestock, and fish production. The port city of Shantou, population 700,000, is Guangdong's second largest city. It is at the center of a prefecture of eleven counties with a total population of 10 million.

Xiamen, population 480,000, is located off the South China coast on a forty-eight-square-mile island of the same name. It is connected to the mainland by a causeway. The most northerly of the four SEZs, Xiamen is well known for its fertile soil, in which tea and fruit are grown. In addition, it is a transportation hub for passenger boats from Hong Kong as well as for trains into China. The whole city was declared a SEZ. Zhuhai, population 138,000, is directly across from Macao and is one hundred miles southwest of Guangzhou. During the 1980s, the former farming community has been transformed into a tourist and industrial center as a result of its waterfront area being declared a SEZ in 1980. Its location has made Zhuhai an important supply base for nearby South China Sea offshore oil platforms. But it has lagged behind Shenzhen because it lacks a rail link to the interior.

In April 1984, following the successful test run of the SEZs, a similar program was started in fourteen more populous coastal cities as well as on Hainan Island in the South China Sea. Running from north to south, the cities designated as "economic and technical development zones" are Dalian, Qintuangdao, Tianjin, and Yantai on the Bahai Gulf; Qingdao, Lianyungang, Nantong, Shanghai, Ningbo, Wenzhou, and Fuzhou on the Yellow Sea; Guangzhou, Zhanjiang, and Beihai on the South China Sea. While the same principles apply to the "open cities" as to the SEZs, there are significant differences.

First, the SEZs are being developed from scratch, whereas in the open cities the emphasis is on modernization of existing facilities. The SEZs also offer more incentives. In these zones, foreigners can invest in everything from industry and heavy construction to agriculture and tourism, although the tax breaks vary. In the open cities, the stress is on infrastructure projects, improvement of factories, high technology, energy, and telecommunications. Hotels and other service-oriented enterprises do not receive any tax exemptions.

In the SEZs, local authorities can approve projects worth up to $30 million; the ceiling is $10 million in the open cities. In the SEZs, 100 percent tax exemptions prevail; in the open cities, only Fuzhou, Qingdao, and Tianjin offer as generous terms, and Tianjin's are only in force until 1990.

Not all the cities receive equal treatment from the government. In June 1985, fourteen months after it "opened" the cities, the State Council scaled down its commitment to concentrate on the four better equipped ones of Dalian, Tianjin, Shanghai, and Guangzhou. Yet the overall thrust remains. In another exhibition of yin and yang, the State Council opened more coastal areas while cutting back on the coastal cities. The new districts are the Yangtze River and Pearl River delta and a southeast portion of Fujian Province bounded by the cities of Xiamen, Quanzhou, and Changhou. The tax incentives are similar to those in the open cities. The emphasis in these areas is on agriculture, forestry, fishing, textile manufacturing, and food processing. Until the October 1986 proclamations, the tax rate, save for special exemptions, was 15 percent in the SEZs, open cities, and open coastal areas. It is now 10 percent.

Here are capsule descriptions of the open cities and Hainan Island. Dalian, population 4.6 million, China's third largest international port, is three hundred miles east of Beijing. It is called "the homeland of apples" because of the wide variety it produces. Heavy industries, including ships, diesel engines, chemicals, and blown glass, are on the outskirts.

Tianjin, population 8 million, is China's third largest city after Beijing and Shanghai. Situated eighty miles south of Beijing on the Hai River, the city is famous for its carpets and for the manufacture of two of China's most prestigious bicycle brands, the Flying Pigeon and the Red Flag. Many heavy industries are in the area, as are large coal mines and offshore oil fields. Grain and fruit are cultivated, too. Tianjin's dynamic 53-year-old mayor, Li Ruihan, a carpenter by trade, has traveled to the United States to drum up business.[2]

Since becoming mayor in 1983, Li's priorities have been to remove Tianjin's "three strange things": three generations of families still living in "temporary" shacks erected after an earthquake in 1976, drinking water "salty enough to make pickles in," and traffic jams. Under Li there has been a boom in residential and road construction, and water from a nearby river has been diverted to Tianjin, since the Hai River, while scenic, is polluted. A superhighway linking Tianjin with Beijing is under construction to replace the existing connection, a bumpy dirt road.

Yantai is a small former fishing hamlet with beaches, orchards, vineyards, and mineral resources. It was selected as a coastal city because 25 percent of China's gold is in the region, as is the country's largest molybdenum mine. Molybdenum, a heavy silver-white metallic substance, is used to harden steel.

Qingdao, population 1.4 million, is two hundred and fifty miles southeast of Beijing. Surrounded on three sides by the Yellow Sea, Qingdao is a major port. China's most popular export brand of beer, Tsingtao, is produced there. The brewery was established by Germans at the beginning of the twentieth century.

---

2. Chinese surnames, like Li, are placed first.

Lianyungang, population 3 million, lies between Qingdao and Shanghai. It is the least developed of the fourteen cities but is regarded as a gateway to China's interior because of its rail connections and deep-water harbor. It is the northernmost point of salt flats that extend for three hundred and fifty miles southward to the mouth of the Yangtze River, the world's longest river after the Amazon and the Nile. Salt processing accounts for one-fifth of its industrial activity.

Nantong, population 7.4 million, is on the north bank of the Yangtze sixty miles northwest of Shanghai. It has a deep-water harbor but lacks road and rail connections to the interior. The chief crop in the district is cotton.

Shanghai, population 11 million, is China's most populous city and largest port. It is the core of China's trade and industry and is foremost among the fourteen coastal cities in its push for modernization. The birthplace of the Chinese Communist party, Shanghai has considerable political clout; traditionally its residents occupy senior party positions. Before the Communist takeover of China in 1949, Shanghai was largely a commercial center. Forty years later, it accounts for one-eighth of China's gross national product and one-third of its exports. The emissions from its iron and steel, car, paper, and electrical equipment factories, petrochemical plants, and oil refineries contribute to a pervasive haze of pollution.

Ningbo, population 4.8 million, is at the midpoint of China's coastal sea lanes. For more than eight centuries it was the exit port for China's silk and porcelain. Today, the emphasis is on oil refining, electronics, and machine building.

Wenzhou, population 6 million, at one time was a major link in China's trade with Japan. It lost its influence to Ningbo and Nantong because of a lack of deep-water facilities and rail and road links to China's interior. Fallen on hard times, it owes its designation as an open city to its proximity to these two rival cities and also to shipping lanes connecting Japan and Korea with Hong Kong and Southeast Asia.

Fuzhou, population 1.6 million, is the capital of Fujian Province. During the April to September monsoon season, typhoons are fairly common. Fujian is known for cork sculptures and lacquerware, television assembly, and food processing.

Guangzhou (Canton), population 5.3 million, is the capital of Guangdong Province, and the leading industrial and foreign trade center in southern China. Its proximity to Hong Kong, one hundred and ten miles to the southwest, has made it the principal choice for investment by Hong Kong Chinese. The congestion and pollution are caused by sugar refining, chemical, automobile, textile, and fertilizer factories.

China business veterans say that the people of Guangzhou, Shanghai, and Beijing have distinctive personalities. Unfortunately, the Cantonese often make an unfavorable impression on foreigners. Peter Ptok, the outspoken president of Garnet Hotels of Toronto, maintains that "to them a contract is not sacrosanct and therefore can be rewritten or broken." Ptok has become familiar with the area as a wholesaler of room reservations for seventy-eight hotels in Asia and as partner in a joint venture hotel in Beijing. He comments: "The Shanghainese are master merchants who know every trick in the book—and some that are not—about negotiating, but they are more straightforward than the Cantonese. As for people in Beijing, it has been my experience that while they are not as outgoing as the Cantonese, you can go more by their word. I have found them straight as an arrow."

Zhanjiang, population 800,000, is the southernmost seaport on China's mainland, traditionally dependent on sugarcane, rubber, and coffee. Its proximity to both the South China Sea and the Gulf of Tonkin have made Zhanjiang a support base for nearby offshore oil exploration. It is also a way station en route to Hainan Island. The thirteen-thousand-square-mile island, population 5.8 million, is rich in natural resources: ebony, rosewood, bamboo, fifty types of minerals—most notably iron and titanium (used to toughen steel alloys)—hydroelectric power, rice, tobacco, and cotton. The Chinese want to develop the island as a tourist resort.

Beihai, population 168,000, is a two-thousand-year-old fishing town reputed to have five hundred species of fish. It also is a source of natural pearls. Because it has ten miles of beach, Beihai, like Hainan Island, has been singled out for tourist development.

Although not included in the government's incentive programs, Beijing, the capital of China, population 9.3 million, rates a brief sketch, too. Beijing officials can approve joint ventures valued up to $10 million. China's second largest city after Shanghai, Beijing is forty-five miles from the Great Wall, the single man-made object visible from outer space. As the political and administrative center of China, the city is home to more than one hundred and twenty foreign embassies and seventy-five news agencies. Although it does not offer the tax incentives that SEZs and coastal cities do, Beijing is a magnet for many large joint ventures, such as Beijing Jeep, due to its large population and ready access to senior government officials.

Because China opened its door only a decade ago, media coverage of business conditions there is often unflattering, and executives, normally at ease elsewhere in the world, are often perplexed as to how to begin. Tod Clare says that research about China's history and customs, as well as its current business practices, is essential for an appreciation of the Chinese style of negotiation. He points out that the long airplane flight from the United States to China provides plenty of time for reading. The flight from San Francisco to Beijing, including a one-hour stopover in Tokyo to change planes, takes fourteen hours. Each member of AMC's negotiating team consulted different books and experts and then shared the information they had gathered.

Advice is also available from the Washington-based National Council for U.S.-China Trade, which charges seventy-five dollars per hour, or a flat fee for more extensive help, for research, consulting, and matchmaking. The fee is lower for member corporations, which have already paid annual dues of twelve hundred dollars for firms with sales under $20 million, to seventy-five hundred dollars for those making $5 billion or more.

The council has a Beijing branch, which provides temporary secretarial services, receives telexes, and assists at meetings and negotiations. A supplementary source in Beijing is the Center for Market and Trade Development, a division of the Ministry of Foreign Economic Relations and Trade (MOFERT), the Chinese equivalent of the U.S. Department of Commerce. MOFERT has final say over approval or rejection of joint ventures. Its market and trade development division conducts market research, identifies potential partners, assists in negotiations, and prepares feasibility studies and other documents.

Some companies prefer to rely on the Chinese connections of their U.S. banks. General Foods, Gillette, and Nabisco turned to the China division of Chase Manhattan, one of the few U.S. banks with such a department. It was established in 1977 by the chairman at that time, David Rockefeller, nearly two years before formal U.S.-China ties were established. The Chase lined up four to eight prospective partners for these companies and provided a Chinese-speaking staff member for the exploratory trips. Subsequently, the Chase's representative office in Beijing acted as the intermediary in unresolved conflicts.

However, like other banks, the Chase found its China advisory business too costly to be profitable and scaled down its activities in 1987. Happily stepping into the breach are for-profit Chinese-American and Hong Kong counselors. An example given by the Chase, which has referred some clients, is TransCapital International of New York, headed by a well-connected husband and wife team of Chinese-born Americans, Albert and Virginia P'an. He is chairman, she is president. They charge a monthly retainer, with a usual minimum time of twelve to eighteen months, and a "success fee"—a percentage of revenue or a bonus. "We want clients whose goal is to be profitable, not those who, caught up in the excitement of something new, are going on a whim," Mrs. P'an says.

Albert P'an's two uncles, now deceased, were on the board of the Bank of China, one of China's four commercial banks and the one that controls China's foreign exchange.[3] P'an worked for W.R. Grace, Pepsico, and the New York Stock Exchange. Mrs. P'an's father was dean of the Jesuit-operated University of Nanking. She previously was a deputy manager at the New York Federal Reserve Board and a vice president in the banking division of American Express. George Waters, the retired president of American Express Travel Related Services, is on TransCapital's board.

According to Mrs. P'an, their background has made her and her husband "streetwise both about China and the United States," an advantage in helping Western clients adjust to the vastly different Chinese business environment. "Most American businesspeople who go to China are senior executives, accustomed to being in control, and in China they are disoriented, often finding it hard to get from the airport to their hotel," she says. "Also, we coach them on how to negotiate in China. Americans prefer to get straight to the point; the Chinese enjoy haggling. We instruct the Americans on how not to give away the store in Round One. In China, Round One is just the appetizer. Americans must learn that by waiting they will win in the end and close negotiations sooner."

Mrs. P'an cites the case of a Chicago confectionery manufacturer as an example of how TransCapital functions. Initially, she identified ten potential partners, visited each plant, took pho-

3. China's central bank is the People's Bank of China.

tographs, and interviewed management. After narrowing the list to three candidates, she told the confectionery company's executives that the time was ripe for them to go to China. "There was no point in their going earlier because all they would have done was attend banquets," she states. From this trip, a partner was chosen that met all of the Chicago firm's specifications: near-national distribution, several trademark brands known across China, and its own plant, thereby relieving the U.S. company of this cost. From investigation to final selection of a partner took eleven months. In the pioneer days of the early 1980s, this process often consumed three years.

When China opened its door in 1978–1979, it had no laws covering negotiations, contracts, and joint ventures. The drafting of these occurred as foreign investment flooded in, and the early arrivals were bewildered by the absence of ground rules. Gerry Gerwirtz, then vice president and general counsel of Otis Elevator, described negotiating and drafting a contract in China at that early time "as very similar to doing the same on the moon." Even now, Chinese laws are not as definitive as in the United States and Western Europe.

Because China has a state-planned economy, joint venture proposals must receive government approval in principle before the details are negotiated. There are three possible approval tiers, depending on the cost of the project. Generally, the local planning commission can give the green light for ventures valued at $5 million and under. Many projects are capitalized at this low level in order not to get entangled in the next two layers. The state planning commission has jurisdiction over projects worth up to $100 million, at which point the State Council, the country's supreme authority, takes over. There are exceptions, though: the Special Economic Zones, Shanghai, and Tianjin have authority up to $30 million.

Besides threading this bureaucratic labyrinth, joint ventures must endure even further examinations. Increasingly, MOFERT reviews all documents. It is keen on ventures that can earn foreign exchange through exports. In addition, joint ventures in which technical renovation of facilities will exceed $10 million must undergo appraisal by the China International Engineering Consulting Corporation. The corporation charges the venture for its work.

China experts caution that delicacy is vital at each stage because one misstep can shatter months of painstaking work. "It takes many people in China to recommend a deal, but just one person can kill it," warns Chase Manhattan vice president R. Barry Spaulding. "It is essential to remember that everything is the government and that at least three levels of bureaucrats are encountered—ministers, deputies, and functionaries. Also, regional government plays an important role and it is incorrect to assume that if the central ministry approves, the regional players will, too, and vice versa." The power struggle between central and provincial authorities peaked during the period 1979–1984, the very years that China began its campaign for outside investment. This made it difficult for the first group of foreign joint venture negotiators to determine whether the agency with which they were talking possessed ultimate decision-making authority. That problem has now dissipated substantially.

During preliminary negotiations, what the Chinese call a protocol and Americans term a letter of intent or memorandum of understanding is signed. Although it merely stands for good faith to meet further and is not binding, a decision not to proceed is regarded by the Chinese as dishonorable and a loss of face. For projects of $10 million or more, government authorities frequently insist on submission of a preliminary feasibility study as a prerequisite for consideration of the proposal. For the most part, manufacturing ventures must get this analysis approved before handing in their proposals, whereas service sector projects such as hotels can present both simultaneously. The report should contain estimates on output, revenue, and costs of production such as energy consumption and raw materials. The Chinese side is supposed to pay for this study.

Following this hurdle, a more detailed feasibility examination is requested. In this case, the bill is split. China veterans say novices should be certain that the wording allows for future flexibility in case operating costs rise. Otherwise, the Chinese may insist that the foreign partner adhere to the original figures even though changed circumstances make them unprofitable. According to the National Council for U.S.-China Trade, a thorough feasibility study covers a general description, market analysis, location, equipment, production plans, and material sourcing.

The general description includes the venture's administrative structure, how much each side is investing, and whether it is in the form of cash, technology, land, or equipment. Loan details must be outlined. The market analysis deals with projected domestic and foreign distribution, local and foreign competition, and past and current trends. Location refers to layout of the plant and required infrastructure improvements. Production plans entail startup and full capacity, quality control, cost of waste disposal, storage requirements, and environmental protection. Material sourcing encompasses parts plus the availability of power and other utility services.

On occasion, the feasibility study is followed by an "agreement" that summarizes the purpose of the venture but excludes the rights and obligations of the partners. Most joint ventures prefer to avoid this interim step and proceed directly to the contract. This document is based primarily on the feasibility study. At the height of the war of words in 1986 over foreigners' grievances about business conditions in China, the U.S. Embassy in Beijing drafted a model joint venture contract that addressed the Westerners' many concerns. The Chinese chose, accurately, to interpret the paper as a commentary, which they used as a guide in framing their October 1986 policies to make life easier for foreign investors.

Final approval of all joint ventures is under the aegis of MOFERT, or of its local branches if a project is within the applicable dollar amounts. In addition to the contract, MOFERT asks for the articles of association and the names of the board members. The Chinese partner must supply written approval from the local government department that has authority over the pertinent industry. The October 1986 regulations promised that the entire complex procedure would take no longer than three months. Within one month of final approval, the venture must apply for a business license at the local industry and commerce government office.

Hopefully, the October 1986 rules will speed up the time required to set up joint ventures in China, preventing recurrences of experiences like that of Otis Elevator, an early investor in China.

> *1978–1980.* Otis sent four teams of six to ten people to China to visit elevator factories. Preliminary discussions were held with possible partners in Shanghai, Beijing, and Tianjin, its ultimate choice.

> *1979.* China issued its first joint venture law following opening its door at the end of 1978 and the establishment of full diplomatic relations with the United States as of January 1979.

*March 1980.* Otis and the First Machinery Bureau of Tianjin, which has jurisdiction over Otis's eventual partner, Tianjin Elevator, started discussions. While their talks were under way, China's State Council, the country's highest government body, developed more joint venture laws pertaining to registration, contracts, loans, and the assignment of labor.

*October 1981.* Otis and the bureau signed a memorandum of understanding and announced that their goal was a joint venture.

*February 1982.* Otis and the bureau formed a two-year "interim" joint venture to perform a feasibility study regarding a manufacturing joint venture and to be Otis's exclusive distributor in China. China International Trade and Investment Corporation (CITIC), the nation's preeminent investment agency, was asked whether it would like to be a minority partner, as it frequently is in joint ventures. It agreed.

*May 1983.* The interim joint venture asked the China International Engineering Consulting Corporation to conduct the feasibility analysis. The agency can undertake such work as well as evaluate studies.

*February 1984.* Otis, the bureau, and CITIC signed a joint venture agreement and took equity positions in Tianjin Elevator's existing operation. Tianjin Elevator was allocated 65 percent, Otis 30 percent, and CITIC 5 percent.

*July 1984.* A thirty-year contract was signed, with provision for renewal. Capitalization was kept to $5 million so that the local planning commission could approve the venture. A bigger commitment would have entailed approval by state, and possibly central government, authorities. Since 1984, Tianjin's authorization level has expanded to $30 million. Tianjin Elevator's contribution was in the form of buildings and equipment; Otis put in U.S. dollars; and CITIC, renminbi.

*December 1984.* China Tianjin Otis Elevator Company began operations six years after the initial discussions about its formation.

CITIC proudly displayed a picture of China Tianjin Otis Elevator's test tower in its 1986 annual report—but the tower turned out to be the wrong choice of symbol. According to William Mallett, general manager of the project, the tower, constructed by the People's Liberation Army and assigned to the venture, is unsuitable for tests because of inadequate power. Until the situation is remedied, Tianjin Otis will not pay for the tower.

The decision to include CITIC as a partner was also made by forty other joint ventures such as the An Tai Bao Mine, in which Occidental Petroleum is the foreign partner, and Guangzhou Peugeot Automobile Company. Yu Yan, vice president and chief engineer at CITIC, states that CITIC plans to double its participation in joint ventures by 1990. In 1986, CITIC and the city of Tianjin signed an agreement for CITIC to establish an industrial base in Tianjin, mainly through joint ventures. Sounding like a Western capitalist, Yu says CITIC's criteria for participation are "projected efficiency and rate of return."

Formed in 1979 with the status of a ministry and headquartered in Beijing's tallest office building (twenty-nine floors), CITIC engages in an eclectic group of activities besides joint ventures: real estate development, defense equipment trading, and finance. It is the most visible Chinese agency outside the country, with offices in New York, Tokyo, Paris, Frankfurt, Vancouver, Melbourne, and Hong Kong. It has substantial investments overseas, too. It owns portions of Cathay Pacific Airways of Hong Kong, the Ka Wah Bank, also of Hong Kong, Portland Aluminium Smelter in Australia, and Celgar Pulp Mill in Canada. Between 1984 and 1986, its assets quadrupled to 8 billion RMB.

CITIC has formed a joint venture merchant bank, China Investment and Finance, with the Royal Bank of Canada, the largest Canadian bank. The joint venture underwrites loans for projects in China and provides advice about joint venture opportunities. It is a competitor to one formed earlier by the Bank of China with First National Bank of Chicago and the Industrial Bank of Japan. The Royal's Alan Bowbyes says, "Getting together with CITIC was very important because it is a leading player both domestically and in overseas Chinese investments." Although more than one hundred foreign banks have representative offices in China, Bowbyes does not foresee many similar linkages. "The Chinese want mutual trust and are extremely selective. The Royal was accepted because its connection with China dates back more than thirty years, long before Canada's 1970 recognition of China," he says. The foundation was laid in 1953 when the bank's chairman visited China.

Although China officially forbids holding companies, CITIC has one (the BC Development Company) with Chicago-based BCI Holdings Corporation, the parent of the Beatrice family of food companies.[4] BC Development specializes in consumer products and claims that joint ventures gathering under its wing can benefit from China's now allowing currency swaps among foreign investors. Beatrice, as a manufacturer, might seem a peculiar partner for a financial joint venture, but China felt indebted because Beatrice was the first U.S. company, as well as the first foreign food firm, to participate in a joint manufacturing venture. Guang-mei Foods Company ("Guang" for its Guangzhou location, "mei" for America) was established in 1981 and makes soft drinks, ice cream, and snack foods.

The attraction of China's large market is luring foreign investors like nectar does bees. How some major corporations got launched in China, including lessons from their difficulties, is detailed in Chapter 6.

---

4. Beatrice brands include Tropicana fruit juice, Peter Pan peanut butter, and Orville Redenbacher's popcorn.

# 6   Some Case Histories of Joint Ventures in China

When Gerardo Rodriguez, vice president of international operations at Nabisco, gave samples of Nabisco soda crackers to workers at Yili Food Factory Company of Beijing, Nabisco's eventual partner, he was nonplussed by their reaction. The crackers were tasty, the workers said, but did the brown on top mean they had been lightly burned? Rodriguez assured them that Nabisco had spent millions of dollars to develop that toasted appearance! What about the chocolate exterior of Nabisco's popular Oreo cookies? he was then asked. Were they burned?

When Gillette demanded prime shelf space in Chinese stores, it expected arguments such as it encounters from North American supermarket owners. But the Chinese, unfamiliar with the concept, readily agreed.

When PPG Industries, the Pittsburgh glass manufacturer, picked a partner, it chose a shipping company. When Garnet Hotel Systems of Toronto wanted to impress the Chinese, it arranged for a visit at a West German IBM computer facility rather than for the customary banquet in China.

Clearly, forming joint ventures in China often involves the unusual. The novelty begins with the search for a potential partner. Firms that are confidently at ease in global expansion elsewhere often find themselves stumbling in China. The conventional resources of business directories, annual reports, and financial newspapers do not exist. Market research is in its infancy, and government statistics are considered unreliable. Moreover, China has set a ceiling on how many joint ventures it wants per industry and the maximum per district. Thus, foreign investors are under pressure to beat their competition in getting settled.

The accepted wisdom is that without *guanxi* (connections) outsiders have no chance of penetrating the Chinese bureaucracy. Yet some have managed with no *guanxi* other than the China Phone Book, found in most hotel bedrooms in that country. Rather than residential numbers, the directory lists the names of Chinese agencies in English and Chinese by city, industrial category, and telex number. The book is available at overseas Chinese government offices or from the publisher, the China Phone Book Company, G.P.O. Box 11581, Hong Kong. The most recent price was fifty dollars.

Some executives plan for joint ventures years in advance, others devote part of their vacations to scouting around. Two examples of well-connected companies are Occidental Petroleum and Hewlett-Packard, although they did not rely solely on *guanxi* but also did extensive preliminary spadework. Oxy's chairman and chief executive officer, Armand Hammer, is acquainted with many world leaders, including China's Deng Xiaoping. They were introduced when Deng visited the United States in December 1978, prior to the establishment of full diplomatic relations between the United States and China. Subsequently, Hammer met China's General Secretary and its Minister of Petroleum and Coal. In 1979, Hammer hired Richard Chen, a native of China who came to the United States in 1961 and worked at IBM and Western Electric, to develop a China department. The department has three people, including Chen, at Oxy's Los Angeles headquarters and another three in Beijing.

Hewlett-Packard's explorations began earlier, in 1972, when the China Machinery Import-Export Corporation (MACHIMPEX) invited William Doolittle, then international vice president, and

Lee Ting, then Far East manager, to explore business opportunities. Their visit was scheduled just months after President Richard Nixon's trip to China. Media coverage of Nixon's trip had been handled by a satellite station outfitted by Hughes Communications, a longtime HP customer. The Hughes technicians had taken along HP's new pocket calculators, which interested the Chinese and prompted the invitation.

Ting, who was born in China, moved in his boyhood to Brazil with his parents and finished his education in the United States. He joined HP in 1970. He was general manager in Taiwan and subsequently Far East manager before taking up his present position of international business development manager. In the latter two capacities he spearheaded HP's excursion into China. HP's *guanxi* impressed the Chinese. David Packard, cofounder and chairman, was well known internationally through his service under Nixon as deputy secretary of defense.

HP's combination of new technology and good connections sparked orders from the Chinese—until 1974, when internal turmoil wracked China. Following Deng's triumph in 1977 over the "Gang of Four" (Mao's widow and her three associates), Packard was invited to visit China. Immediately after the Carter administration announced normalization of relations with China in December 1978, Ting proposed that the firm be allowed to send technicians to Beijing to conduct five week-long seminars. The logistics were daunting. HP was the first foreign company to take technical know-how plus equipment to China. Because high-technology items were involved, a U.S. export license was required. It arrived just days before departure, and the visas from China's office in Washington came on the last day. As before, HP dispatched high-level officers. This time, the representatives were president John Young and executive vice president Dean Morton.[1]

Their trip occurred in June 1979. Two months later, the Chinese invited Packard to return. He was accompanied by Chining Liu, a native of China who by then had worked at HP thirteen years. He is now president of the joint venture, China Hewlett-Packard. Packard and Liu toured computer and integrated circuit factories. Packard reciprocated by inviting some Chinese he had met for a stay at his ranch. In 1980, HP launched negotiations to establish a representative sales office in Beijing, which was opened

1. HP's cofounder, William Hewlett, is vice chairman.

a year later. It was 100 percent owned by the China Electronics Import and Export Corporation (CEIEC), designated by the Chinese government as its official channel of cooperation. CEIEC, a foreign trade association within the Ministry of Electronics Industry, represents two thousand electronics enterprises in China.

Pleased with annual compounded growth of 60 to 70 percent, HP asked CEIEC in 1983 to alter the arrangement into a 50:50 manufacturing, marketing, and research and development joint venture. Formal agreement was reached in 1984. The next fourteen months were devoted to technology and product transfer, training of staff, and preparation of the necessary documents for government approval. The venture officially opened in June 1985, thirteen years after HP's initial overtures. HP officials say the careful cultivation netted good results. HP's is the first high-tech joint venture to which China granted multifunction status. "For high-technology enterprises to do well, all three functions must be integrated," Liu emphasizes. By the time the venture started, an experienced sales organization was in place. "The interim stage was very important because by the time the final venture emerged, one hundred people were trained who could work together," Liu adds.

China Hewlett-Packard (CHP) was the first joint venture allowed to recruit in Chinese colleges and to advertise in Chinese newspapers. Eighty-one percent of its employees are university graduates. They are young; their average age is twenty-eight. Liu points out that all these factors have already placed CHP on a par in sales with HP's operations in South Korea and Taiwan, even though it only assembles two HP products. The bulk of its revenue comes from distribution of items made elsewhere. Like other companies with business in China and Taiwan, HP has no intention of withdrawing from Taiwan and has not let the recognition dispute between the two countries interfere with its ties to either place.

Whereas Oxy and HP eased their way into China, Garnet Hotel Systems, a much smaller company, went from initial visit to contract for a Beijing hotel in eighteen months, a shorter period than customary in joint venture negotiations. Garnet executives had no contacts in China. During a holiday there, one of them flipped through the three-hundred-page China Phone Book and singled out CITIC as his target. His choice was fortunate because CITIC's mandate is to provide foreigners with a "one-stop shopping facility." To do so, it provides market data and lists of companies. A courtesy call was paid and then, as often happens, there was silence. Like many foreigners, Garnet executives assumed that they were at a dead end. Their assumption was incorrect; the Chinese were merely weighing their next step. It was not at all what Garnet expected, but it was typical—a test of the sincerity of Garnet's "friendship." The Chinese regard friendship as essential in their dealings.

Garnet president Peter Ptok recalls: "I received a telex from CITIC that one of its vice presidents would be visiting Siemens in Germany and while there would appreciate my arranging for him to visit IBM's facilities on a Saturday, his only free day." The request did have a peculiar logic: Ptok knows IBM executives through Garnet's use of computerized systems to wholesale reservations in Asia. Ptok telephoned IBM World Trade's chairman, an acquaintance, who agreed to arrange the visit. To further prove his friendship, Ptok flew to Germany and chauffeured the CITIC man from city to city, refraining from an outright sales pitch. "The trip was worth every penny because it obligated the Chinese," he explains—and he was right.

CITIC became Garnet's "godfather." It arranged for a driver to meet Ptok at Beijing's airport, contacted potential partners, provided a translator, handled preliminary negotiations, and shepherded Garnet through MOFERT against ninety-six competitors. Garnet's edge was that the son of the head of MOFERT worked for the CITIC vice president who was Garnet's direct contact. The deal was approved and the venture was incorporated within four months—very rapid for China. Of course, what helped was Garnet's canny choice of location next to the Cultural Palace of Nationalities. The Palace is an exhibition hall in honor of China's fifty-five nationalities and Garnet pledged that the decor and staff would reflect this diversity.

Whereas Garnet courted the Chinese, Gillette was pursued by them, but happenstance also played a role in its success. Early in 1979, MACHIMPEX, the agency that had earlier contacted Hewlett-Packard, told a British traveler to China that it had telexed Gillette requesting a quotation for razor blade production machinery but had not received a reply. The Britisher was kind enough to inform Gillette U.K. of the apparent Chinese interest, and that division then notified Gillette's world headquarters in Boston, which had no record of receiving the telex.

Shortly afterward, Gillette's then international affairs vice president contacted MACHIMPEX while he was accompanying the Boston Symphony Orchestra, of which Gillette is a sponsor, on a tour of China. He told the Chinese that Gillette never sells its proprietary, made-in-house equipment but that it was interested in exploring other ways of working together. During his visit, he toured China's four small razor blade factories as well as twenty plants potentially capable of making other Gillette items. Gillette's product range includes White Rain shampoo, Dry Idea deodorant, Paper Mate pens, Liquid Paper typewriter correction fluid, and Braun appliances. Ultimately, Gillette settled on razor blades for its joint venture because they are comparatively simple to make and were considered most suitable for China in its early stages of modernization.

Gillette preferred Shanghai as a site but quickly lost interest because the local manufacturer was only agreeable to spinning off part of its business. It wanted to retain the rest, and this would have made it a competitor to the joint venture. Also, the Chinese government was eager for Gillette to locate elsewhere, since Shanghai already had plenty of light industry. The Chinese never stated baldly that Gillette would not otherwise gain entry, but they did promote as a site Shenyang in northeast China, which at that time had no joint ventures. One hour by plane from Beijing, Shenyang is China's fourth largest city and its Pittsburgh.

The government wanted light industry, such as razor blades, to counterbalance Shenyang's concentration on heavy industry and steelmaking. Foreign investors were avoiding Shenyang because it is harshly cold in the winter and grittily dusty in the spring. Moreover, there is nothing of sightseeing interest nearby, nor much in the way of evening relaxation. The Chinese believed that if world-famous Gillette were to select Shenyang, other foreign investors would follow. This has been the case.

China's eagerness to establish this venture enabled Gillette to obtain several concessions that were difficult to get in those early days. Of most significance to Gillette is that although it shares ownership 50:50, the Chinese agreed that Gillette could make most of the operations decisions and run the venture—Shenmei Daily Use Products Company ("Shen" for Shenyang, "mei" for America)—"in Western style." This phrase is the code expression for differential pay according to skill and position, incentives for productivity, quality control, power to dismiss employees, and a ceiling on the number of workers assigned. The factory that Shenmei Daily Use Products took over had 260 employees. At that time, Chinese authorities still firmly espoused their theory of jobs for life, identical salaries, equality of workers, and respect for seniority. Gillette believed the factory had too many employees to be profitable. It insisted that the Chinese lay off personnel or there would be no deal. "We said we wanted the sixty best people and we got our way, because the Chinese are more interested in technology than preservation of jobs," says Rodney Mills, executive vice president, Gillette International. "When it comes to a choice, technology always wins." Shenmei's work force has since grown to 104 people, but that number covers three shifts and is enough to handle expansion in production, according to deputy general manager Kelvin Tam, a Gillette representative.

Other sweeteners were granted, too. The Chinese appointed top personnel to the project. The director of Hardware Bureau Number Two of the Ministry of Light Industry, the department with jurisdiction over Shenmei, was designated the project's initial chairman. Shenmei's materials manager had previously been general manager of the factory that Shenmei acquired. The controller had been a senior official in the Ministry's Shenyang office, and the personnel manager had been section chief at the Shenyang Municipal Daily Use Company.

Gillette also struck a fine bargain on accommodations for the four expatriates stationed in Shenyang. Most foreigners in China live at hotels and the Gillette people are no exception. However, they have their own building at the Shenyang Friendship Hotel. Designed as a house, it has seven bedrooms, a living room, a game room, and a kitchen. The rate is only double the cost of one bedroom in the nearby hotel. Moreover, Gillette's staff has fixed up the building in the style of a college dormitory. It is modest by American standards but vastly improved since Gillette moved in. New plumbing and air conditioning were installed; before that, mosquitoes had swarmed in through screenless open windows, necessitating netting over beds.

Through its capitulation with regard to location, Gillette manipulated unpalatable circumstances in its favor. Otis Elevator's experience is a modern version of the tortoise and the hare. Otis was beaten into China by its chief competitor, Schindler, because the Chinese with whom Otis was negotiating laid down unacceptable conditions, but through its refusal to be bullied, Otis wound up with the better deal. Also, since its investment of $1.5 million was far smaller than Schindler's $4 million, Otis recouped its money faster.

Unlike many foreign joint venture investors, Otis is not a newcomer to China. It began operations there in 1919 and remained until the Communist takeover in 1949. It is easy to understand why Otis wanted to return. First, its technology was superior to China's thirty-year-old machinery. Second, annual demand for elevators in China was forecast to climb from twenty-six hundred in 1980 to five thousand by 1985 and seven thousand by 1993. Although most office and apartment buildings are not allowed to install elevators unless they have six or more floors, the government is expected to have to permit high-rise construction because of China's housing shortage. China Tianjin Otis Elevator is confident it will have close to 30 percent of the market by 1993, compared with 18 percent in 1985, its first year of operation.

While enthusiastic about the potential, Otis also considered the disadvantages, chiefly the existence of 160 domestic elevator manufacturers. But it was unconcerned, because the market was fragmented and Otis's prospective partner, Tianjin Elevator Company, established in 1956, had a 16 percent market share. Until 1981 only the government apportioned elevators to buildings. From 1981 to 1983, manufacturers had carte blanche to sell to any buyers. Since 1984, the government has assigned 80 percent of the elevators produced and the companies sell the rest freely. Elevators are in such demand that high-priority buildings can wait for an installation for up to a year and low-priority structures for several years.

Eager to begin, Otis readily entered into negotiations with the first Chinese agency that approached it. Unfortunately, that agency, the state capital construction commission, did not represent China's entire elevator industry—for instance, factories in Shanghai and Tianjin, the two places of most interest to Otis. Shanghai was appealing because Otis had had a large business there before it left in 1949. Tianjin was attractive because its elevator company was successful, a prime consideration if the joint venture was to fare well.

Moreover, the commission tried to take advantage of the rivalry between Otis and Schindler, with which it was negotiating simultaneously. It pledged exclusive rights in China in return for a commitment to export $165 million worth of equipment in the venture's first decade. Apprehensive that the elevators might not be of international quality, Otis refused. When Schindler agreed, Otis believed it had wasted three years in useless discussions, but because of the rivalries within China, it soon learned its fears were groundless. In China, the competition between Shanghai and Beijing is outdone by that between them and Tianjin, and Tianjin had elected not to join the Schindler joint venture. Tianjin officials insisted that the central government revoke Schindler's exclusivity. Then they invited Otis to form a joint venture in their city.

That marked the conclusion of round one. The next round of problems arose from a power struggle between politicians and civil servants, which placed the venture in limbo. Once again, Otis reacted by playing tough. Its negotiators told Tianjin's vice mayor, a proponent of the project, that they would abandon the talks unless he brought to heel the "shadow bureaucracy." The vice mayor then took twenty men to a meeting with Otis, said that they were the shadow bureaucracy, and ordered them to cooperate. Ten days later the contract was signed.

Otis soon had more cause to celebrate. It found that Schindler's apparent advantage—factories in both Shanghai and Beijing—was actually a disadvantage. The contest for glory between the two cities dashed Schindler's hopes of allocating the entire production of different lines to achieve economies of scale. Stubborn about maintaining face, both factories asserted they wanted to make the same items. Moreover, a dissident group at the Shanghai factory formed a rival company. As yet, Otis has no joint venture competitor in Tianjin, whereas Schindler does in Shanghai. After rescinding Schindler's exclusivity, the central government admitted Japan's Mitsubishi Corporation, which formed an elevator joint venture in Shanghai, too. But, although China Tianjin Otis Elevator is the sole joint venture elevator manufacturer in Tianjin, Mitsubishi elevators were installed in the Hyatt Tianjin Hotel. This is one reason why Otis expatriates moved from the Hyatt to the Crystal Palace Hotel, run by Swissair, when that establishment opened in 1987: the Crystal Palace has Otis elevators.

As evidenced by Otis's ordeal, selecting the correct authority to approach in China is laborious, and even the most sophisticated firms can err. According to the National Council for U.S.-China Trade, the decisive factor is the product's end use. For instance, it advises, it may be best for an electronics manufacturer to deal with the building and machinery ministry instead of the electronics department if its potential customers are under the former's jurisdiction.

One firm that was detoured is Xerox. "Because the copier factory that initially approached us was under the purview of the shipbuilding department instead of the light industry ministry, we were assigned low priority," says James Shapiro, in charge of the company's Far East operations. "When we learned we were in the wrong church, we suspended negotiations in a friendly manner." Xerox's chairman then consulted a senior official at the People's Bank of China, who made no specific suggestions but provided a list of places to investigate. From this list Xerox selected China's leading copier manufacturer, located in Shanghai, where Xerox wanted to be because of the city's many parts manufacturers.

Food and beverage companies were among the earliest entrants into China. Four of the firms—Beatrice, Heinz, General Foods, and Pabst Brewing Company—are in the Guangzhou area. General Foods is in another joint venture in Tianjin, and Nabisco's project is in Beijing. Pabst is the first U.S. beer to be brewed in China, and the company employed a novel approach: whereas most foreign investors either build or renovate factories on site, Pabst dismantled two U.S. plants and shipped the parts to China for reconstruction. Charles Diodosio, Beatrice vice president, China development, still expresses exasperation when he recollects the difficulties in getting Guangmei launched. "It took two years to receive all the necessary approvals and to drain the swampland site," he says.

Nabisco undertook what Gerardo Rodriguez describes as a "dog and pony show" to locate a partner. Accompanied by another Nabisco executive and a Chinese-speaking representative from Nabisco's bank, the Chase Manhattan, Rodriguez conducted community meetings in Beijing, Shanghai, and Tianjin. He showed a film about Nabisco with a Chinese language sound track and distributed samples. He found the Chinese more receptive to the technical presentation than to the samples because they are not accustomed to "giving anything away free." Although the person Nabisco had hired to run the joint venture, a former executive of a Hong Kong food company, urged years of market research and distribution of samples, Rodriguez decided two years was long enough. "You can't test and research forever but must make a decision," he states.

Nabisco aligned itself with the Yili Food Factory Company because Yili already knew how to make biscuits American-style. That knowledge had been acquired from the donation of a bakery by the American Bakery Institute as well as from the training of some Yili employees by the institute. Because Chinese homes are small and lack room for storage, Nabisco judged it best to make biscuits that occupy little shelf space and require no refrigeration.

As its dowry, Yili offered Nabisco an old ceramics plant that it said could be converted into a factory and expanded, if necessary. Nabisco accepted on the condition that it not contain contaminants. Nabisco quickly learned that certain American facilities are not needed in China. "When I showed Yili's managers a model of the plant, they immediately pointed at a big square adjacent to the building and asked what it was. When I explained it was a parking lot, which all U.S. factories have, they said all they required were some bicycle racks," Rodriguez recalls. He also emphasizes that what is taken for granted in the United States should not be in China. "You cannot assume that you will get an empty field beside a highway, as at home, nor that there will be good roads and abundant power supplies," he warns. "None of these are readily available."

In North America, factory blueprints usually receive rapid zoning approval, but this is not true in China. Nabisco had to send structural engineers to prove to the China Design Bureau why certain restructuring and enlargements were necessary. The company was also startled by the casual Chinese attitude toward the state-of-the-art machinery they had insisted that Nabisco supply. "During construction of the plant, they did not place canvases over the window openings to protect the equipment when it rained," Rodriguez recalls.

Whereas Xerox, Gillette, Nabisco, and Hewlett-Packard formed joint ventures with logical partners—firms in the same industry—the logic of the match between the glassmaking company PPG and China Merchants Steam Navigation Company, an old shipping firm, is not so evident. However, the pair is really not an odd couple. Their association combined a powerful local agency desirous of a big foreign partner with a powerful foreign partner searching for an influential Chinese associate.

Established in the 1800s, China Merchants not only survived but thrived during the many political upheavals in China. It opened a Hong Kong branch and, best of all for foreigners, held substantial foreign exchange reserves. The Deng regime allocated responsibility for the development of Shekou, a small community in the Shenzhen Special Economic Zone, to China Merchants. Although Chinese authorities, impatient for modernization, believed China Merchants was too conservative, under its supervision Shekou grew in population from a mere fifteen hundred in 1979 to twenty-five thousand by 1983, the year it signed with PPG. As part of its mandate to be more aggressive, China Merchants decided to concentrate on products for buildings, like glass.

Meanwhile, gaining entry to China had assumed paramount importance in PPG's global strategy. As George Crossett, vice president, primary glass, explains, PPG already was well positioned in North America and Europe. It exported to the Far East but felt an on-site presence was essential to tap the market more fully. At the same time, PPG was nervous about joint ventures because it had not engaged in any. Evidently, it has grown to like them: in addition to its China venture, it now has joint ventures in Taiwan, where it is building that country's largest chlorine-caustic soda plant, and in Korea. The Korean project indirectly links PPG and General Motors through their respective joint ventures. The PPG venture makes automotive coatings for Daewoo Motor Company, a GM associate that produces cars for GM to sell worldwide.

Through a process of elimination, PPG selected China as the best entry point into Asia. "The rest of the Pacific Rim—Korea, Taiwan, Japan, Thailand, and Australia—had high-quality manufacturing facilities," Crossett says. "If we were to build a plant in Japan, for example, it would be hard to do well against the keen competition. As for Hong Kong, it is strictly a distribution center." PPG concluded that China was ripe for such a plant. As management saw it, China would become a leading economy in much less time than the twenty-five years it had taken Japan to do so, because China's modernization is occurring in an era of much more advanced technology. Although China already had many glass plants, PPG felt that Chinese technology was outdated, leaving the market open for PPG's superior methods. Elsewhere in the Pacific Rim, PPG would have been up against equally advanced glassmakers.

Although PPG knew what it wanted, it endured considerable trial and error before it settled on China Merchants. The time span was much longer than anticipated. Because the glass plant would cost $80 million,[2] PPG desired a "soft landing" in a Special Economic Zone, with tax breaks and permission to hire and fire at will. It reached this conclusion after four years of fruitless trips to the interior of China. "Several proposals were made by local building material enterprises, but they all faded into the bureaucracy," Crossett remembers.

PPG's troubles were exacerbated by the construction of a joint venture plant in Shanghai by its chief competitor, Pilkington Brothers, the United Kingdom's largest glassmaker. Pilkington was proceeding nicely while PPG was still having trouble getting started. Finally, PPG concluded *guanxi* was the only answer. Its *guanxi* was a chance acquaintance—a Thai glass executive acquainted with China Merchants through its Hong Kong branch. But when he introduced the companies, PPG did not immediately perceive China Merchants as the solution.

PPG executives first investigated an alternative site near Guangzhou. However, they finally settled on Shekou, which, like Guangzhou, is in Guangdong Province. They were swayed by China Merchants' *guanxi*. In a country where it is a struggle to obtain even one bulldozer, China Merchants had rounded up many, as well as an able construction crew. Also, in contrast to China's generally poor infrastructure, China Merchants had developed power, sewage, and road facilities in Shekou.

A firm does not have to be large to prosper in China. Small firms can fare well also, as demonstrated by United Tire & Rubber Company of Toronto. Its annual sales are equivalent to two days' sales at Goodyear. To date, the major tire manufacturers—Goodyear, Uniroyal, Firestone, Michelin, Dunlop, and Pirelli—are not interested in exploring the China market because car and truck ownership is slight and automotive joint ventures there are only in their infancy. But United Tire took the opportunity to enlarge its international business in a noncompetitive environment.

Tire making is a capital-intensive industry. The minimum investment required for a small factory is $50 million, and United

---

2. Seventy percent was debt financed. First National Bank of Chicago was the lead bank, and seventeen others participated.

Tire's annual revenue is only slightly higher. Established in 1944, United Tire was a distributor for its first twenty-six years. From 1958 until 1971, it was the single Canadian distributor for Japan's Bridgestone Tire Company, taking on the assignment when it was still difficult to sell "made in Japan" products in North America. The two parted after a disagreement, and United Tire then branched into production of "off-the-road" tires, huge tires used on forestry, mining, and construction vehicles. Eventually, the firm had two small plants, one at its headquarters and another about sixty miles east.

But its manufacturing ambitions were a financial drain. Many years were devoted to in-house technology and design tests before a model was ready. By the time production problems were overcome, United Tire realized that it lacked the large amount of capital necessary for developing a world-class facility and that it would be unable to compete in the tough pricing rivalry that characterizes the tire industry. Furthermore, with sales stagnant in Canada's mature market, United Tire had excess capacity.

Another factor that made United Tire receptive to a joint venture was management's dissatisfaction with the lack of productivity at its plants. "We were torn between sharing the overall concern of Americans and Canadians that overseas joint ventures in effect export jobs and dissatisfaction with the performance of many workers," says vice president Robert Sherkin. "The tendency was to goof off fifteen minutes before coffee breaks. Moreover, coping with union rules regarding bumping was difficult. Bumping entails replacing a person who leaves with the employee next in line. There is a domino effect—as each person is promoted to a vacancy, he or she leaves again a position that likewise must be filled."

Thus, United Tire was a company desperate for a solution. When it did come, it was from an unexpected source—China. One day, Sherkin received a telephone call from the Toronto branch of a Hong Kong trading house, Trinity Development Company, which acts as a partnership broker between the Chinese and North Americans. The representative asked Sherkin a question that reflects China's urgent need to retool 40,000 factories that still use 1930s technology. "Would you like to sell a factory to the Chinese?" he inquired. In return, he said, Trinity would want a piece of the venture if it were consummated.

Sherkin's immediate reaction was, "This was just another weird and wonderful request that firms receive when they conduct international business." But he did not dismiss the idea, "because you can't win a race unless you run it." He requested a list of clients from the broker, and when they expressed satisfaction with its work, Sherkin told the firm to proceed. It identified prospects and roughed out a deal with Tianjin Rubber Industrial Company and Tianjin International Trust and Investment Company. Tianjin Rubber was a good choice because it controls twenty-five rubber companies. From these it suggested Tianjin Tire Company as a prospective partner, since two of its three factories made off-the-road tires. The third produced tires for trucks, cars, wagons, and carts.

The very problems that concerned United Tire—the cost of development, excess factory space, and fierce international competition—were precisely what made the firm of interest to the Chinese. They urgently needed tires for mining, forestry, and construction transport. They also wanted to reduce their dependence on imports from Japan, but not through joint ventures with Japanese firms or large Western multinationals. They feared these companies would refuse to export substantially because that would eat into their existing overseas sales. United Tire, by contrast, agreed to export half of production, although it stipulated this would not occur until the tires reached international standards.

Having lined up the Chinese side, the broker advised Robert Sherkin and his father, Charles, who is United Tire's president, that it was now the proper time for them to visit China. The Sherkins were introduced, Robert recalls, "to a tremendous number of people—key players and others from the political bureaucracy who monitored the proceedings. Initially, there were so many people we didn't know who the real decision makers were." The Sherkins stayed two weeks, during which time they signed a letter of intent to pursue negotiations. Thereupon, the Chinese visited the firm's factories and eventually bought the equipment of the plant that was sixty miles from Toronto. The $14-million assessment of the value of the machinery and technology was considered sufficient for United Tire to have a 20 percent equity interest. Subsequently, it closed the shell of the factory and consolidated operations at its headquarters.

Concluding the partnership took two years of difficult negotiations, which typify the physical and mental endurance tests foreign investors sometimes undergo in China. The Sherkins traveled to China four times, which was hard on their budget. The lowest round-trip fare from San Francisco is about thirteen hundred dollars (U.S.), and from Toronto to San Francisco, about four hundred dollars. Hotel rooms in China cost at least one hundred dollars per night. Although tipping is prohibited, the hotels have a 10 to 15 percent service charge, as do their restaurants. Meals are no cheaper than in North America. Robert Sherkin also had a memorable encounter with a taxi driver when he tried to arrange to go to Tianjin from Beijing by car, having missed the train. "The driver wanted to charge by the meter rather than a flat rate and to take a friend along for a free ride," he recalls.[3]

These were passing annoyances. What tried the Sherkins more was the ordeal of the negotiations. Sherkin remarks, "The Chinese never stop negotiating. They keep chipping away to wear you down. One tactic they employ is to say talks will take eleven days when you have allotted only five. They figure that by the end of the eleven days you will be so fatigued and concerned about the additional expense, your resolve will have weakened. The Chinese also establish overriding principles, and every time there is a hitch they maintain it contradicts the principles. In North America, negotiators only go to the mat over meaty issues. They are prepared to make concessions on small matters. But with the Chinese, every point, big or small, counts the same. Consequently, what takes six months to negotiate in North America can take three times as long in China."

Sherkin also discovered that a lawyer is persona non grata at negotiations. "No North American executive in his right mind would negotiate without a lawyer; indeed, the lawyer is the first person called when a deal is proposed," he says. "But the Chinese dislike lawyers. They focus more on the principle of working together for mutual benefit than on the printed word. Our lawyer prepared a contract for us to take over, but the Chinese said they preferred to work from their draft.

"They insist on adherence to certain clauses even if circumstances dictate a deviation. For example, we had said we would ship our equipment in one 'break' bulk lot. But when the time

---

3. Chinese taxi drivers often display the profit motive. I was charged two different flat rates to Beijing's airport. The third time, by the meter, was cheapest. Taxis are the prime method of transport for visitors. If prearranged, they will wait for however long your appointment takes, then return you to your starting point at one-and-a-half times the fare.

came, it was cheaper to send the smaller items by container and the big ones in bulk. The Chinese argued that we had stated there would only be one shipment; we replied that it was a single shipment being sent on two boats. They took a week to deliberate, then agreed, provided they did not have to pay more—which we had never suggested."

Other battle-scarred veterans of negotiations in China also have interesting observations and valuable advice. James Shapiro of Xerox says a common error of foreigners is to classify all Asians as homogeneous in their business conduct when in reality they are diverse. "The Chinese and Japanese are as different as the French and Germans, or as New Yorkers and Chicagoans," he says. "The Chinese are less reserved than the Japanese. They are very questioning and cautious, wanting everything proved. But this same 'show me' attitude is prevalent in the United States, too."

Shapiro further points out that outsiders should be aware that the variety of Communism in China is unlike that in the Soviet Union. Indeed, Chairman Deng has set China on a course toward Socialism. Shapiro says: "In China you can buy *The Wall Street Journal, Time,* and *Newsweek,* and travel freely to most cities. In Russia you often are convinced you are being tailed, and all the publications are Russian."

A Chinese proverb says, "A good beginning is half the success." Negotiating sessions in China, as elsewhere, commence with protocol etiquette. The chief negotiator is seated in a prominent position, and the flags of each side's country are placed on the table. Then the outline of the talks may deviate startlingly from the norm. Instead of immediately getting down to details, the foreign side often finds itself spending several days teaching the Chinese the meaning of various capitalist concepts, like profit and loss statements, targeted returns, and the formula for proceedings at directors' meetings. When the discussions finally begin, the Chinese do not follow the usual U.S. practice of discussing several points simultaneously in vociferous conversations; they prefer a more decorous item-by-item progression.

"You can't throw out three or four scenarios as you would at home because the Chinese are uncomfortable with this method," explains Roger Clough, director of licensing and export sales at PPG's glass division. He was PPG's chief negotiator for its Shekou plant. "The Chinese dislike taking the initiative. They also are reluctant to tell you something they believe you won't want to hear, as they don't wish to offend you."

To underline his message, Clough cites two analogies: "The difference between their approach and ours resembles the contrast between Chinese checkers, in which strategy is based on territorial moves, and chess, where individual pieces are shifted. Or they argue that the entire contents of a deal are altered once one item is eliminated, the same way that the appearance of a table is transformed when a cup is removed. They further maintain that once one item is rewritten, they are free to modify another one, put something else on the table, or change something to which they already agreed. It is at such times that I suggest people remember what we were advised: the three most important items are patience, patience, and patience."

Another critical ingredient is shrewdness, which both sides possess. Clough proudly cites PPG as a useful case history. "We negotiated the technology agreement, articles of association, by-laws, shareholding split, management, sales agreement, and feasibility study before we agreed to form the joint venture," he says. "We were certain that if we were to leave all these items to chance, we would have no negotiating clout. We signed our memorandum of understanding in 1979, the shareholding agreement in 1982, and the financial and technology terms in 1984.

"Ordinarily, feasibility studies are a prerequisite for government consideration of joint venture proposals. Because we were wary that the Chinese might use our material to shop around for another partner, we refused to conduct a feasibility study until the agreement was signed. Only then did we show our blueprints. Of course, we did tell them the general concepts in advance, but we never divulged specifics about the technology or construction methods."

One of the thornier issues is the Chinese insistence on matched salaries. They demand that, for each expatriate, one Chinese should receive the same amount of money. But foreigners see no reason why a Chinese should earn the $50,000-plus wage of an expatriate, since the Chinese person only receives a small portion of the stipend and the government absorbs the rest. The foreigners protest that equal payment for the Chinese employee is really a form of taxation.

Their claim is justified, because salaries are low in China. The average wage is 70–100 RMB ($19–$25) per month. It is said that even Chairman Deng earns under $150 per month. Still, thanks to government subsidies, the Chinese are not as badly off as it might seem. About 40 percent of their expenses, including housing, food, and medical care, are subsidized. A one-bedroom apartment costs 2 RMB per month, two-bedroom, 5 RMB, and three-bedroom, 10 RMB. Consequently, the Chinese have money to spare for discretionary purposes.

Foreign negotiators skirt the wage issue in several ways. Schindler recalled most of its expatriates rather than acquiesce. Some, like PPG, forestalled any conflict by negotiating a lump sum for management services. Hewlett-Packard arranged for expatriates' compensation as well as workers' wages, plant location, and sourcing of components to be excluded from its joint venture contract. That left China Hewlett-Packard's manager, Chi-ning Liu, free to do as he saw fit.

William Mallett, general manager of China Tianjin Otis Elevator, was particularly resourceful. When he assumed his position in June 1986, eighteen months after the venture's startup, he discovered that vice general manager Wang Yun Qi had yet to receive the salary increase from 275 to 700 RMB[4] per month promised him in 1984. The delay was due to objections by the First Machinery Bureau of Tianjin, which has jurisdiction over the project. The bureau argued that 700 RMB would be far in excess of Chairman Deng's stipend. It also reemphasized that China has rigid pay guidelines to make salaries equitable, regardless of whether a person is a waitress or a computer programmer. Rebuffed but uncowed, Mallett suggested that Wang be paid 350 RMB and that the other half be set aside in a credit union account for him to draw on. The bureau rejected this proposal, too. Finally, Mallett hit on incentive compensation, since the venture's contract permits bonuses.

The subject of sourcing of raw materials and components is also a cause for disagreement. The Chinese prefer purchases to be made in China, but foreigners remain skeptical about the extent to which China can supply goods of suitable quality at competitive prices. Thus, most joint venture contracts are vague on this matter. They state that the project will use local materials and parts "wherever feasible" but do not mention specific quantities. Otherwise, negotiations can bog down. "The Chinese say they can build the equipment, and the other side replies it is uneasy about how well

---

4. Income tax in China applies to 800 RMB and higher. The Chinese claim that only a handful of people make this amount.

the Chinese will do it, and this happens piece by piece," PPG's Clough says. "If your side is not careful, it can wind up nickeled and dimed over everything or, out of frustration, it may tell the Chinese to forget the whole deal because it refuses to accept the Chinese technology."

Sourcing locally is frequently a headache because parts are either out of stock or substandard. Dieu Eng Seng, the first Gillette expatriate appointed manager of Shenmei Daily Use Products, recalls the struggle he underwent to obtain simple bolts and valves.[5] When he insisted on top quality, he was told, "Because your project is under the light industry ministry, it is only entitled to Grade D ones." Perhaps Dieu should have expected this obstinacy. After all, he had had to appeal to Shenyang's mayor for approval to buy furniture because such a provision was not in Shenmei's contract.

Quiet and self-controlled, Dieu quelled his frustration by conducting Sunday Christian prayer meetings. He also is determined. "You must fight over everything like an icebreaker, even if to prevent being encased in ice necessitates educating fifty bureaucrats," he says. Finally, Dieu wound up speaking to the governor of the province in which Shenyang is located. "Imagine having to take up the time of the governor of a province with millions of people over a normally inconsequential matter of bolts and valves," he comments.

Next, there is the dilemma of how to balance foreign exchange needs. There is no official conversion rate between Chinese and other currencies but unofficially it is 3.7 RMB to the U.S. dollar. China is unique in having two forms of money in identical denominations. Normally, when one converts money in another country, one gets that nation's pounds, marks, or yen. China allows only Chinese to use its renminbi. Foreigners receive foreign exchange certificates that are the equivalent of renminbi. Taxi drivers sometimes fob off renminbi as change on greenhorn travelers. The unfortunate passengers then find that other Chinese refuse to accept the renminbi "because foreigners aren't supposed to have renminbi."

Expatriate managers familiar with this ploy have an effective counterstrategy. Most employ secretaries from Hong Kong. At a quick glance, the women resemble mainland Chinese, and they

5. Dieu is now regional general manager of Gillette's Asia-Pacific Group.

get rid of the unwelcome renminbi when they take a taxi. Joint ventures hoard their precious forex by arranging to pay the hotel bills of their staff in renminbi rather than in the foreign exchange certificates tourists must use.

Ventures that double as distributors for their foreign parent receive a commission in hard currency. Unfortunately they are squeezed between U.S. and Chinese regulations. Eighty percent of American goods must obtain an Individual Validity License from the U.S. government. Subsequently, the Chinese authorities must approve purchases involving expenditures of foreign currency. Clearance has become more difficult because of the clampdown on imports caused by China's concern over its shrinking foreign reserves and widening trade imbalance. All the red tape places the joint ventures in a ticklish spot. The Chinese want state-of-the-art goods, but by the time the licenses are received and the foreign currency approval obtained, two years often have elapsed. By then the product can be obsolete.

Some ventures have Chinese approval to make items strictly for export in order to generate forex. For example, Gillette designated Shenmei Daily Use Products as the Asian manufacturer of brushes for Gillette's Liquid Paper typewriter correction fluid. Shenmei ships the brushes to Gillette's Australian and Thai plants, which insert them in the containers that they produce. Additionally, Shenmei snaps together the heads and handles of Gillette's disposable razors for export to Thailand. The brushes and razors are an inexpensive way for Shenmei to earn forex. Only one machine and one operator are required to make the brushes and only one person to assemble the razors.

As vexing as the forex problem is the scarcity of renminbi, according to Yoshiaki Fujiwara of Mitsui. "Ever since the government devalued the renminbi from 2.79 to 3.7 per U.S. dollar in 1986, companies have been squeezed by shortages of both local and foreign currencies," he says. The tight money situation also affects Chinese managers of joint ventures when they travel abroad. If they are on their own, the government curtails their hotel expenditures to fifty dollars per night to prevent a drain of currency from China. Good hotels charge far more, so if the Chinese accompany Western expatriates, they are allowed extra to show they are equals.

Another danger to foreign investors, remarks Fujiwara, is that China lacks bankruptcy reorganization laws. "In theory, your mortgage is your guarantee, but there is no saying what will happen to you if you try to exercise it," he comments. Indeed, the foreign community is dubious about the strength of all China's commercial statutes, despite the government's constant issuing of new ones. "What China means must be inferred, because the content is vague," William Mallett of Otis notes. "Because the language in the Chinese version of a contract is more ambiguous than in the English one, it is important to include a clause that both the English and the Chinese translations are applicable."

Each side generally starts out not understanding the cultural differences that motivate the other, but a sense of humor can alleviate the tension. Like people everywhere, the Chinese enjoy a joke. They were amused when executives from Gillette wanted to use the company's Paper Mate ballpoint pen to sign documents. However, as China only accepts documents signed by fountain pen, they asked Gillette to forego its product loyalty. Nabisco's negotiators had a hearty laugh over the Chinese response to Nabisco's concern about whether their joint venture would be profitable. "That's no problem—just raise prices," said the new capitalists.

Nabisco encountered Chinese obduracy leavened by kindness. Their contract discussions were held in Tokyo (other negotiations often take place in Hong Kong), and when it came time to prepare the document in Chinese, the only typewriters available were from Taiwan. "To use these machines would have insulted the Chinese, and we feared we were roadblocked, all because of typewriters," Nabisco's William Seidler recalls. "But one of the women on the Chinese team came to the rescue. She volunteered to write out the contract in longhand."

The discussions are also hallmarked by hospitality. The foreign partner invites the Chinese to tour its facilities in Asia, back home, or both. In China, the two sides host each other, plus many local government officials, at fourteen-course banquets with many toasts in mao tai, the potent Chinese wine. At some groundbreaking ceremonies, the Chinese symbolically pour mao tai into the earth to drive out evil spirits.

"Wise foreign investors are flexible and forbearing," says Virginia P'an of TransCapital International. "American chief executives tend to be authoritative, autocratic, and in a haste to make a deal, whereas the Chinese have a longer perspective. I urge Americans to prepare their stew and then wait, because they will close the deal sooner and give away less than if they rush. Patience indicates to the Chinese that you are not a patsy."

Like the memory of the agony of a toothache, the pain of negotiations fades as time passes. Most firms portray their initial joint venture as a bridge into this emerging nation. Soon, as is the experience in eating Chinese food, they are hungry for more. The trouble is that the second time around is often as bad as the first. For example, Gillette would like to export chemicals and plastics employed in making razor blades at Shenmei. But the Shenyang bureaucracy is opposed, not because it disapproves of the concept but because Shenmei is under the jurisdiction of Hardware Bureau Number Two and the other products would be covered by another department. "Many bureaus compete with one another, or they don't know what the others are doing," Gillette's Rodney Mills comments.

In 1987, three years after its Tianjin joint venture was launched, Otis Elevator suggested that China Tianjin Otis Elevator embark on a joint venture in Suzhou (Soochow) in southern China. Travel literature describes Suzhou as the Venice of the East because of its many canals. Settled more than three thousand years ago, it was once a leading silk center. In principle, Chinese members of the Tianjin joint venture favored Otis's proposal. So did Tianjin's mayor—such expansion would raise his national profile.

However, Otis then encountered an unexpected stumbling block—the pride of the Tianjin Chinese. As Otis's original Chinese associates, they wanted to impress Suzhou with their primacy. They thought the best way to do this would be for Otis to charge Suzhou a higher royalty rate for its technology. Suzhou, on the other hand, wanted to pay less, and Otis was agreeable. It figured it could afford to levy a smaller fee at first in order to win the contract and gain access to another large segment of China's population. Then it would raise the rate. The bickering between the Chinese and the Americans over what was actually one-quarter of a percentage point difference stalled the negotiations for two years. The impasse finally was resolved when Otis offered China Tianjin Otis a portion of the royalty assessed Suzhou.

One final piece of advice from the China veterans: After the negotiations are settled, do not expect any special greeting. "Once you are partners, you are treated as casually by the Chinese as they treat one another," Nabisco's Rodriguez says.

# III

# Running the Venture

# 7 Living and Working Conditions

"Back to the Future"—the title of a popular science fiction movie—is the sardonic catchphrase that expatriates in China employ when they go on leave to their homes in the United States, Hong Kong, the United Kingdom, Europe, Japan, or Canada.

Planners of international joint ventures must take into account a host of factors besides the manufacturing process. On the personal side, the cost and availability of groceries and accommodation, and the quality of medical care, must be taken into consideration. On the business front, the availability and cost of office space, what language will be spoken, distribution and marketing, and the state of transportation, communications, and utilities must be weighed. While the emphasis in this chapter is on China and Japan, some reference is also made to India, which is gaining popularity as a locale for international joint ventures.

The car best symbolizes the gap between lifestyles in industrialized and developing countries. Most people in North America,

Japan, and Europe own a car. In developing countries, the car is a scarce commodity and expatriates must struggle to get one. In China, the effort assumes heroic proportions. For example, there was a long verbal battle between PPG and the Shekou bureaucracy over this matter.

Although Shekou has rapidly metamorphosed from a fishing hamlet into a city of broad streets, apartment buildings, schools, and hospitals, it still bears little resemblance to modern metropolises outside China. "It has a convenience store, of which the city is very proud and which it terms a supermarket, but unlike in the United States, there are no clothing or shoe stores where one can window-shop," George Crossett of PPG explains. "With a car, however, our people figured they at least could go for a short drive, perhaps to a scenic or historic attraction.

"We bought one car for our six expatriates and hired a Chinese driver. But he was not necessarily available when our people had time free. So the six of them applied to the local licensing agency for driver's licenses. 'Why do you want six licenses for one car?' they were asked. They had a very hard time explaining they might want to go out individually. Then their wives decided they, too, wanted licenses. That was too much for the Chinese and they said no."

In China the first two numbers on license plates denote the city where the plates were purchased. White plates indicate that permission is required from the local authorities to leave a province, while owners of red plates, including joint venture personnel, may do so without clearance. In Tianjin, a city of 8 million, only one hundred cars are registered. Thus, when China Tianjin Otis Elevator increased its fleet from five to eight cars, the Tianjin motor registry department dropped a bombshell. "You have too many cars, so we'll take three," the officials said. Since China is Communist, everything technically belongs to the state; thus government divisions can appropriate whatever they wish. Otis reacted by registering its cars through other authorities.

Most joint ventures buy imported air-conditioned Japanese minivans and automobiles, rather than cars made by the joint ventures in China—Beijing Jeep, Shanghai Volkswagen, and Guangzhou Peugeot. Otis has a mixture of cars from Japan and Shanghai Volkswagen. As expatriates are chauffeured around, the highest-ranking Chinese representative insists on equal treatment. At Gillette, the first Chinese manager caused an uproar when he demanded a Cadillac. "In China form often is more important than substance," remarks Dieu Eng Seng, Gillette's initial senior expatriate. Gillette overruled the Chinese person on the grounds that forex should not be spent in this way.

In North America, Japan, and Europe, car owners take for granted the abundance of dealerships, service centers, and gasoline stations. In China, gasoline stations are so scarce that tour guides point them out as sightseeing attractions. In large North American cities, no consumer knows how many gasoline stations there are. In Shenyang, a city of 4 million, the precise count—twenty—is cited. Because stations are so few and far apart, taxi drivers tend to switch off their car engines at traffic lights to conserve gas.

As for dealerships, Donald St. Pierre, president of Beijing Jeep, wryly says, "There will be no dealerships in China in my lifetime and probably not in my son's either." A few service centers do exist. Beijing Jeep has appointed fourteen as its representatives. But, says St. Pierre, "service, generally speaking, is a big problem in China—there is virtually none and they do not really care that there is none." Foreigners rely on the mechanic at their country's embassy for repairs.

Appalled by the high cost of overseas postings, most foreign companies do not assign more than half a dozen staff to a joint venture, usually one per specialty, such as production or quality control. In Japan, because of the swollen value of the yen, the U.S. dollar can only buy half what it did a few years ago. Consequently, a high salary in U.S. dollars translates to barely a living wage in Japan. It is estimated that it costs $300,000 to $400,000 annually to keep one expatriate in Japan.

Houses in the Tokyo area sell for 100 million yen—about U.S. $725,000. Apartment rents are expensive, too—an average of $1,200 per month in Tokyo. Utility charges are about $140 per month. Meals at department stores are a bargain, at under $10 for lunch or dinner, but grocery store prices are far steeper than in the United States. Some shops charge $8 for a steak, $4 for a pint of strawberries.

The only consolation for expatriates is that they are in the same predicament as the average Japanese family of four, which on an annual income of $50,000 from salaries and bonuses also cannot afford to live in Japan. Although the Japanese boast of having the world's highest saving rate, most Japanese do not believe that by retirement at age 55 or 60 they will be able to put aside the 15 million yen—about $110,000—that the government says is the bare minimum for this period of their lives. Most Japanese, therefore, try to hoard some of their money by living in small apartments or houses. Almost one-third of the houses lack flush toilets.

Although China is poor, it is one of the most expensive places in the world in which to do business. The average annual cost of maintaining one expatriate there is $150,000 to $200,000. The price tag for five or six people often equals or surpasses the amount the foreign partner invested in the project. Office rent is extra, ranging from $25 to $50 per square meter per month. Because there are few office buildings, most foreigners rent a hotel room and convert it into an office. In Beijing, the fee runs from $50,000 annually at the older Beijing Hotel to $125,000 at the newer Great Wall Sheraton.

In Beijing, more than one hundred blue-chip corporate foreign tenants in the city's newest office tower (its twenty-three floors make it the second tallest in the city) have been caught in the middle in a dispute between the Chinese and Canadian owners of the building. The conflict delayed completion of the tower by six months in 1987, the tenants subsequently did not know to whom they should pay their rent. Earlier they had been enraged when the developers demanded a furniture rental fee even if tenants had their own furniture. The Chinese were so angry over the conflict that they removed the Canadian partner's name from the office tower in January 1988.

The crux of the dispute concerned what had been planned and what was actually constructed. According to the joint venture agreement, the Canadians—Reginald Noble and Josephine Chong of Toronto—were to finance and build a complex of offices, apartments, a hotel, and an exhibition center. Instead, only the office tower was built. Because the Chinese partner—an affiliate of the state science and technology commission—had been planning to pay for the tower's operating expenses with revenue derived from the rest of the complex, it was left with no source of money to fulfill this obligation. Consequently, the Canadians paid the operating bills.

The Canadian partners maintained that it did not make sense to proceed as originally planned because a glut of housing, office, and hotel space had occurred between 1980, when the agreement was signed, and 1987, when the first phase—the tower—opened. Noble and Chong contended it had taken excessive time to complete the tower, since they had had to deal with four Chinese organizations, each with different ideas. Also, they had had to pay for new housing for those displaced by the project as well as for a school and a nursery.

In "hardship" zones like China, expatriates are generally not posted for longer than two or three years. Because they work from 8 a.m. to 5 p.m. six days a week and go to bed by 9 or 10 p.m., expatriates have scant free time. Sundays are devoted to laundry and shopping (stores are open every day). The expatriates do not want more spare time, as there is little for them to do by way of diversion. Going for a walk is enervating because of the heavy pollution. Also, parks are scarce in China; where they do exist, they attract enormous crowds. Most expatriates try to live in hotels with individual kitchen facilities. Some hotels have installed tennis courts and bowling alleys.

Travelers' initial impressions of Chinese hotels categorized as first class are that they are no different from those at home. The lobbies are large and lavishly decorated. The main dining room serves continental European cuisine to the accompaniment of a classical or jazz pianist or a tuxedo-clad string quartet. Huge buffets with pancakes and croissants are laid out at breakfast. Club sandwiches and hamburgers are on the lunch menu. The bars serve martinis, gin and tonics, and diet soft drinks. The bedrooms are furnished Western-style and there are packages of bubble bath and shampoo in the bathrooms. American movies are shown free over each room's television set.

But closer inspection often reveals serious faults in construction and service. For instance, much criticism was directed at the $75-million, twenty-two-story, 1,004-room, glass-mirrored Great Wall Hotel in Beijing. Built in 1983, the hotel gained international attention the following year when President Ronald Reagan entertained Chinese leaders there. In 1985, Boston-based Sheraton Corporation beat two other U.S. chains—Holiday Corporation (which operates the nearby Lido) and Hilton Corporation—as well as two French ones to win the management contract. Previously, the Chinese had been in charge, drawing a chorus of complaints.

Sheraton inherited a hotel with a magnificent facade, an attractive atrium, and a problem-riddled interior. Corridor wallpaper was already peeling. Bathroom sinks became detached if people leaned on them while washing their hands. Water shortages made it impossible for a guest to shower if the person above was bathing. Electrical wiring was exposed in bedrooms. Because there was no computer reservations system, it was not unusual for guests' bookings to be lost. "When our worldwide network was installed, it recorded fifteen hundred bookings in its first hour of operation due to pent-up demand," says Joseph Cotter, executive vice president at Sheraton.

Sheraton worked hard to reconstruct the hotel. But the structural problems paled next to those concerning service. Cotter sighs as he recalls that front desk staff "brushed their hair in front of customers" and that chambermaids "did not know how to operate vacuum cleaners." Service in the restaurants was slow and brusque. To transform the place, Sheraton sent eighty hotel operations experts, including twenty from Sheraton, to start training programs in every department. Theirs was a massive assignment; the Great Wall Sheraton has sixteen hundred employees.

"It was a very painstaking process, requiring masters of repetition rather than volatile people with short fuses who could be set off by the frustration," Cotter remarks. "The burnout factor was high. The expatriates refused to stay longer than two-and-a-half years and needed frequent trips away from China to refresh themselves." Sheraton was powerless to dismiss local employees despite the severity of their misconduct. For example, when two cooks, one a Hong Kong expatriate and the other a Chinese, pulled knives on each other, the hotel's Sheraton-appointed manager fired both. But six months later he was forced by Beijing authorities to reinstate the local man. All he could do was demote the cook and lower his pay.

Sheraton endured all the difficulties because it gained concessions that it regarded as important to its future in China. It was the first international chain allowed to put its name on the hotel it operates. Also, the Great Wall Hotel was a staging ground for Sheraton's expansion throughout China. It opened the $70-million, 1,000-room Hua Ting Sheraton in Shanghai in July 1986, fifteen months after taking over management of the Beijing property. As in Beijing, it is the manager, not an owner, in keeping with its corporate philosophy for worldwide expansion. It now manages hotels under the Sheraton name in more than sixty countries. Next on Sheraton's China agenda is the historic city of Xi'an, which was the capital of eleven dynasties. Ultimately, Sheraton plans to operate eight to ten hotels in China.

Until the influx of American, European, Japanese, and Hong Kong chains, hotels in China were grim. Most were erected hastily by the Soviet Union in the 1950s and 1960s. They all bore the same name (Friendship Hotel), looked dingily alike, and had poor plumbing and cracked plaster. One expatriate who was enthusiastic about his new modern hotel, called his old former abode a hovel because it had split plaster and dirty windows that did not close in winter. When I later referred to the place as "modest," he emphatically corrected me: "It was a hovel."

Because of the living conditions, including an absence in most cities of English-language schools for their children, expatriates tend to leave their families at home. The wife of an expatriate factory manager who accompanied her husband at Shenmei Daily Use Products during his two-year assignment, says she cried for days because she felt so lonely and isolated. Then she instituted a daily routine: she taught the hotel kitchen staff to make soft-boiled, scrambled, and fried eggs; performed daily exercises; learned Mandarin, the official Chinese dialect, from a chambermaid; read; and baked treats for her husband and his colleagues.

The availability of good medical care is one of the first items checked out by foreign companies in determining where to locate their joint ventures. Gillette sent its company doctor to investigate the water purity and hospital facilities in Shenyang before proceeding with its negotiations. He deemed both adequate, and his opinion was borne out when an expatriate who suffered a heart attack was treated at the Shenyang hospital and recovered. Gillette's doctor also gave the expatriate team a copy of the American Medical Association's family health guide and a large supply of commonly required medicines.

Other firms keep an open plane ticket to Hong Kong for each expatriate, to be used in the event of a medical emergency. They also keep a supply of disposable needles. The needles originally were intended for allergy or insulin injections. Now they are also being used to comply with China's decree that foreigners be tested for AIDS (acquired immune deficiency syndrome).

The drivers hired by joint ventures perform several functions besides chauffeuring. They pick up customers and other guests from airports or train stations and purchase plane and rail tickets, a time-consuming process caused by long lines and small wickets. Many joint ventures hire secretaries from Hong Kong, whose language has many similarities to mainland China's. When the secretaries go home on vacation, they frequently purchase stationery supplies for their employers because of dissatisfaction with the quality of Chinese paper and printing. Fine paper requires latex content, and China's latex production is only now gearing up. Newsprint, however, does not use latex.

Customs officials are apt to levy a duty on imported computers and typewriters equivalent to the cost or to impound them for a month. Joint venture veterans say the problem generally vanishes after a few dinners for customs officials. Ingenious transformation of existing furnishings can be helpful. For example, one expatriate at China Tianjin Otis Elevator converted an old safe into a filing cabinet. Maintenance is another problem in view of the damage created by the oppressive atmospheric dust and the dearth of manufacturers' agents or repair shops to fix breakdowns.

Distribution and marketing in Asia and India differ radically from U.S. methods. In the United States, merchandise travels from the manufacturer, either through a wholesaler or directly, to the retailer. The system operates on a nationwide basis, and each link in the chain warehouses inventory at strategic regional locations. This method is rarely used in Asia or India.

Japan's manufacturers have gained international attention—and are being emulated—for their insistence that suppliers deliver parts "just-in-time," that is, the right quantity precisely on time at every step in the production process. In this way, the manufacturers require far less storage space than their U.S. counterparts. Each manufacturer also has its own family of suppliers, effecting greater reliability in delivery and closer supervision of quality control.

But Japan's distribution system is uncoordinated, convoluted, and rooted in age-old loyalties. Goods wind through at least four tiers. The bottleneck intensifies at the local level because distribution for a product has been controlled by one family in each community for centuries. This decentralization makes it difficult for foreign investors in Japan to break into the inner circle.

But it is not impossible. Fuji Xerox found that the solution was not to tackle the existing system but to form its own supply and distribution channels. To ensure a constant flow of business machine parts, Fuji Xerox purchased five manufacturers of components. Besides ensuring supplies, having one's own family of suppliers reduces costs, explains Yoichi Ogawa, managing director of the joint venture.

"In-house production is less expensive than purchases from outside vendors," he points out. "This is extremely important in our business because parts comprise 70 to 80 percent of the cost of our machines. Thus, if we can reduce the price of our parts, we can do the same with the final product."

In addition to having its own sales representatives, Fuji Xerox has built up a family of distributors through a web of twenty-six marketing joint ventures that it has spun throughout Japan. Xerox vice chairman William Glavin says these affiliates account for 40 percent of Fuji Xerox's sales. "Fuji Xerox could not have afforded the number of salespeople necessary to cover all of Japan," Glavin states.

Fuji Xerox's partners must meet three criteria: be powerful in their district, be in a different business, and have a range of customers from big to small. Sometimes the partner is in a related field. For example, the Tokyo associate is a book company, and the one in Kyoto deals in paper products. In other cases, there is no relation. For instance, Fuji Xerox's Osaka partner is Suntory Company, Japan's leading distiller. It was the best choice, Ogawa says, because "it is headquartered in Osaka and is a strong power in western Japan."

Fuji Xerox's situation today is much improved over that of its first ten years, 1962–1972, when it made an ill-judged attempt to transplant American sales methods into Japan. Xerox insisted that the infant joint venture lease rather than sell copiers, even though leasing was an unknown concept in Japan in the early 1960s. The Japanese considered it illogical to rent rather than buy smaller, cheaper copiers. Finally, Xerox took Japanese consumer preferences into account and permitted Fuji Xerox to follow an optional sales policy. Small copiers are now sold or leased; big ones have always been leased.

Another difference between U.S. and Japanese distributors, according to John Chappell of SmithKline Beckman, is that the Japanese settle outstanding bills more slowly. "There is no risk about not getting paid, but they do take close to six months, two to three times longer than what happens in the United States," he comments. "Consequently, there always is a significant amount of outstanding debt, and working capital is less than it otherwise would be. One recourse is to discount distributors' promissory notes at banks."

Breaking into a foreign market is a formidable challenge for a venture when the competitor is a powerful local monopoly that brooks no competition. The nine-year struggle, from 1977 until

1986, by a joint venture formed by Gillette to penetrate India's razor blade market testifies to how rough the fight can be. Gillette proceeded because India is the world's largest blade market, in unit terms. Moreover, through India's numerous bilateral trade agreements with East Bloc countries, Gillette obtained access to nations where it previously had sold spasmodically or not at all.

Although the Indira Gandhi government in the 1970s generally rejected foreign investment in consumer products, in this instance it encouraged Gillette as well as a competitor, Wilkinson Sword of England. The government's support reflected its determination to break the local razor blade monopoly, the House of Malhotra, whose dominance contravened the country's Anti-Monopolies and Restrictive Trading Practices Act. Established in the 1940s, Malhotra had an 85 percent market share in India by the 1970s. Its monopoly served to make it the world's second largest razor blade manufacturer in units sold. Gillette is the leader in volume and revenue. Malhotra, however, did not knuckle under to the government's pressure. Instead, it elected to fight Gillette through the courts and through efforts to prevent merchants from carrying Gillette's blades.

The episode began when House of Poddar Enterprises, an Indian family conglomerate with interests in tea plantations, steel mills, jute, textiles, and chemicals, approached Gillette about the possibility of a joint venture based in New Delhi. Because India limited foreign ownership to 40 percent after becoming independent in 1947, a joint venture was Gillette's only path into the country.

Reflecting on the troubles Gillette and Poddar suffered, Gillette's Rodney Mills points out with dry humor that the initials of the Indian firm's name spell HOPE. "As we underwent our many years of trying to get our product launched, we all agreed this was a most appropriate set of initials," he remarks. Poddar and Gillette each own 25 percent of the venture, called Indian Shaving Products Ltd.; the rest is publicly held, a common procedure in India.

Malhotra sought to stalemate Gillette through a series of court cases over Gillette's and Poddar's plans. Gillette and Poddar countersued. Eventually, they were embroiled in seven legal battles. The resulting media coverage delighted Gillette because the articles chastised Malhotra for irregular practices. "We got so much publicity that we used to joke with Poddar that we would never have to spend on advertising or public relations," Mills recalls.

Indian Shaving Products' inquiries about purchasing existing production facilities were blocked by Malhotra, which owned most of them. The government then stepped in and provided the venture with a site in a new industrial park. It also provided generous tax and investment incentives and arranged for power and electricity connections.

Indian Shaving Products avoided an immediate confrontation with Malhotra by first building up a base in areas where Malhotra was less strong. Because Malhotra is strongest in central India, Indian Shaving Products deemed it best to start distribution in northern India, then in southern India, and finally in central India. Also, to prevent a hostile reception toward its salespeople by merchants fearful of Malhotra's wrath, the venture began by piggybacking via Thomas Lipton's sales force. Lipton, entrenched in India for many years prior to Gillette's arrival, had extensive distribution contacts. Theoretically, the venture could continue to rely on Lipton but Mills says the venture's preference is to build an independent sales network which will also monitor new opportunities.

Although India is little more than half as large as the United States, distribution was not twice as easy. Actually, it was far harder. As a nation of small shops, India presents two problems to manufacturers: how to reach all the stores, and if that is accomplished, whether there will be ample shelf space for their products. Consequently, like Indian Shaving Products, most joint ventures concentrate on one region. The small size of the stores forces manufacturers to be inventive in their packaging. General Foods, for example, placed its Ju-C crystallized juice in narrow envelopes that could be affixed in strips from store ceilings in the manner of flypaper. "They don't occupy much space and are easy to see," John Manfredi says.

When a foreign company is not a joint venture partner, the Indian government treats it less enthusiastically, as American Motors discovered. In the 1960s, AMC began to sell Jeep technology under a licensing arrangement to Mahindra of Bombay, a large Indian car producer. The government permitted one renewal of the agreement but rejected a second one in the early 1980s, maintaining there was no reason why Mahindra should pay royalties ad infinitum. Also, the government reasoned that if, after twenty years, Mahindra had not mastered the technology, it probably never would.

AMC bowed to the government's logic, since it was permitted to retain its 8 percent investment in Mahindra. "The Jeep name is still kept before the public because Mahindra builds thirty-five thousand Jeeps annually," Tod Clare says. "That is a far better way of remaining known than building a new plant which could cost $300 million or more." With the exception of once-a-year discussions, Mahindra is on its own.

Joint ventures in China encounter the same problems in marketing as in India and Japan—small shops and complex distribution channels—plus poor transport, lack of warehouse facilities, substandard packaging materials, and intraprovincial rivalries that make it difficult to penetrate new markets. All these factors limit the scope of the ventures; consequently, they tend to cluster around China's populous cities, where they can reach consumers more readily.

One company that does cover most of the country with service representatives is China Hewlett-Packard, with the exceptions of hard-to-reach Tibet and its neighboring provinces of Xinjiang and Qinghai, as well as parts of Inner Mongolia. However, because of China's erratic airline schedules, CHP's contracts stipulate that its speed of response depends on the first available flight. Chinese and foreign travelers sarcastically refer to China's airline, the Civil Aviation Administration of China (CAAC) as "China's Airline Always Cancels" or "China's Awful Airline Corporation."[1] What makes matters even worse is that only one-way tickets are available within the country. Because the return ticket must be purchased at the other end, there is no assurance as to when one will get back to one's starting point.

Manufacturers must cope, too, with a complete reversal of the U.S. system in which suppliers deliver raw materials to manufacturers' plants. In the United States, the finished goods are sent from the plants to the principal warehouses of retailers, who then distribute the merchandise throughout their chains. In China, the manufacturers are responsible both for picking up components from suppliers and distributing to customers.

1. Unlike most airlines, where travelers can check in at any counter, CAAC designates one or more counters for all passengers headed for a certain destination.

Substandard packaging materials are a major concern for joint venture food manufacturers. Chinese glass bottles tend to shatter in high-speed production lines, and the cardboard for boxes is too weak. The ventures do not want to import materials because that would drain precious forex. But at the same time, they are anxious for their products to remain fresh over a long shelf life and for the wrapping to be attractive to gain customers' attention. When they can, the manufacturers use polypropylene laminations, which combine flexibility with strength.

Because few grocery stores have freezers, Guangmei Foods Company, the Beatrice joint venture, substitutes milk powder for fresh milk in its ice cream. There is no danger of the ice cream melting from lack of refrigeration. Instead of packaging it in cartons, Guangmei scoops it into cones or single-portion containers, which kiosk operators then load up on their bicycles and take to their stands.

Eastman Kodak, concerned that photographic chemicals produced in China do not match the purity of Kodak's in the United States, ruled out a joint venture in China. Nonetheless, Kodak wanted to be active in some way in China, to reach both the large domestic market and the many tourists. In 1984, Kodak sold equipment and technology to the Chinese for a color film plant in Xiamen in southern Fujian Province. The factory is the second largest undertaking in China by U.S. companies, next to Occidental Petroleum's coal mine. It is the first color film plant in China. China's plants make only black-and-white film.

Kodak officials say the technology it provided is of "excellent quality" but a "generation behind the state-of-the-art products manufactured in the West and Japan." Because the Chinese lack sufficient forex to import raw materials, local ones are being used that Kodak executives characterize as "not as consistently good as in the United States." Even in the United States, Kodak's quality control department examines one out of every two hundred rolls of film and shuts down production no matter how small a defect is detected.

The film can be contaminated without proper packaging, and finding that is difficult in China. "To prevent scratches of 35-mm film, it is threaded over a slim piece of velvet in the cassette, and we spent weeks trying to find appropriate material," says Richard Skow, general manager of Kodak's Asia-Pacific division. Kodak trains teams of Chinese at its Australian operations about raw materials management and inventory control. "We want to prevent slippage from the best to good enough," Skow emphasizes.

Although Kodak's name does not appear on the box of film, purchasers are aware of Kodak's involvement, Skow points out. "Most of the customers are government agencies, which know we provided the technology," he says. "Also, the big thrust in China is on updating technology, and whenever we send over technical news releases, they are printed verbatim by China's technical publications. At first, we gave away copies of the *National Geographic*. The pictures appealed to the Chinese yearning to take photographs and the text to their thirst for knowledge and desire to learn English."

For amateur photographers, imported Kodak color film is available under its brand name at hotels and government-run Friendship stores, which cater to tourists. Indeed, Kodacolor film and Coca-Cola were the first American consumer products to be sold in China after the country opened its market to outsiders in the late 1970s. However, the film's local circulation is hampered by its sale being restricted to people with forex. Also, Kodak faces stiff competition from Japan's Fuji Photo Film.

The current senior Gillette expatriate at Shenmei Daily Use Products, deputy general manager Kelvin Tam, learned about marketing through teaching. A lecturer on Western marketing methods at Shenyang's university, he has used the opportunity to query his students about China. One obvious difference is what constitutes a department store. In the United States, Europe, and Japan, a department store can occupy a square block, is many stories high, has a variety of merchandise, is well lit, has eye-catching displays, and has several restaurants. In China, the typical department store has one floor, often of uncovered stone, its lighting is dim, and the merchandise is stacked in glass cases. Displays are above eye level and therefore out of the line of vision. Also, there are no city, regional, or national chains.

Manufacturers and retailers do not advertise, set sales targets, or pay commissions. They must submit new packaging designs and price change proposals to the government for approval. They do not conduct sidewalk or telephone market research surveys. They wait for customers to come to them rather than drum up new business.

Gillette decided that Shenmei Daily Use Products would not adopt the Chinese practices but instead would stick to hard-sell

American techniques. At the end of 1985, two years after its start-up, Shenmei began advertising on television. Radio commercials, point-of-purchase posters, and display racks were introduced in 1986. It also printed hand-out posters about its sponsorship of the world soccer championship; the Chinese are avid soccer fans.

Tam, a native of Hong Kong who served initially as Shenmei's marketing manager, trained a young English-speaking Chinese, Jeffrey Wang, to succeed him. Formerly, Wang had worked in Shenyang's gardening bureau. When he joined Shenmei, he apprenticed for several years as a salesman and also was sent to Gillette's Hong Kong office for six months' training. He has adopted a Madison Avenue style in dress and manner. Of the Chinese executives I met at Shenmei, he was the only one in a Western-style pin-striped suit. The others wore the customary Mao suit of trousers and jacket.

Shenmei's sales force is on straight salary augmented by monthly and quarterly incentive bonuses if targets are exceeded. In China, pharmacies sell only medicines. Razor blades are sold at cosmetic and vegetable shops. Wang is proud of how he instructed his sales staff to conduct street-corner market research to ascertain how many passersby had seen Shenmei's television ads or its display racks at retailers. "I tell them to write clear reports on any problems," he declares. Retailers are invited to tour the factory.

Distribution in China is as cumbersome as in Japan. In China, the merchandise travels from a big wholesaler through two tiers of smaller wholesalers before it reaches retailers and customers. Some joint ventures circumvent this maze by going directly to consumers. This is convenient for manufacturers of large industrial equipment but not for consumer products manufacturers like Shenmei. Hence it continues to use the traditional channels. But it has not been hesitant about raising prices. Joint ventures are exempt from government pricing controls. Once Shenmei made market inroads, Gillette maintained that as the only stainless-steel blade manufacturer in China, it was entitled to charge more than its competitors. The current price is based on Gillette's overall profit margin parameters.

Most joint ventures, however, do little advertising, since demand exceeds production output. "I try to do as little as possible because my production is presold months in advance—and I have the money in the bank," Beijing Jeep's Donald St. Pierre comments. "I try to do only image or brand advertising and that not too much." One prime location where Beijing Jeep has a large billboard is at the entrance to the Temple of Heaven in Beijing, where the emperors worshiped. Other joint ventures have billboards at major street intersections.

Foreign investors must also adjust in developing nations to a severe lack of infrastructure. It is unrealistic to expect a duplicate of America's well-serviced industrial land adjacent to four-lane highways and close to good rail and air freight connections. Instead, conditions resemble those of the nineteenth-century American frontier. Although statistics vary from nation to nation, the basics of the situation in China are similar throughout the Third World: transport, communications, and utilities are woefully inadequate.

Over the past thirty years, the Chinese government has laid 32,000 miles of railways and 560,000 miles of road. But most of this construction was for political rather than economic reasons. The rail lines were built in remote mountain and desert areas rather than between the country's resources in the center and west or near the bulk of the population and factories in the east. Rail mileage has doubled since the Communist takeover in 1949 but has been outpaced by passenger volume, which has soared by 800 percent, and by freight volume up by 1900 percent. Double tracking is under way, but it is a slow process; consequently, four-fifths of the lines remain single-track.

Three-fourths of China's locomotives are still steam-driven and based on forty-year-old designs. Since half of all freight and passenger transport is by train, the stations are jammed. They are also poorly lit and maintained. Passenger comfort is minimal. Ventilation is slight. First-class compartments have "soft" seats compared with "hard" seats in other sections, but the white slip-covers are soiled and the floors are sticky and stained from spilled drinks.

Because China's aircraft industry is still in its infancy, the country expects it will have to buy its aircraft from foreign suppliers for at least the next thirty years. Although air travel in China is growing at the fastest pace of any Asian country, it could grow even faster if the country's airports were in better shape. Only 10 percent can accommodate jumbo jets, and only half have capacity for medium-sized planes. There is no unified traffic control network. Ground facilities like warehousing and refrigerated storage are scarce.

So far, road transport is not a satisfactory alternative because only 2 percent of roads in China are paved or asphalted highways. Major neighboring cities are linked only by dirt roads. However, an ambitious road construction program is under way, including the country's first four-lane expressway connecting Shanghai and its suburban Jiading County.

Regardless of the temperature outside, those buildings that have furnaces turn on the heat on November 15th and turn it off on April 15th. Expatriates quickly learn to wear sweaters. Power shortages are not as easy to solve. China has allotted priority to development of power projects, but their completion is years ahead. The main one, a hydroelectric plant on the Yangtze River, known as the Three Gorges project, will be the largest of its type in the world. However, the $20-billion venture, which also will assist in flood control and improve navigation of the river, will not be finished until early in the twenty-first century. Meanwhile, to conserve energy, the government shuts off the power on a rotating basis one day a week. Joint ventures have their own generators for these occasions. A smart choice of location helps, too. For example, China Hewlett-Packard, whose computer-equipped Beijing office depends on an uninterrupted flow of electricity, located its headquarters in a former watch factory because it received abundant electricity.

Yili-Nabisco Biscuit and Food Company was not as lucky. Biscuit baking requires ovens, and ovens require an energy supply. The amount of electricity available at the venture's location in Beijing, an area of narrow streets, low-rise brick housing, and small shops, is inadequate. The sole option was gas, although the equipment installed can be converted to electricity in the event that some day enough becomes available. Unfortunately for Yili-Nabisco, its confidence in a ready supply of gas was ill founded.

During the two years the factory was under construction, the joint venture had no assurance it would ever get a gas connection. On the contrary, there was the unpleasant prospect that the building would be a white elephant, unable to bake a single biscuit. Beijing authorities blamed the delay on traffic and weather conditions. Beijing's streets are crowded with bicycles during the daytime, confining road work to after dark. Also, the officials

said, nothing could be done during the winter because the ground
is frozen. Finally, construction of a bypass to Yili-Nabisco was
started in the spring of 1987. The connection was completed in
August 1987, eight months after the factory could have opened.[2]

In industrialized nations, the telephone is ubiquitous. Executives have one in their offices, washrooms, and cars. Pay telephones are available on almost every street corner and in hotel
lobbies. Many households have a separate line for the children.
By contrast, telephone installation in China is in an early stage.

Under China's sixth Five-Year Plan (1981–1985), the nation
produced 40 million TV sets, but only 2.7 million telephone lines
and 4 million telephones. The government's seventh Five-Year
Plan (1986–1990) calls for triple the number of telephones and 3
million more lines. The goal for the year 2000 is 34 million telephones, or 2.8 telephones for every 100 people, still a far cry from
the coverage in the United States.

There also are ambitious plans for expansion of direct long-
distance dialing, which was instituted as recently as 1986 and remains limited to a few cities. The program provides an immense
opportunity for global telecommunications giants, many of which
are already engaged in projects in China, but until the plans are
realized, communications will remain a headache. Furthermore,
there are no post boxes nor automatic sorting of mail.

What will be the official language of the joint venture—English, the native tongue, or a combination—must be ironed out,
too. While some foreign partners assign Japanese-Americans to
Japan and Chinese-Americans or Hong Kong natives to China,
other ventures send over unilingual Westerners. All such expatriates whom I met were diligently studying Japanese or Chinese,
but the task is formidable, since each language has tens of thousands of written characters but far fewer syllables with which to
pronounce them. One sound can represent more than one hundred
characters. The only differentiation lies in the tones, and speakers
whose native languages do not rely on tone differentiation find
tones exceedingly hard to master.

Some English words, especially high-tech jargon, have no
translatable equivalents. It is hard to find interpreters capable of

2. By contrast, only two months elapsed before Kentucky Fried Chicken received its joint
venture license and another six until the completion of its first restaurant, a five-hundred-
seat outlet overlooking Beijing's focal point, Tienanmen Square. KFC forecasts weekly
traffic of 45,000 customers at the restaurant.

handling both technical terms and colloquialisms. When one is found, joint ventures either place the interpreter in the same room as the senior English-speaking and Chinese or Japanese officials, if they share quarters, or in an office between the two executives.

Some joint ventures elect to teach their workers English, the officially recognized international business language. They believe translation of all the data would be prohibitively expensive, so they leave all technical documents in English or shortlist key items in the local language. However, not all joint ventures subscribe to this approach. Beijing Jeep, for instance, translated its numerous manuals on quality control standards into Chinese for the reason given by quality control director Ernest Regehr, an AMC expatriate: "We wanted to propel the Chinese through thirty years of technology as quickly as possible."

Young Westerners who are fluent in Chinese or Japanese can leapfrog over their colleagues at U.S. companies to the managerial ranks through an executive appointment at an Asian joint venture. For example, SmithKline's senior person in China is a twenty-five-year-old American who speaks Chinese. "In the land of the blind, the one-eyed man is king," comments John Chappell.

# 8  Management: Japanese Partners

Japanese companies are known for the team spirit they develop through extracurricular activities organized for employees. For the sake of camaraderie between Americans and Japanese at Tokyo-based Japan Communications Satellite Company ( JCSat), the Hughes-Itoh-Mitsui joint venture, managing director Fred Judge is happy to act as the company's unofficial social director. At employees' requests, he started a bridge night and a conversation club (for which JCSat provides coffee) and paid for employee memberships in a nearby swimming and tennis club. He gladly goes on company skiing expeditions. But he draws the line at participating in night climbs up Mount Fuji in order to witness the sunrise from the summit. The Japanese, in turn, humor Hughes's custom of twice-a-year parties for employees and their families. Normally, spouses and children are excluded from corporate social events in Japan. Judge says that few Japanese wives and children attended at first, but that their number is increasing.

Management of joint ventures between Japanese and Western partners is characterized by a delicate mix of diverse cultural customs and management styles. The Japanese generally are more preoccupied with seniority and with consensus management, in which decisions are made at the middle level and rubber-stamped at the top. They also are content with long-term paybacks. The Western emphasis is usually on short-term results and on clear lines of authority leading to the chief executive officer.

Troubled ventures suffer from N.I.H.—not invented here— syndrome, a reluctance to accept the other side's way of doing things. In these instances, the venture's purpose of yielding economies of scale through shared production is destroyed by each participant's adherence to its own system. In effect, they remain competitors despite their agreement to collaborate.

Three essentials for the success of joint ventures are mutual trust, the ability to compromise, and a good business climate, says William Glavin of Xerox, a partner in Fuji Xerox in Japan. "If the senior executives at the parents and venture trust one another and have confidence in one another, their subordinates will perceive it and behave similarly," he adds. "Without outright ownership, the ability to compromise is important because you can't order a joint venture to do something. Instead, you must be careful as to what you ask.

"That sometimes frustrates managers at the parent companies because they are accustomed to telling people to do this or that. My response is—that would be the beginning of the end of a joint venture because when orders must be given it is a sign that a business is not working. Finally, favorable business conditions are vital in the venture's formative years. Thus, if tough times arise later, the venture has the strength to survive. Fuji Xerox, for example, commenced in good times, and all the fundamentals were in place before fierce competition arose."

Glavin also stresses that Fuji Xerox does well because it does not step on the toes of other Xerox operations. "Although single-site world mandates are not possible since some countries call for manufacturing capability in order to sell there, Xerox works hard to avoid duplication," he says. "For example, Fuji Xerox makes a small copier known as the 1012, which it ships to the United States and the United Kingdom. For the copier to sell in the European Community, it must contain some European content; therefore, a few components are installed in the United Kingdom. But in the United States no alterations are necessary, as there is not a similar requirement for local value-added parts."

Technically, Rank Xerox, the Xerox joint venture with the U.K.'s Rank Organization, is Fuji Xerox's Western parent. But Rank takes no part in the management of Rank Xerox or Fuji Xerox. "After the first eight months of Rank Xerox, the Rank person running it concluded he did not like working for Americans; consequently, Xerox sent an American to London to run Rank Xerox," Glavin explains. Subsequently, in 1974, when Glavin became head of Rank Xerox, he suggested that Fuji Xerox report to Xerox in the United States instead of to Rank Xerox. His reason was that because Fuji Xerox was in the process of enlarging its manufacturing capability, it made more sense for it to deal directly with Xerox, which had the essential resources. Ever since, as Glavin has moved up the Xerox hierarchy in the United States, Fuji Xerox has reported to him for the sake of continuity. In addition, he encourages the development of close ties between Xerox managers and their Fuji Xerox counterparts to foster cooperation at all levels.

Glavin says that the root cause of Fuji Xerox's success lies in Fuji Photo's willingness to allow Xerox to be in charge. It does so even though both own 50 percent and despite the contract giving it the authority to appoint Fuji Xerox's chief executive officer. It exercises this power but otherwise stands aside. Surrendering control to Xerox reflects a pragmatic recognition that Xerox is both the source of the venture's technology and its chief customer.

Established in 1934, Fuji Photo has become one of Japan's top twenty manufacturing companies but, as its name indicates, its principal interest is in photography. Consequently, of Fuji Xerox's two parents, Fuji Photo had less to contribute in technology. "For a joint venture to get started, both parents must have a need, but after it gets going, one partner must be willing to allow the other to work more closely with the venture," Glavin comments.

Whereas Fuji Photo and Xerox amiably resolved the issue of operational authority, Austin Rover and Honda were locked in a tug-of-war in the initial stages of their joint manufacture of certain models of cars. They differed over the structure of parts as well as over inspection and testing standards. "On the one hand, Honda's engineers might be certain that one centimeter thickness was enough for a component; on the other, Rover's were equally adamant that two centimeters were necessary," says Kiyoshi Ikemi, deputy general manager, international planning, at Honda. "If agreement was not reached, each used different components, which made it difficult to attain economies of scale."

Ikemi stresses that conflict was "more the exception than the rule" but does admit that 20 percent of the disagreements ended in the partners going their separate ways. Because the two companies were working from different drawings for the same components, perhaps it is surprising that there were not more disputes. In any event, both learned a lesson. On their present collaborative effort, they are using the same blueprints which, as Ikemi dryly remarks, "maximizes commonality."

Whether the Japanese travel to North America or Europe to form a joint venture, or its partners cross the Pacific Ocean, the basic management objective is to interlace the ranks with capable executives from both sides. "Our approach at Kodak Nagase is coeducational; each side understands and appreciates how the other thinks as a result of the cross-fertilization of backgrounds and ideas," says David Biehn, executive vice president of the joint venture.

Biehn also suggests that Westerners, whether they agree or not, should respect the importance the Japanese attach to seniority and status. For instance, Biehn, in his early forties, cautions that "it is inappropriate to send over a thirty-year-old to head a Japanese-staffed company whose managers are fifty or sixty years old." His observation is based on the highly structured nature of Japanese society, in which there are unwritten rules on how to behave in the presence of superiors, peers, and people of lesser status.

"The Japanese custom of exchanging business cards on introduction reflects the importance to them of rank," Biehn continues. "The cards are a nice way to judge status without pointedly inquiring about it. The Japanese can then act accordingly. It's hard for Westerners to fully comprehend this. I've been here several years, and while I feel I have a positive understanding, I can't believe it's complete. The Japanese do forgive foreigners for breaches, but not their countrymen, because they believe Japanese should know better. Therefore, in setting up the management of a joint venture with the Japanese, seniority must be taken into account."

Kodak Nagase practices what it preaches. The president is Japanese. He was the former manager of Nagase's Kodak division. What to designate Biehn was a problem. The term "vice president" in Japan does not signify the number two spot. By adding the prefix "executive," Biehn achieved the requisite status. The rest of Kodak Nagase's management chart consists of a buddy system of Japanese and expatriates. So that the Japanese do not lose face, they hold the senior title and the foreigners act as assistants.

JCSat has a triad of senior executives. The presidency and vice presidency are held by Japanese. The managing director and chief operating officer, Fred Judge, is American. Save for one American, all the departmental managers are Japanese. As at U.S. companies, they can authorize expenditures up to approved levels. After that, JCSat practices *ringisho* (management by consensus). Judge warns that this is where clashes can arise between expatriates and the Japanese. "In the United States a company's president makes the ultimate decision, but in Japan the consensus method sorts out matters at lesser levels," he explains. "Lower managers make decisions and request the pro forma approval of their superiors.

"A young kid will walk into a senior executive's office and say, 'Trust me. Sign. I'm in a hurry.' The process of signing underlines this difference between Japan and the United States. In the United States, managers must personally affix their signature or initials. In Japan, approval is stamped with a chop (seal) bearing the executive's name. Young people are granted wide latitude in using that stamp when the executive is absent."

Judge has made certain that this will not occur at JCSat. He keeps the president's chop in a safe. He also insists on direct involvement in the steering of JCSat. Staff are requested to prepare summaries of their visits to government officials and customers to ensure consistency. Judge admits he must rely on what the personnel report back because he is still learning the complex Japanese language. JCSat board meetings and minutes are in English, with a Japanese translation of the proceedings, as required by law.

He also concedes that he can enforce the U.S. way because the Japanese partners lack Hughes's experience in running a satellite business. "After ten years, or maybe just five, it will be harder to prevent a reversion to the Japanese customs, since by then the Japanese will be as expert as we are," Judge says. "Consequently, they will be less dependent on the expatriates."

Office layout at joint ventures is a hybrid of Japanese and American styles. The typical Japanese corporation has a vast lobby, as in the United States. Some give an entire floor to the chairman and president, separating them with corridors of art works. But between the opulent ground and upper floors is a far different world. Most of the staff in a Japanese company work in uncarpeted offices at desks jammed next to one another. There are no plants or baffle screens as at U.S. offices that have open office landscaping. Visitors rarely get a glimpse of these conditions because they are ushered into conference rooms lining the perimeter of most floors. These lack long meeting tables; essentially, they are sitting rooms with deep comfortable chairs arranged in a rectangle. The clerical staff wear uniforms, and the receptionists leap to their feet to greet guests.

Because Western expatriates are uncomfortable with the Japanese style, joint ventures strive for a compromise to make both sides happy. The floors are carpeted, there are many plants, and desks are spaced. Since the Japanese are accustomed to working, living, and socializing in groups, some joint ventures have no partitions. If they do, they select low ones so people can peer over or walk around easily. Managers are given their own offices, with a door for privacy. The clerical staff do not wear uniforms; the women wear dresses and skirts (no slacks) of their choice. Receptionists are courteous but remain seated.

The nucleus of the staff at joint ventures consists of employees reassigned from the parent companies. They have little option but to transfer; nonetheless, the joint venture wants them to feel secure and to give the venture their loyalty. Kodak and Nagase made it a point to inform Nagase's personnel of the formation of their joint venture well before it became public knowledge. To indicate the significance both companies attached to the venture, each called upon its most senior officials to explain why and how the procedure would be handled. To nurture a Kodak Nagase corporate culture, dinners and parties were held and awards were instituted.

Because the Japanese regard "root binding" between employees as vital for team spirit, the Kodak expatriates adopted the Japanese custom of senior and junior executives meeting for after-hours drinks. The behavior at the office remains structured, whereas these outings encourage outspokenness. "It's important to do this, because you find things out more quickly," Biehn says.

In addition to fostering good will, Kodak taught the former Nagase employees about Kodak's barometers for judging success.

"Whereas at Nagase the Kodak division concentrated primarily on sales as an indicator, we have introduced other guidelines pertaining to profitability, such as the costs of distribution, advertising, and administration," Biehn states. A joint venture treads a tightrope between its structure as a separate company and its affiliation with the worldwide organization of its parents. Of Kodak Nagase's parents, only Kodak is a global business.

Biehn explains that considerable thought was given to how the joint venture would fit into Kodak's "worldwide framework of manufacturing, marketing, and research development." Kodak Japan K.K., established in 1984, oversees all Kodak's Japan operations to ensure they mesh with what the company does elsewhere. This is achieved through Kodak's stipulation that all planning, ranging from overall strategy to capital expenditures, and annual operations be developed with the assistance of the Kodak-supplied executive vice president.

In addition to winning the loyalty of Nagase employees, the joint venture had to persuade customers that Kodak Nagase would be an improvement over Nagase's Kodak division, with which they were well satisfied. Again, a number of strategies were employed. Senior executives at client companies were invited for a preannouncement conference. Subsequently Kodak undertook an extensive public relations campaign. It listed its stock on the Tokyo Stock Exchange; sponsored judo, soccer, and junior tennis championships; advertised during televised baseball games; placed announcements in newspapers; distributed sales brochures; and posted five neon signs in Tokyo, including one in the Ginza, famous for such displays. But its most talked-about advertisement is a huge blimp that floats over the downtown office towers. It is painted yellow, with Kodak's name superimposed in red letters, the same design as that on Kodak's film boxes. The emphasis of the program was on Kodak, but Kodak Nagase also benefited from the publicity.

In their recruitment of staff, joint ventures in Japan are handicapped by the reluctance of Japanese managers to forgo the security of working for long-established Japanese firms. However, Yoshio Terasawa of Nomura Securities maintains that a joint venture has an advantage over an American subsidiary because "there is less apprehension about job loss when there is Japanese participation. Whereas Americans may withdraw if they do not do well, in Japan the pattern of lifetime employment remains important, and thus employees are more confident of job security at joint ventures."

The chief attraction that joint ventures cite in their hiring campaigns is that they offer the opportunity for faster advancement than at Japanese companies. SmithKline and Fujisawa, for instance, advertised sales positions at their venture as a fresh start for managers eager for a mid-career change. Thirty percent of its representatives belong in this category.

College graduates are the main source of new employees. In Japan, the scramble for the brightest begins immediately after students finish university on April 1st. The interview process can be time-consuming. JCSat, for example, annually interviews thirty applicants, of whom it hires five.

JCSat's Fred Judge claims that joint ventures located in Japan have an advantage over those elsewhere because the Japanese are imbued with the concept of lifetime loyalty by employees to employers (and vice versa). Thus, he says, "it is much easier in Japan to develop a personal sense of responsibility toward a business. Beneath their confident surface, the Japanese still feel that because their nation is poor in natural resources, its success could slip away."

Japanese companies play on these feelings of insecurity to encourage employees to work hard to guarantee the success of their company. On the other hand, the chances of vaulting over one's peers at large Japanese companies are remote. Because the youthful joint ventures provide an avenue for more rapid advancement, they overcome the traditional Japanese preference to work for long-established corporate giants. "We pay them more than their counterparts make, and offer the opportunity for many to become vice presidents while still young," Judge says.

JCSat has attracted several talented women to its staff by offering opportunities for career promotion. However, in this, it is an exception among joint ventures. Usually, women are relegated to dead-end secretarial or tea-serving jobs, reflecting the still widely held perception in Japan that women's roles should be subservient to men's. Even JCSat, which was prepared to have executives fetch their own coffee (as they do for the most part in the United States), found it could not Americanize its office to this extent. Having been taught that it is courteous to bring beverages to the boss or to visitors, JCSat's secretaries asked that they be allowed to continue doing so. Despite the lower status of women in Japan, visiting female executives from the U.S. parent company are accorded the same deference as their male colleagues.

Yokogawa-Hewlett-Packard's executive vice president, Toshio Muraoka, believes that joint ventures depend on two factors to flourish—good products and good management. "Joint ventures thrive more when they have freedom in their management than when U.S. companies impose American rules," he maintains. It also helps if the U.S. company empathizes with Japanese management practices. Muraoka says this definitely is the case with Hewlett-Packard. "HP wasn't and isn't a typical American company," he explains. "I regard Ford as a type A company—strictly American in style; Mitsui as type J—strictly Japanese; and HP as type Z. I classify it differently because what the firm calls the 'HP way' is much like the Japanese way. Whereas it is normal in the United States to change employment frequently, HP has always emphasized its appreciation of long service. It marks every five years of employment with an award such as a tie clasp. Such programs are popular in Japan, too.

"HP does not rely on contractual work by temporary workers. When times are tough, it does not lay off workers, the same policy as in Japan. Instead, it cuts salaries, including those of the top executives.[1] HP also is proud of what it calls its 'management by wandering around.' By that it means it follows an open-door policy. For many years, only founders David Packard and William Hewlett had their own offices. All other key managers did not, because HP believes communications increase and conflicts decrease if there are no doors or walls separating people. Japanese companies do the same."

Although HP officials in the early stages of Yokogawa-Hewlett-Packard believed the Japanese side, Yokogawa Electric Works, transferred far too many workers to the fledgling venture, Muraoka, who was one of the managers sent to the joint venture, paints a happier picture. He feels that the important point is that HP agreed to the staffing of YHP by Yokogawa Electric workers rather than hiring outside management, as U.S. companies tend to do. "Many U.S. firms hire people on the basis of their fluency

---

1. In 1986, because of a soft market affecting the entire computer industry, HP implemented voluntary severance and a voluntary early retirement program, which fifteen hundred employees accepted.

in English or their graduation from an American university, even though neither guarantees talent in management and technology," he states. Although he speaks English well, Muraoka stresses that Westerners who establish wholly owned subsidiaries or joint ventures in Japan "must keep in mind they are doing business in Japan."

Like Kodak Nagase, YHP plays the status game with titles because of the importance attached to rank by the Japanese. This is most evident with YHP's sales force. In Japan, the term "salesperson" has a lowly status equated with sellers of door-to-door consumer goods and life insurance. "Inasmuch as almost all our salespeople are engineers who make sales calls on other engineers, we call them field engineers," Muraoka says. "When you hope to sell big systems worth as much as one million dollars, what you label your sales representatives is very important psychologically." From its inception YHP has relied on its own sales force rather than on Yokogawa Electric's, because each manufactures different equipment.

The good and the bad of what happens when the Japanese are the foreign parent in a joint venture are exemplified by New United Motor Manufacturing, Inc. (NUMMI), the General Motors-Toyota venture, and by National Steel in Pittsburgh. NUMMI was selected in 1986 by the U.S. Department of Labor as a case study on "positive labor-management relations" for the International Labor Organization. By contrast, National Steel has had heavy staff turnover. Shortly after its 1983 startup, the president, vice president-general manager, and vice president of operations left. The president, a thirty-year veteran of the U.S. parent, National Intergroup, was asked to take early retirement. He was replaced by the senior managing director of the Japanese parent, Nippon Kokan, who had thirty-five years' experience.

Both ventures have one thing in common, however—they were the only recourse in a troubled industry. The U.S. automobile industry's problems intensified at the beginning of this decade. Because of combined losses of more than $5.5 billion in 1981 and 1982, GM, Ford, Chrysler, and American Motors laid off hundreds of thousands of United Auto Workers. To their dismay, the four firms discovered that mid- and large-sized cars, which they had emphasized, were not what U.S. consumers wanted. Their preference was for Japanese compact and subcompact vehicles that cost several thousand dollars less. By the 1980s, the Japanese were selling one out of every three vehicles worldwide. Between 1970 and 1985, their exports multiplied five-fold. GM wanted the link with Toyota so as to learn how to make small cars competitive in cost and quality with Japanese automobiles.

GM's plant in Fremont, California, which became NUMMI's home, typified the slide of the U.S. auto industry from a supreme position to a jeopardized one. When the 3-million-square-foot factory was built in 1962, the U.S. auto industry was unchallenged. The Japanese were not as yet big exporters. GM spared no expense in keeping the factory technologically competitive, spending millions of dollars on state-of-the-art equipment. Yet by 1982 it was one of four car plants permanently closed in California. Indeed, only one auto factory remained open in that state.

GM's Fremont plant, which is painted gray, was dubbed "the battleship" by workers because of dismal labor-management conditions. During its twenty years of operation, there had been four shutdowns. The United Auto Workers' local at the plant regarded management as "authoritarian and inflexible." Management viewed the union as "militant and rowdy." Community leaders in Fremont (population 141,000) were apprehensive, because the plant was the city's largest industrial employer.

Fortunately for the factory and its workers, they were rescued by the aspirations of the very Japanese whose exports to America were causing U.S. car makers to seek protectionist tariffs. Whereas Honda and Nissan had established their U.S. operations prior to the imposition by the United States of "voluntary" quotas on Japanese car makers, Toyota had failed to take this precaution. It was anxious to establish a manufacturing presence in the United States, but first it wanted to make certain that its production and labor philosophies could work in that country. Thus, when GM suggested a joint venture, Toyota was presold on the idea.

Like GM and Toyota, the UAW regarded the joint venture as vital to the future. It was in disarray in the early 1980s. Not only were many of its members unemployed but the outlook was bleak. Disenchanted with the adversarial nature of labor-management relations, U.S. car makers were shifting many of their operations outside the country. Either they sourced parts elsewhere or they manufactured the entire car in cheaper labor markets. Both Honda and Nissan had nonunion work forces at their U.S. operations. For the UAW to survive, it realized, it had to prove to both U.S. and Japanese firms that it was cooperative and noncombative.

Although GM and Toyota each own 50 percent of NUMMI, Toyota is in charge of management. It seconds about forty managers, all of whom speak English, for three-year postings. To underline the importance attached to the venture, Toyota appointed Tatsuro Toyoda, the son of Toyota's founder, as NUMMI's first chief executive officer. GM contributes sixteen people on a rotating basis. Their prime function is to soak up Toyota's methods and disseminate the information throughout their home company.

Because Toyota is responsible for daily operations, NUMMI's management system is Japanese. The chief distinction is that Toyota employs a team approach, in which one person performs several assignments, instead of the customary U.S. assembly line, in which a worker does only one task. The Japanese system is considered more demanding and productive than the monotonous U.S. method.

Shortly after GM and Toyota signed their contract, NUMMI began discussions with the UAW. The company agreed to hire the majority of its workers from the pool of laid-off GM employees, thus enabling the same UAW local to continue as bargaining agent at the plant. Eighty percent of NUMMI's twenty-two hundred employees are former GM people. At its peak in 1978, the GM plant had seven thousand Fremont workers; when it closed in 1982 there were five thousand. The remainder of NUMMI's employees come from closed Ford and Caterpillar factories. The company also consented to pay prevailing U.S. auto industry wages and benefits.

The positive labor-management climate referred to by the U.S. Department of Labor in its 1986 submission to the International Labor Organization has its cornerstone in the preamble to the NUMMI-UAW contract: "Both parties are undertaking this relationship with the full intention of fostering an innovative labor relations structure, minimizing the traditional adversarial roles, and emphasizing mutual trust and good faith."

The theme of NUMMI's labor contract is joint union-management resolution of issues, a concept absent from previous

U.S. auto industry contracts. The contract includes the following clauses:

- Joint union-management commitment to deal with problems through consensus rather than confrontation.

- Joint union-management efforts to improve quality, productivity, and cost controls.

- Advance consultation regarding layoffs, production schedule changes, major investments, and other matters normally the preserve of management.

- Joint union-management review of suspensions or discharges of workers.

- The strongest job security ever given to the UAW. Management must reduce its own salaries and reassign subcontracted work to NUMMI as ways to avoid layoffs. The first test of this clause occurred in 1987 when sales of the Chevrolet Nova failed to meet expectations. Instead of taking the customary U.S. recourse of layoffs, NUMMI cut back production by about six cars per hour.

A letter accompanying the application form sent to the three thousand ex-GM workers who applied to NUMMI reiterated the spirit of the contract. It stated that NUMMI's purpose was to develop a new "environment based on mutual trust, respect, and cooperation." But it also warned that the high absenteeism and poor quality work of the past would not be tolerated. Whereas U.S. car plants at the time generally hired people who walked in off the street, NUMMI subjected each applicant to a three-day assessment of simulated production functions, individual and group discussions, and written tests. Those who passed attended a four-day orientation program in which Japanese production and labor-management systems were explained.

For its part, the UAW agreed that NUMMI, as a new company, was not bound by the work rules and eighty-five job classifications of the GM regime. Instead, NUMMI has only four job ranks: except for one hundred employees, the workers are "team members," that is, production line workers. The remainder are "skilled trade" workers, that is, maintenance, tool and die, and tool and die tryout. All are paid hourly and are represented by the UAW. A team leader is appointed over every four to eight team members. Approximately three teams are placed under a group leader, who is a salaried supervisor. As in Japan, each team member is trained to do the work of the rest of the team plus his or her own job.

Each team is expected to practice Japanese workplace principles. *Kaizen* (continuous improvement) calls for workers to detect waste in machinery, materials, labor, or methods of production and to suggest how to solve the problem. *Jidoka* (quality control) entitles workers to stop the assembly line by pulling a rope or pressing a button if a defect is spotted. (In U.S. plants, halting the assembly line can result in disciplinary action.)

In May 1984, NUMMI hired its first group of employees. The following month these four hundred group and team leaders were sent to Toyota's facilities in Japan for three weeks of classroom instruction and on-the-job orientation about *kaizen* and *jidoka*. Each NUMMI employee worked beside a Toyota trainer on the assembly line. These people then trained others in Fremont.

NUMMI started production in stages, commencing in December 1984 with seven hundred workers. Only two cars a day were produced as team members built and rebuilt cars according to the precept of *kaizen*. New staff and output were added gradually, until full production was reached in October 1985. NUMMI began by making Chevrolet Novas for GM. The 200,000th was produced in August 1986, and the next month the first Toyota Corolla FX rolled off the assembly line. Once again, the car plant, which has a payroll of $75 million, is the leading economic player in Fremont.

There have been no strikes since the inception of NUMMI. When the contract came up for renewal in July 1987, it was harmoniously approved. Grievances have shriveled from thousands per year under GM to a few dozen, and absenteeism is one-seventh of what it used to be. GM has absorbed valuable production and personnel techniques. The "hardware" lesson it liked most was the building of car doors next to the main assembly line instead of in a separate plant.

GM was impressed by *kanban,* an information system that underlies Japan's famous just-in-time system for parts delivery by suppliers. *Kanban* is a card designed to prevent overproduction and surplus inventory. The Japanese maintain that its proper use makes possible cost-efficient plant layout and scheduling and exposes inventory and quality problems that otherwise might remain undetected. As a result of *kanban*, NUMMI occupies only 40 percent of its space. The rest is for storage until NUMMI expands; this is not imminent, considering the present softening in car demand.

But the most important revelation for GM was that the Japanese had accomplished their gains through emphasizing people rather than technology. Hitherto, U.S. companies were convinced that the Japanese surge arose from using more automation than the United States employed. "GM restructured its thinking on how to integrate man and machine so that it now leans more on people," NUMMI spokesman Thomas Klipstine says. The UAW was elated, too, because NUMMI's success proved that the union was a plus and not the minus that critics charged it had become. NUMMI is less automated than the newer plants of U.S. car makers, yet it boasts improved productivity.

Said the UAW in its magazine, *Solidarity:* "The key to NUMMI's high productivity is the fully informed worker, not the semi-smart machine. . . . To develop fully informed workers with a broad range of skills, the UAW agreed to just one job classification for all line workers and just three for the trades. Critics say this historic reversal of protective job demarcation exposes NUMMI workers to the whims of management. But the UAW fought for the more than one hundred job classifications in traditional auto assembly plants precisely because workers had no control over job content on the shop floor. At NUMMI they do. If the lone job classification is a concession to Toyota, it is even more emphatically a concession to the age-old thrust of American workers for creativity, flexibility, and a degree of job control." Following the initial euphoria, there have been some rumblings of discontent about too hard a work pace and tension caused by peer pressure. But these are minor.

Notwithstanding the serene coexistence of management and labor at NUMMI, the venture has not proved to be a guidepost for most other joint ventures or for Japanese car makers' wholly owned subsidiaries in the United States. Few choose to agree in advance to union representation. The most prominent exception is Mazda in its planned marketing association with Ford. Mazda's acquiescence is understandable because it is moving into a former Ford plant in the Detroit area, the stronghold of the UAW.

Satisfied by NUMMI that its production principles were suited to the United States, Toyota subsequently built a plant in Kentucky at which it did not give the UAW prior recognition as it had at NUMMI. Neither did Diamond-Star, the joint venture between Chrysler and Mitsubishi. Chrysler plans a more active role in Diamond-Star's management than GM takes at NUMMI. While all NUMMI's senior officers are Japanese, Diamond-Star's chairman, executive vice president, and chief financial officer are Chrysler appointees. Still, daily operations are to be under a president from Mitsubishi.

Besides its innovative labor contract, NUMMI set a pattern for automotive joint ventures in being strictly a manufacturing joint venture. It cannot sell its cars; that job must be handled by its parents, according to a decree of the Federal Trade Commission. Otherwise, the FTC feared, collusion might arise from GM and Toyota joining forces in marketing as well as manufacturing. The Chevrolet Nova and the Toyota Corolla FX, the two cars that NUMMI makes, are essentially alike. The Nova is a clone of Toyota's Sprinter subcompact, sold only in Japan and patterned on the Corolla. The main difference between the Nova and the Corolla FX is that the Nova has four doors and the FX two.

The FX sells strongly in the United States, as do imported Corollas, which compete directly against the Nova. The Nova has not done as well and as a result, for some months in 1987, NUMMI was forced to trim production from six hundred and fifty to six hundred cars per day. GM's difficulties in selling the Nova were attributed to both internal and external factors. Chevrolet was faulted by automobile analysts for ending dealer incentives and for inadequately distinguishing between the Nova and two subcompacts Chevrolet itself makes. Also, unfairly or not, U.S. car buyers perceive Japanese small cars to be of higher quality than American ones.

The FTC's marketing restrictions keep NUMMI executives from discussing the sales tactics of GM and Toyota. However, Thomas Klipstine does note that GM's problems are not isolated but reflect the "overall softening of the car market." He adds, "NUMMI is around where it wants to be in terms of production numbers," and points out that fleet sales of the Nova to car rental agencies are strong.

Just as most automotive joint ventures are reactions against tougher industry conditions, National Steel is a response to troubles in the steel industry in both the United States and Japan. The first steel company to share U.S. and Japanese parentage, National Steel began in 1983 in harsh times. On average, U.S. prices had dropped from nearly $525 per ton a year earlier to $475. Prices continued to plunge after the venture's formation. By 1986, the average price was down to $450 per ton, and three companies— LTV Corporation, Wheeling-Pittsburgh Steel, and McLouth Steel Products—were involved in bankruptcy proceedings. Several other firms were in precarious financial shape. Over 250,000 workers had lost their jobs, and membership in the United Steelworkers of America was down 50 percent from the late 1970s.

Once the world's most flourishing steelmakers, the Japanese corporations are suffering, too. In 1986, they recorded their worst performance since the end of World War II. To prevent their financial results from sinking even lower, they resorted to selling part of their investment portfolios. The outlook for U.S. and Japanese steelmakers remains grim. Japanese exports continue to decline because of the strong value of the yen and the hostility of other countries toward steel imports. In the United States, output remains at about 72 percent of capacity and prices are still low. Whereas Japan frets about falling exports, the United States is perturbed that imports from Japan and South Korea still account for close to 23 percent of the domestic market, above the government's target of 20.2 percent.

Fortunately for them, National Steel's parents have both embarked on ambitious diversification programs to decrease their reliance on steel. Through its 1986 acquisition of Fox Meyer Corporation, National Intergroup became the third largest U.S. pharmaceuticals wholesaler. Nippon Kokan has branched into the production of silicon semiconductors. It bought an Arizona facility in 1985 and constructed another in Oregon, scheduled to begin production in 1988. The concern at National Steel is that these businesses will deflect its parents' interest in it. Although on the upswing, National Steel is concerned whether demand and prices will slacken again, causing it to slide back into losses.

National Steel is a joint venture whose union is content but whose management has been wracked by discord. The workers are pleased because of a precedent-setting labor agreement. During the company's initial years at least, much of management was miserable because of different reporting procedures and uncertainty about the future. They were also suspicious of whether their paperwork stopped at the desks of National Steel executives or was actually intended for Nippon Kokan's use, which, in effect, would make them Nippon Kokan employees. The Japanese have sought to allay these concerns.

To start with the positive, the labor pact reached in April 1986, hailed as a "milestone" by *Business Week* and as "one of the most creative labor accords ever" by *The Wall Street Journal,* contains several historic clauses pertaining to management-labor co-operation and job security. These terms are highly similar to NUMMI's labor contract, which garnered similar praise. National Steel's arrangement is not termed a contract; instead, it is a "co-operative partnership agreement."

In one long sentence the preamble reads: "The management of National Steel Corporation and the United Steelworkers of America jointly recognize that in order for the corporation to meet the immediate challenge of survival and the need for long-range prosperity, growth, and secure employment, both parties must now work closely together in a joint partnership that extends from the shop floor to the executive suite to solve problems quickly and in a cooperative manner." Subsequently, National Steel took another historic step. It included a two-page "letter from labor" about the agreement in its 1986 annual report, a first for U.S. steel companies.

The letter makes clear that the preamble's reference to survival is not melodramatic: "As we sat down to the bargaining table, it was clear that the survival of the company and the preservation of the jobs of our members demanded a new approach: a cooperative effort between two equal partners, management and labor. After decades of disagreement, we finally agreed on one thing for certain: 'business as usual' would mean no business at all. It was in our membership's interest that National Steel survive and become profitable, but neither the union nor National Steel could do it alone. We needed a commitment from both sides."

Like most steelmakers, National Steel wants to slash overhead in order to be cost-competitive. It regards a reduction in its work force as the answer, because slackened demand has made many workers superfluous. National's goal is a 30 percent decrease. Unlike other steel firms, however, it has not laid off employees but has vowed that personnel will shrink only through attrition or sweeteners for early retirement. In return, the union agreed to a one-dollar-per-hour wage cut to preserve more jobs than otherwise would have been possible.

To encourage the remaining staff, profit sharing and incentive pay tied to productivity were introduced by management, and the union agreed to fewer job categories. "Hitherto, four people were necessary to change a motor in a mill—two mechanics and two electricians," explains Sosuke Doi, who served as executive vice president from 1984 until mid-1987, when he returned to Nippon Kokan. "One mechanic loosened the bolts and the other tightened them after the motor was fixed. One electrician disconnected the wiring and changed the motor; the other stood by in case of a mistake."

Despite its financial woes, National Steel could better afford the concessions it made than its competitors could. Its customers, car and appliance manufacturers, were still placing strong orders, and it had improved its cost efficiency through installation of modern equipment. The media gave much of the credit for the contract to Nippon Kokan for taking an active role in the contract talks so that the labor climate would be modeled on harmonious relationships in Japan. However, former vice chairman Richard Smith emphasizes that although the contract is worded in the Japanese style, National Intergroup worked on the contract for a year-and-a-half in advance. Doi says Nippon Kokan's main contribution was to ask the union to increase productivity, which would make it possible for fewer workers to turn out a ton of steel.

The atmosphere in the executive suite was far pricklier and placed the Japanese side in a no-win position. Some of the Americans complained that the Japanese interfered; others said that the Japanese were bystanders and made no effort to be active participants in management. It took some time until a compromise was reached. Those at National Steel, angered by what they regarded as far too much paperwork, were typified by a mid-level manager: "It started slowly, with one report form, and ultimately became several hundred pages," he said. "They reasonably asked, 'Don't you think we ought to?' If you rejected them outright, they responded, 'Don't you think we ought to at least discuss it more?' Of course, you had to be fair and say 'Yes.' Then they would say, 'Could you set up the meeting?' There were a number of theories amongst the Americans as to why the Japanese wanted the information. We were uncertain whether they wanted us to do the work on their behalf, which they would then forward to Tokyo, or whether they were trying to change our management style to focus more on details.

"It was no use turning to National Intergroup for help because the Japanese side was more persistent. To me it is analogous to a father asking a child to dust and vacuum when the mother has asked only that the youngster pick up his or her own clothes and put them in the hamper. The mother isn't upset if the extra work is done.

"I was concerned, though, because to complete the paperwork involved overtime, for which management is not paid. Twenty people work for me, most of whom were already working hard, and I disliked having to press them further. People work more for fulfillment than for titles, salaries, and perks, but they like to come up for air sometimes. With the volume of paperwork, it seemed to me as if the light at the end of the tunnel was a train.

"Confrontations with Japanese executives are more trying than with Americans. American executives may be gruff when employees speak up, but usually they will listen. In Japan, the proper procedure is for superiors to initiate discussions and for subordinates to accept what they say and patiently wait until they wind up in their boss's job to change things. Thus, when we protested, the Japanese reacted in a roundabout fashion."

While most of his anger was directed at the Japanese, he also considered National Intergroup's administrative charges exorbitant. National Steel occupies five floors of National Intergroup's Pittsburgh headquarters. To save on computer charges, National Steel planned to farm out its work to a data-processing center. However, National Intergroup, which had performed this function, felt that such a switch would deprive it of substantial revenue.

There also was a misunderstanding between the Americans and the Japanese as to the extent of Nippon Kokan's involvement in operations at National Steel. The Americans anticipated learning a lot from the Japanese firm, which, besides being Japan's second largest steelmaker, owns the world's biggest producing steel plant. The mill, Fukuyama Works, has an annual capacity of 16 million tons—almost four times National Steel's output in 1986.

"It took some time for each of us to understand the other," says Richard Smith. "We hoped there would be more of an operating interface early on through their sending over more people than they did at first. However, no numbers were specified in the joint venture agreement." Initially, the Japanese assigned seventeen people to National's plants; three years later, it upped the number to fifty. Doi says more were not dispatched earlier because "there was no use sending them unless they knew they would be welcomed."

Smith says the Japanese taught the Americans a great deal about "blocking and tackling problems. In the United States, engineers fix something but do not set up corrective standard operating procedures; if the problem recurs six months later, they fix it again. By contrast, the Japanese have a problem-solving process and therefore the quality of their production is more reliable."

Initially, the Japanese suggested spending $1.4 million on new equipment, but when National Intergroup pointed out the amount was unwarranted in view of excess capacity, the Japanese agreed to halve the expenditure. They are assisting National to reduce scrap and rejects. "In Japan, under 10 percent is lost as scrap or rejects, but in the United States more than 20 percent is," Doi says. "If we can improve this rate, we will save a lot of money."

Doi attributes the turnover in managers, and the grumbling by some who remained, to differences in culture. "The Oriental religions of Confucianism and Buddhism teach the importance of constant improvement of oneself and of learning the truth," he explains. "So when you tell Orientals they should undertake self-examination in order to improve, it's a natural thing to do. But in the Western culture, human beings regard themselves as being an image of God and therefore nearly perfect. Thus, if one tells them they need to improve, they are offended."

Under the terms of the agreement signed by National Intergroup and Nippon Kokan, National Intergroup can sell its shares to its partner as of 1989. In the event of a hostile takeover attempt of National Steel before 1989, National Intergroup must buy out Nippon Kokan. What happens to the venture depends largely on whether its rebound to profits in 1987 continues.

If the venture should suffer losses, Nippon Kokan would not want to purchase National Intergroup's stake. That would leave National Intergroup with the alternatives of selling its shares outright to the public or selling to its existing shareholders on a pro rata basis, possibly a half share of National Steel for one of National Intergroup. But if National Steel were to slide back into the red, it would probably be hard to find takers.

As joint ventures between the Japanese and other industrialized countries increasingly make sound economic sense, more are likely to start up. Like their predecessors, they will have to realize that astute management and labor relations are as important for success as skillful production and marketing.

# 9 *Management: Chinese Joint Ventures*

In 1986, when William Mallett became manager of China Tianjin Otis Elevator, he was conducted on a tour of the joint venture's facilities. All was fine until Mallett reached the paint shop where, to his amazement and fury, he saw a worker asleep at 3 p.m. "Wake him up," Mallett demanded of the factory supervisor who was his guide. The supervisor's answer both flabbergasted and incensed Mallett further: "If I wake him, he will ask me why I did." That did not deter Mallett. The slumbering employee was awakened.

Mallett's encounter exemplifies the bewilderment, exasperation, and frustration that Westerners can feel in the far different world of management in China. Problems of recruitment, training, discipline, productivity, quality control, marketing, service, and inflexibility on the part of government authorities cause foreigners to declare China one of the most troublesome places in the world in which to work. Many classify it as *the* most difficult. However, those who master the intricacies of joint venture survival in China are well prepared should they decide to set up joint ventures in other Communist countries, most notably in the Soviet Union.

On average, Westerners or Japanese in joint ventures in China say, because of the many drawbacks they expect to have their own people in charge in China for at least five years. Some maintain twice as long is necessary. "It takes two years to get a joint venture going in Indonesia and ten in China," claims Dieu Eng Seng of Gillette. Chi-ning Liu of China Hewlett-Packard adds: "It takes us eighteen months to train a person, whereas HP in the United States needs only six months."

The Chinese have some justifiable grievances, too. Their chief complaint is that foreigners have unrealistic expectations about the ease of obtaining English-speaking college graduates knowledge-able about both high technology and management. Such jewels are rare, for two reasons.

First, under China's planned economy, the Chinese are nor-mally assigned to the same work unit for their entire careers. Even though government authorities say joint ventures are to receive cooperation when they want workers, getting a work unit to release workers is not easy. Other members of the unit become envious that one of their group has the chance to earn more money. Some Chinese enterprises demand financial compensation for the release of workers. According to the National Council for U.S.-China Trade, such payment has been as high as three thousand dollars. In other instances, the workers' former employers refuse to transfer their "work dossiers" because retention of these files enables them to recall the workers at any time. As a result, joint ventures can abruptly lose talented staff.

On average, salaries at joint ventures run 20 to 50 percent higher than at Chinese enterprises. Most joint ventures pay 50 percent more. However, to avoid an across-the-board commit-ment, they stipulate an *average* of 50 percent more, based on merit. That gives them maneuvering room to go above or below if they wish. They do have the delicate task, though, of rejecting relatives of employees who want to make the same good money but lack the ability. Other joint ventures agree to pay a basic salary plus a multiple, which can run as high as 300 percent. Whichever ap-proach is followed, the monthly salary works out to be about 300–350 RMB (about $82–$95 at the 1986–1988 rate of 3.7 RMB to the U.S. dollar).

Second, skilled managers are scarce because the 1966–1977 Cultural Revolution denied young people of that era the requisite education. These Chinese are now in the age bracket from which middle managers usually are drawn, but there is no such pool. Very briefly, Mao Zedong intended the Cultural Revolution to overcome the stagnation caused by bureaucracy in education, industry, and agriculture and to promote egalitarianism, which is supposed to be the hallmark of Communism. But what was meant to be a peaceful step forward degenerated into violence and chaos under the very group Mao had designated to provide leadership— the Red Guards. During this turbulent decade, intellectuals were exiled to farms to perform manual labor. They were forced to change places with farmers and peasants, who were made college professors. These poorly educated people were only capable of teaching the dogmas of Communism and Mao.

Until some time after the Cultural Revolution ceased, China had no business schools. Today, a race to catch up is under way. The State Economic Commission, which ranks higher than a ministry, has established nine management schools, where Americans, Europeans, Japanese, and Canadians lecture. For example, the Management Center for Economic Cadres, established in Beijing in 1979, has twenty full-time professors and fifty part-time instructors recruited from Europe's leading business schools. The nine main schools are supplemented by seventy-six Enterprise Management Institutions.

The State Economic Commission claims that by the year 2000 a total of 12 million students will have graduated from these institutions. Meanwhile, there is a constant stream of new management through joint ventures. Expatriates are replaced every two to three years, because they refuse to stay longer. Chinese trained as managers also depart quickly because authorities pull them out for promotions.

In all fairness, say some expatriates at joint ventures, the foreign partner must bear some of the responsibility for management woes in China. "Because Westerners are good managers does not mean they are automatically good trainers," says Kelvin Tam, deputy general manager of Shenmei Daily Use Products. With the problems still being sorted out, joint ventures place a premium on a partner with a good track record. Mallett of Otis advises: "Foreign investors shouldn't try to resurrect worthless organizations. They should link with ones that were strong financially, because that will provide a good foundation." Otis's partner, Tianjin Elevator, had four factories, a modest research center, and a nationwide network of marketing and service affiliates.

According to Mallett, China Tianjin Otis Elevator's 1986 net income of $10 million was equal to 60 percent of the profits of the fifty joint ventures in Tianjin. That is quite an accomplishment, considering several other prominent projects are there. A Sino-French winery produces Dynasty white wine, of which it exports 80 percent to France, the United States, Japan, and Hong Kong. In 1984, Dynasty won a gold medal at a world wine-tasting competition at the Leipzig International Fair. The company plans to branch into champagne, brandy, and other wines. A Tianjin joint venture involving Wella AG of West Germany makes shampoo and hair conditioner. Yishang Trading Company of Hong Kong and a Tianjin garment factory produce clothing fiber. However, none has as many employees as the 2,450 at Tianjin Otis. The Wella venture has ninety-eight workers and the Hong Kong one eight on its assembly line.

While linking with a proven company can ease the work of expatriate managers, because they inherit a plant and staff with at least partial knowledge of the industry, there are highly successful undertakings that started from scratch. A leading example is China Hewlett-Packard. "We began from ground zero," recalls general manager Chi-ning Liu. "We had to find our own facilities, which is no simple matter in China since there are no commercial leasing agents. We also had to recruit all our staff. On the one hand, that was a plus because we avoided the problem of what to do with unsuitable people. But on the other hand, there is no open labor market in China and arranging a transfer of workers from their present jobs isn't easy."

Even though China Hewlett-Packard was the first joint venture allowed to recruit at universities and to advertise in Chinese newspapers, it still had problems getting the type of worker it wanted. In its first year, it had 906 applicants, of whom it interviewed two hundred. Eighty were offered positions and half accepted. Part of the venture's recruitment difficulty lay in its insistence that it would only consider those who spoke English. "The cost for translating Hewlett-Packard technical documents would have been too high, so we had to make this stipulation," Liu comments.

Often, China Hewlett-Packard was frustrated in its hiring by the refusal of Chinese work units to release people. In one fifteen-month period, thirty-five engineering applicants were interviewed out of the more than one hundred who took the venture's English test. Offers were made to six, but none joined because their work units would not agree to their transfer.

Because the Chinese are unfamiliar with conventional management methods, Liu says, he spends half his time on issues that managers in the "mature environment" of U.S. companies do not encounter. "I have to bridge the cultural differences between the United States and China, smooth out the expectations of both the American and Chinese partners, deal with Chinese regulations, expedite the transfer of people, settle salary issues, and handle such everyday matters as maintenance," he points out.

Since China has an urgent need for elevators and the machines take months to assemble, Tianjin Otis does not have one problem that plagues many joint ventures—far too much output. By May 1987, the company had presold 65 percent of its planned 1988 production and even had orders lined up for 1989. Other foreign investors, however, complain that the Chinese do not understand the basic economic concept of demand and supply. Consequently, they have a habit of building inventory just to show how much they are able to produce.

One company that had this problem is Parker Hannifin Company of Cleveland, the largest U.S. manufacturer of hydraulic seals for automobiles, construction equipment, and machine tools. Parker's interest in China evolved from a 1979 trade mission by Ohio's governor and a group of businessmen to Wuhan, the capital of Hubei Province.[1] Wuhan is strategically well located in the center of China, equidistant from Beijing, Guangzhou, Shanghai, and Chongqing, the most important industrial city in southwest China. Wuhan was a logical city for the Ohioans to visit because, like Ohio, it is noted for its machinery production.

In 1980, a Hubei delegation visited Ohio, where the first deal it negotiated was with Parker Hannifin. The Hubei Parker Seal Component Factory came into existence eighteen months later. Capitalized at $9 million, it is 49 percent owned by Parker and 51

1. Wuhan is a contraction of three city names—"Wu" from Wuchang and "han" from Hankou and Hanyang. The three communities are at the confluence of the Han and Yangtze rivers. Wuchang is on the east bank; the other two are on the west bank.

percent by the Hubei Auto Industry Company. The venture's duration is for twenty years, and during the first seven Parker is to receive $50,000 as a technology transfer fee. Before the venture's formation, China imported seals for its planes, cars, ships, and industrial and agricultural equipment, since Chinese-made ones were of inferior quality. That caused a significant drain of forex. Thus, the Chinese were delighted at Parker's participation.

At the outset, Parker was pleased, too. True, its partner had never made seals but their manufacture is relatively uncomplicated. Also, Hubei provided an empty building and did a good job of manufacturing production equipment from Parker's specifications. So confident was Parker that these factors guaranteed clear sailing that it relied totally on local management recruited by Hubei Auto from within its own ranks rather than send over Parker expatriates.

"In retrospect, that was a grave error," states George Stevens, president of Parker's intercontinental group. He can easily make this admission since someone else held his position at the time. Without direct supervision by Parker, the Chinese did what they normally do: produce as much as they could rather than tailoring supply to the forecasted demand. "There was a large surplus—not a catastrophic amount but far, far in excess," Stevens says. "The Chinese lack sophistication in marketing. They do not compile historical data on which to base production forecasts. Their concept of marketing is to produce to full capacity and then try to sell everything. In other words, they are capacity-driven rather than sales-driven like U.S. corporations.

"We had no warning signs because we had nobody at the site. There was a reporting system but it was not followed. Trying to place calls or send telexes into the interior of China is difficult. Finally, we flew over and laid down the law. We demanded that they manufacture no more than orders totaled and that they submit reports regularly." Stevens concedes this system could idle machinery, but he stresses this is "only a short-term concern" and therefore the worry of surplus inventory is more significant. Stevens says Parker realized it could not pursue a hands-off approach, as it does in countries where the principle of supply and demand is ingrained. "Before, the factory made all 150 items constantly; now they follow a formalized structure we supplied," Stevens states.

Parker is not the only firm that learned that lack of skilled management in China limits the rate of growth. Japan's Mitsui Company made a similar discovery. International Leasing Company, which Mitsui cofounded in 1985, got off to a rapid start. Capitalized at $3 million, International Leasing did $50 million worth of business in each of its first two years and $100 million in 1987 to become China's second largest leasing company. In all, there are fifteen joint venture leasing firms in China, mostly between the Chinese and Japanese or Germans.

Yoshiaki Fujiwara, general manager of business promotion at Mitsui, with responsibility for International Leasing, maintains the venture "easily could have signed one hundred million dollars in contracts in its first year." International Leasing supplies industrial machinery, for which there is a pent-up demand caused by a chronic lack of new factory equipment in China. Nevertheless, Mitsui recommended that the rate of growth be deliberately controlled because of the scarcity of skilled management. "International Leasing is short-staffed with twenty people because of the difficulty of finding the proper workers," Fujiwara says. "We asked our partner—China National Technical Import Corporation—to find employees for simpler jobs such as receptionist, driver, and canteen operator. But as it is hard to fire workers, we wanted to carefully select the rest ourselves to make certain that the choices were appropriate."

Part of the recruitment problem stems from foreign partners using the same interviewing techniques about career aspirations as they do at home. Unaccustomed to such questions and wary of repercussions that could result if they are candid, the Chinese reply cautiously. "When asked their objectives in life, they will answer 'To serve Socialism' or 'To serve the four modernizations,' because they are afraid to state personal ambitions," says K. K. Ng, general manager of Yili-Nabisco. The purpose of the "four modernizations" program, announced in 1978, is to transform China into a "powerful Socialist economy" by the year 2000. Its fourfold focus is on agriculture, industry, national defense, and science and technology.

Many of the management vexations at joint ventures erupt from Chinese unfamiliarity with standard Western practices like organization charts and management by objectives. In Western corporations there are many horizontal layers of management known as line authority. In China, officialdom is arranged vertically, and nobody is willing to be decisive, since an incorrect judgment can result in criticism from Communist Party officials. Thus, matters that are resolved within hours in Western corporations are lobbed from bureaucrat to bureaucrat in China as if each was trying to pass on a live grenade.

The first action by expatriates when they enter into a joint venture with the Chinese is to draw up a simple organization chart, usually consisting of three levels. Those of China Hewlett-Packard and Shenmei Daily Use Products, in which Gillette is the foreign partner, are shown in Exhibits 9.1 and 9.2.

China Hewlett-Packard has nine senior officers; Shenmei has fourteen. By contrast, in the United States, Hewlett-Packard has twenty-seven and Gillette has thirty-nine. Noticeably absent from the lineup in China are a corporate counsel and a public relations officer. Most legal and publicity matters are handled by the U.S. parent, although China Hewlett-Packard, for example, is anxious to develop a public relations division of its own for broader coverage of the vast Chinese market.[2]

Joint ventures in which the Japanese are the foreign partner reflect Japanese management principles. An example is Fujian Hitachi Television Company, the first Sino-Japanese electronics joint venture. Established in 1980 on $2.4 million, the enterprise manufactures both black-and-white and color television sets. Hitherto, the Chinese partner, Fujian Electronic Import and Export Corporation, was capable of producing only black-and-white TVs. The Japanese insisted that the plant be run their way. To ensure this they demanded control over manufacturing, product testing, and quality control. The plant was cleaned up and machinery rearranged to improve traffic flow. In addition, Chinese technicians were sent to Japan for training.

Because so many managerial differences must be overcome in China, it is imperative that the senior foreigner and the Chinese person who serve as general manager and deputy get along well. Although some confess that they often yell at each other in private, as top executives do around the world, in public they make certain they give the semblance of agreeing. "It is essential that expatriates and Chinese think of a joint venture as their company, rather than align into separate camps of us versus them," Mallett of Tianjin

2. Unlike in Japan, women in China hold senior executive positions, including at joint ventures.

Exhibit 9.1
China Hewlett-Packard
Organization Chart

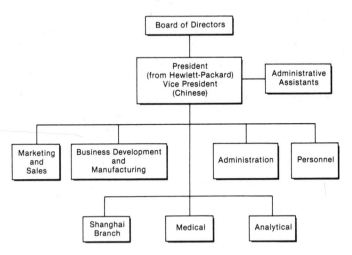

Exhibit 9.2
Shenmei Daily Use Products
Organization Chart

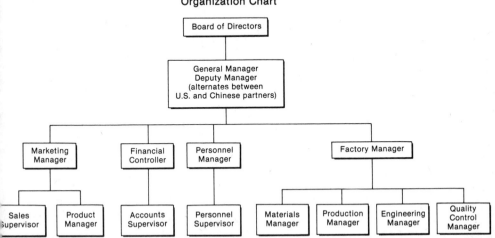

Otis advises. He and the Chinese deputy general manager, Wang Yun Qi, have worked out a winning routine whereby Mallett deals with the Chinese bureaucracy and Wang tackles the hierarchy at Otis to obtain concessions. For example, Chinese managers at joint ventures can sidestep Party criticism by saying that the foreigners "instructed" them to do what the officials are questioning. Thus, Mallett "instructed" Wang to use a certain car.

Since the Chinese do not understand why managers should have their own secretaries, Mallett also "instructed" Wang that he was to share the secretary-interpreter Mallett had hired. "At first, I had to emphasize that she is *our* secretary—both his and mine," Mallett says. One of the first memos Wang dictated was a request that Tianjin Otis supply soft drinks three times daily in the summer. Initially annoyed at the $60,000 budget, Mallett later agreed that Wang was correct because Tianjin is hot and dusty then.

On the other hand, Wang willingly intervenes when Mallett runs into opposition at Otis. For example, at one point, Otis toyed with the idea of creating a new vice presidency at headquarters to whom Tianjin Otis would report. The person under consideration for the position was a Chinese-American but otherwise he had no relevant qualifications, in the opinion of Mallett and Wang, who did not want to deal with him. When Otis dug in its heels, Wang, after consultation with Mallett, wrote a letter saying he refused to deal with the proposed appointee. He insisted that Tianjin Otis continue reporting directly to the president of Otis. The stratagem worked because the bottom line at Otis is never to offend the Chinese.

Most of the time, however, Chinese managers are reluctant to sign memos, letters, or telexes for fear government officials will see the contents and react critically. Mallett indicates he had to "train managers to correspond with the outside world. At first, Mr. Wang would demur, saying I knew Otis's procedure better. But I convinced him that he should, too, in case I might be away."

Mallett also had to school Wang in Western bureaucracy, most particularly in intracompany correspondence. "The Chinese approach is to send a telex that reads 'X arriving on such and such a date. Please train," Mallett says. "We have to tell them the usual procedure is to send an inquiry as to when it would be most convenient for them to go, assuring the other end that Tianjin Otis will pay expenses and outlining what training is required."

Senior Chinese at joint ventures profess to like the Western style of clear-cut lines of decision making at each level of authority. Wu Zhi Peng, general manager at Shenmei Daily Use Products, explains: "Because joint ventures are newborn babies in China, we can learn much from outside management practices. Western management is very advanced and worth promoting and popularizing. The one aspect I find most distinctive is that there seldom is interference with managers' decisions. Personnel matters are the responsibility of the personnel manager and technical ones of the factory manager. Therefore, everyone can work efficiently and fully use their talents and abilities.

"However, the management techniques should be adapted to the local context. For example, before this factory became a joint venture, there was no open recruitment. We had to pioneer this in Shenyang." Wu's comment minimizes Shenmei's problems of recruitment. When local work units refused to release people Shenmei deemed acceptable, Shenmei's managers had to turn to Shenyang's mayor for help.

But Shenmei's personnel manager Chen Pei, admits that while Shenmei's one hundred and four workers include eighteen college and technical graduates, "the overall quality can't be compared with companies abroad." But, Chen hastens to add, "the quality is good for China." He says that on average he interviews ten people per opening, and "even then we may still not have the ideal candidate or his work unit will not release him."

Another area where Western management techniques required modification at Shenmei was the incentive system, Wu says. "Incentives are common in China; if they are not paid, workers are not at ease," he explains. "A successful incentive system combines Western philosophy with Chinese practices. Most Chinese enterprises do not have as detailed a system as Gillette's." Unlike the U.S. custom of recognizing individual merit plus overall productivity, Shenmei's is tied to aggregate results.

What follows is a comparison by Shenmei's materials manager, James Wang, of how his department is run Western-style versus the traditional Chinese methods. Wang was manager of the razor blade factory that Shenmei acquired. "There are eight people in my department and most have dual responsibilities, whereas they would not at Chinese enterprises," he says, "Dual responsibilities increase efficiency. Because people are always busy, there is no passing the buck, as can happen when there are extra people.

"For example we have three drivers. One picks up the Western managers at their hotel, takes them back, and also transports guests. The minitruck driver is responsible for the purchase and delivery of goods, both for domestic sale and exports. He must work on holidays and Sundays if the train is booked for then. The sedan driver mails letters and parcels, purchases train and plane tickets, and chauffeurs the Chinese general manager. Our drivers also act as handlers, if necessary, unlike at local companies, where there are people especially assigned. The others in the department also assist in loading and unloading when required."

Wang is proud of the large-scale responsibility his staff has in handling "one thousand materials that meet ten thousand specifications. They range from carbon and stainless steel to polypropylene wrapping, lacquer, lacquer thinner, printers' ink, grinding wheels, rubber stamps, press tools, and spare parts for machines," he says. "At the outset, we relied on imports, but now we are sourcing more and more materials locally. That shortens lead time and diminishes costs."

The Chinese also have had to adjust to such foreign management principles as flexibility in job assignments, advancement on the basis of merit rather than seniority, bonuses to induce greater output, management by objectives, and penalties for waywardness. The motivation of workers was almost destroyed during the Cultural Revolution. Since he became Chairman of China in 1977, Deng Xiaoping has endorsed the concept of *duo lao, duo de* (more work, more pay) as a cornerstone of the country's "four modernizations" program. But his enthusiasm has yet to penetrate all levels of China's bureaucracy. Many Chinese cling to another catchphrase, "the iron rice bowl"—job security no matter how little work a person performs.

Until the October 1986 reforms in which foreign companies were given carte blanche over compensation, hiring, and firing, the foreigners were often blocked by local officials hostile to Western management techniques. The bureaucrats maintained that personnel matters were internal and therefore off limits to foreigners. Because the personnel manager assigned to most joint ventures was usually a senior Communist Party official, foreign managers had little leeway.

Prior to the October 1986 changes, the primary recourse for foreigners concerned about the common practice of featherbedding was to insist on either a freeze on new workers or reductions through attrition. Occasionally, joint ventures were able to dictate exactly how many workers they wanted. Nevertheless, horror stories abounded among foreigners about Chinese sleeping on the job or whiling away the time by drinking tea, playing cards, and reading newspapers. In addition, the Western concept of a meritocracy, in which the best and brightest rise to the top regardless of age and are richly rewarded, clashed with China's traditional respect for elders. Thus, there was resentment when young Chinese in their twenties and thirties were appointed supervisors over people more advanced in years who had been their superiors by virtue of age even though they might lack the intelligence and talent to warrant their positions.

Gillette is one foreign partner that placed ability ahead of hurt feelings. C. I. Li, a twenty-four-year-old Chinese engineer, was Gillette's choice for quality control manager at Shenmei Daily Use Products. Jeffrey Wang became Gillette's marketing manager at age thirty. Shenmei's deputy general manager, Kelvin Tam, who is not much older, says that young people like Li and Wang, while recruited and trained by Gillette, "still need a lot of seasoning and on-the-job experience. We and they are eager for them to mature quickly but this can't be achieved through impatience. Because of their cultural background, the Chinese find it tough to be authoritative and supervise, and they dislike confrontations."

Gillette does try in some measure to assuage the sensitivity of older people through paying them more when they occupy the same positions as younger people. Other joint venture foreign partners try to be tactful, too. If a youthful de facto manager goes on a training course at an overseas branch of the foreign partner, his nominal supervisor is sent along for at least part of the time so he will not lose face, the worst possible embarrassment in Asia.

In addition to a basic salary that is up to 50 percent more than at state enterprises, joint ventures provide bonuses scaled to profit if the plant meets or surpasses its target. Some ventures pay the extra money monthly, others quarterly or annually. The standard practice is 10 percent extra if the goal is reached, another 5 percent if the target is exceeded by 10 percent, and 10 percent more if there is a 20 percent or greater overachievement. Performance evaluations are generally conducted after the first four months and thereafter annually at year-end.

In addition to the financial bonuses, workers get free lunches and allowances for tea, sugar, and haircuts. Many plants have bathhouses, for which soap and towels are provided at no charge. For the three-day festival celebrating the Chinese New Year, some joint ventures present employees with food baskets of chicken, shrimp, and other items. The Chinese New Year occurs in January or February in conjunction with cycles on the old Chinese lunar calendar. China's other statutory holidays are January 1, the New Year; May 1, International Labor Day; and October 1 and 2, the anniversary of the founding of the People's Republic of China.[3] China now adheres to the standard Gregorian calendar. The ancient Chinese calendar reckoned days and years in cycles of sixty.

Just as there are rewards for good conduct, there are penalties for misbehavior. However, enforcement is not easy because the ultimate weapon, firing, is anathema to Chinese officials. They prefer to fine and demote workers. The list of possible infractions is long: tardiness, absence, sleeping on the job, neglect of duty, abusive language, having pornographic literature, smoking in prohibited areas, spitting, picking one's nose, littering, improper use of equipment, damage to blueprints, and inattention to safety rules.[4] When misconduct occurs, a progressive series of punishments snaps into place.

The relevant department manager reports the infraction to the personnel manager. The latter speaks to the worker and then drafts a memo to the deputy and general managers for further action. For lesser offenses, they issue a "warning." The next stages in the severity of reprimands are "serious," or "yellow," followed by "red" warnings, which include token salary deductions. Repeated violations are subject to a fine, usually 10 percent of wages, plus a wage reduction of 10 percent.

Workers who do not reform can be fired but because of the difficulty in getting local government officials to approve firings, joint ventures encourage people to leave. Those Chinese at joint ventures who are conscientious say they approve of the Western system. "Here at Shenmei, we say that no iron rice bowl exists," personnel manager Chen Pei says proudly. "Because Shenmei has these regulations, most workers have a good attitude."

---

3. Those wishing to do business in Japan en route to or from China should avoid Golden Week, covering April 29 (the Emperor's birthday), May 3 (Constitution Memorial Day), and May 5 (Children's Day). Japanese businesses close during this period, and usually several days' more vacation are added at either end.
4. It is estimated that 80 percent of Chinese males smoke. However, CAAC has banned smoking on domestic flights. The government posts signs at cultural and historical attractions prohibiting spitting and littering. But it is not uncommon to see children urinating in public view as their parents take them through these places.

Ironically, one of the few disagreements between Shenmei's senior expatriate, Kelvin Tam, and senior Chinese, Wu Zhi Peng, arose when Tam wanted to retain a person who "resigned" and Wu did not. Tam thought the individual should have a second chance because he was a "gifted university graduate." Shenyang's labor department also urged that he be kept "because of the good opportunities at Shenmei." Consequently, Wu relented.

Office layout plays an important role in fostering greater worker effort. The typical quarters of Chinese officials are a shock to Westerners accustomed to the comfortable and frequently palatial decor at corporate headquarters outside China. Since elevators are not allowed in low rises, visitors normally have to climb many flights of concrete stairs. On each landing there are spittoons, often former chamber pots, filled with water for the disposal of cigarettes. The Chinese are hospitable, serving tea from vividly painted thermoses, but their offices are sparsely furnished. Windows often are unwashed and covered with torn plastic or threadbare curtains.

Plant layout is also very different. Unlike the vast hangarlike U.S. factories, Chinese plants are filled with cubbyholes in which workers can sleep unnoticed. Thus, foreign managers place the remodeling of facilities into brightly lit open spaces high on their agenda.

China Hewlett-Packard, for example, is a replica of Hewlett-Packard's open office landscaping, even to the rose color of the partition screens and the pearl gray of the frames of the fluorescent lights. Chi-ning Liu says it took forty-five days to transform the building. When not enough light frames could be found in the desired shade, the China Hewlett-Packard team painted them.

"Traditionally, the Chinese workplace is very structured, with Indians and chiefs who have their own cubicles," Liu remarks. "By contrast, one could describe HP as a socialistic-capitalistic company run as a classless society, since it has open office landscaping, and employees can speak to one another without appointments. Also, they are on a first-name basis.

"We wanted to set up a similar system in China from the outset so the Chinese would see we meant what we said about HP's credo of 'management by wandering around,' " says Liu. He deliberately located his office midway on the floor so that employees would feel free to drop in and chat with him. He also made the personnel department highly visible so that staff could readily look in when walking to and fro. "I did this to remove the mystery that the Chinese tend to assign to Personnel," Liu explains. Completing his tour of the U.S.-style layout, he grinned and said, "See, it can be done."

Chinese cooperation also is more likely if the Chinese see that the expatriates receive no special treatment. For example, when William Mallett arrived at Tianjin Otis, he was distressed to find that the expatriates had placed a sign outside their office saying "experts' department." He immediately slotted them into their respective divisions at the factory, either training the Chinese or reporting to Chinese managers. When one expatriate protested, Mallett sent him home. To underline his message, Mallett turned to that symbol of power in China—the car. All the senior Chinese managers were given new automobiles.

Considerable attention is devoted by foreign joint venture managers to quality control as a way to increase efficiency and output. The Chinese term for this is *jishu gaizao,* literally "technical reformation" but better known as "civilized management." The mission of the Chinese in joint ventures is to acquire state-of-the-art technology, whereas the more mundane goal of the foreigners is to start at the beginning by upgrading the factory and existing machine tools. The factories occupied by joint ventures are usually thirty to forty years old. Normally, their layout is unrelated to natural production flow. Maintenance and cleanliness are poor.

Although their facilities are not equal to the gleaming, brightly lit, spacious factories of North America, in a few years joint ventures in China have made tremendous strides. Most have undertaken some landscaping even if the small entrance only permits a few forsythia bushes, petunias, or pansies. Some courtyards also contain a basketball hoop as well as a painting of the Great Wall done by an employee. Inside, the heat or air conditioning may be inadequate by Western standards, some tools may lie on the floor where people can trip over them, and the production line may not be quite as dust-free as in Japanese, American, or European factories but still the clutter and grime of the typical Chinese factory is absent.

The first step toward "civilized management" is painting yellow lines to demarcate clear passages for walking. Previously, containers and equipment spilled all over the place, making crossing the floor hazardous. Equipment used to become scratched or rusted from being dumped close together on the uncovered floor. Now it is stacked on racks, and the racks are placed in squares outlined by white paint so that people do not stumble into them.

Color coding distinguishes between wiring for electricity and heat. This identification system is also used to differentiate between cabinets for various tools and to indicate heavy loading machinery.

"Civilized management" in this form is both easy to implement and inexpensive because it applies to layout and not people. Extension of the concept to workers is a slower process but of greater significance, since the quality of what is produced determines whether the joint venture will become an exporter or be confined to domestic sales. When the foreign partner puts the importance of quality control in this context, the Chinese are more prepared to listen.

How quality control is implemented is well illustrated by Beijing Jeep. The front lawns of the numerous buildings that constitute the automobile factory are covered with many signs in Chinese and English, exhorting better quality and service. They read: "Quality first, customer first" "Strive to speed up localization of the XJ" "Build a civilized factory" "Develop top management, top products, top employees." To achieve these goals, Beijing Jeep has a comprehensive set of quality control standards for its four thousand workers and for its suppliers.

These standards are an adaptation, rather than an exact replica, of those of the U.S. cofounder, American Motors. Quality control director Ernest Regehr, an AMC veteran, emphasizes that what works in America cannot be transplanted completely into China but must be tailored to local production volumes and Chinese sensitivities. "In the United States, where about forty cars are made an hour, it is cost-efficient to run several tests a day on expensive equipment to determine the strength of body welding sheets through efforts to tear them apart," he explains. "But in China, where only one or two cars are assembled an hour, such experiments could destroy a far greater proportion of production. Moreover, the far smaller output does not justify the purchase of such a test device. Thus, we examine the durability with available machinery."

As in U.S. car plants, inspectors are stationed along Beijing Jeep's assembly line. They check what the worker has done against the job instruction sheet. For example, are the fuel and brake lines installed in the right place and the connections secured? Or is a part loose, damaged, or the wrong one? Regehr concedes that as yet quality control is not at the point where defects are automatically detected and corrected where they occur.

Consequently, Beijing Jeep still follows an AMC recommendation that after each item on the checklist is approved, a color coded sticker be attached to the vehicle. When a sticker is applied, it triggers the next step in the assembly sequence. AMC still trains Beijing Jeep workers in the United States for six to fifteen weeks. At the height of the launching of the venture, it stationed twelve expatriates "permanently" (for several years) at Beijing Jeep and assigned thirty temporary experts for the first three months. Forty percent of Beijing Jeep's workers were formerly employed at AMC's partner, Beijing Automotive Works.

Tact, patience, and perseverance are also essential for communicating the importance of quality control measures, Regehr advises. "The Chinese approach to resolution of problems differs sharply from that of Americans," he cautions. "The Chinese are much less confrontational than Americans. In the United States, it is not unusual to employ crude, angry language in telling employees that what they have done is unacceptable. The Chinese are just as objective-oriented, but they do not mind traveling around the mountain to achieve their purpose rather than through it, as Americans are apt to do.

"Those Westerners who are accustomed to slamming their fist on the desk to get action would thereby upset the Chinese and, as a result, would not achieve their purpose nor last long in China. Foreigners must be willing to spend the requisite time to reach a compromise between the two extremes of American and Chinese cultural values. It is vital that they do so, because although the Chinese want our technology and our type of financial results, there are limits to how far they will accept our methods."

AMC criteria also are used in the selection of Chinese suppliers. When a company asks to be a vendor to Beijing Jeep, the venture sends a quality control technician along with the purchasing representative to investigate the firm's worthiness. They take a questionnaire patterned on AMC's U.S. system. Its contents cover the average skill of the workers at the prospective supplier, the state of its workshops, its ability to design new items, and the quality control organization.

To gauge the record of the quality control department, Beijing Jeep's people query its size, to whom it reports, if it has a quality control manual, a separate out-of-the-way area for scrap, process documents defining each production step, and accurate calibration instruments. Should the prospect subcontract its work, Beijing Jeep puts the subsuppliers through the same review.

Satisfactory completion of production merely carries managers halfway through the often tortuous process of doing business in China. They must subsequently grapple with how to merchandise their wares in a country unfamiliar with Western marketing notions. North American, European, and Japanese manufacturers tend to offer "full-service" packages that include installation and after-sale checkups. Generally, they derive more money from this work than from the original transaction.

By contrast, under China's state-planned economy the relationship between supplier and customer ends with the conclusion of the deal. The government allocates products to the end users and also designates the installers. The only way joint ventures can break what is tantamount to a monopoly is to threaten not to supply machinery unless they are permitted to put it in place as well.

Western managers who believe merchandising is merchandising no matter where, quickly realize this is not so in China. To the Chinese, the American habit of sounding out consumer needs and preferences by means of surveys and then designing suitable goods is an alien concept. Consequently, joint ventures have no reliable historical data as the foundation for targeting sales.

Another merchandising headache is what joint venture managers term "phantom boundaries" between provinces, caused by centuries of competition. This rivalry thwarts attempts to sell nationally even when China's primitive transportation and distribution systems are working. Overcoming these obstacles through advertising is difficult because merchandising promotion is in its infancy in China. During the Cultural Revolution, China banned advertising on the grounds that it was capitalistic. But Chairman Deng canceled the prohibition as part of his overall campaign to reverse the policies of the Cultural Revolution. In 1987, Deng underlined his approval of advertising when he invited many of the world's largest advertising agencies to Beijing for talks.

Because there are few pages in general-interest Chinese newspapers, there are long waits to purchase advertising space. An exception is the specialty *China Advertisement and Information,* a semiweekly that primarily consists of ads, including color supplements, interspersed with inspirational stories on Chinese entrepreneurs.

Television advertising is an alternative, since many Chinese now own television sets. However, Chinese advertisers have yet to adopt Madison Avenue's techniques of bombarding viewers with commercials throughout shows and of matching the content to the audience. Instead, advertisements are bunched at the end of programs, and commercials about children's toys are apt to be run late at night, while those for machine tools accompany afternoon cartoons.

In 1985, China published an advertising code which prohibits criticism of state policy as well as "reactionary, obscene, evil, or superstitious materials." Pretty girls may be used as models but blatant sexual images are taboo. Advertisements of foreign businesses must receive government approval.

It is apparent that the task of joint venture managers in China is arduous. But thanks to the pioneers of the last decade, the next wave of foreign joint venture partners will likely have less cause for frayed nerves. Moreover, despite periodic outbursts in China against "bourgeois liberalism," the leadership is committed to modernization of the country's thousands of antiquated enterprises. Also, many more joint ventures are likely to start up in China because its basic appeal remains: it has the world's largest population.

# *10*   *The Europeans*

Volkswagen, Western Europe's largest car manufacturer and Number Four globally, and Ford, Number Two globally, are in a joint venture in Latin America that ranks among the world's ten biggest passenger car enterprises. Pilkington Brothers of England, the world's largest glass manufacturer, parlayed a seemingly mundane joint venture in ophthalmic glass into the production of holographic instrument displays for the American F-16 fighter plane and the development of bifocal contact lenses. International Computers of England, whose existence is crucial to the country's being a leader in the world's computer industry, is alive today largely due to a joint venture begun in 1981 with Fujitsu.

Varity Corporation, the world's largest tractor and diesel engine manufacturer, which changed its name in 1986 from Massey-Ferguson, views a small joint venture in the Philippines that leases farm machinery as a laboratory experiment for how the greening of Africa and Asia can be achieved. George Wimpey, Britain's largest building company, and Tishman Realty & Construction Company of New York, among the top five U.S. construction managers, have formed a joint venture of brain power. Based in London, the collaboration is going after the high-tech, high-rise market created by the influx of foreign investment dealers and banks into England's financial services industry as well as by the burgeoning demand for shopping centers.

While this book concentrates on joint ventures from the viewpoint of North American and Asian participants, the rest of the world cannot be ignored. Therefore, this chapter describes the ventures of some prominent European companies whose successes or failures provide universally applicable lessons about the merits and difficulties of hands-across-the-ocean partnerships.

The reasons for the Europeans' entry into joint ventures reflect those of companies elsewhere: new growth opportunities, a desire for the latest technology on cost-effective terms, and the demand of developing nations for partly domestic ownership. Furthermore, they believe that in gratitude for their direct investment, local governments very likely will freeze out imports or erect stiff tariffs against them. Either action would aid joint ventures in those countries.

The setbacks the Europeans have encountered also mirror those of their counterparts in other nations: seemingly propitious circumstances turn sour or the partners clash. Consequently, some prominent firms remain wary of joint ventures, relegating them to last place in their corporate strategies. Siemens, the West German telecommunications giant, feels this way. Jörg Wehr, senior director, contract department, at Siemens, says: "The purpose of joint ventures is to produce the equivalent of ham and eggs. But while the chicken only has to lay an egg, a pig must be slaughtered to produce ham. Thus, the pig does not want to make its contribution. The same is true in a joint venture—neither partner wants to be the pig."

The Volkswagen-Ford alliance, Auto-Latina, which operates in Brazil and Argentina, has received relatively little attention compared to the joint ventures between American and Japanese, British and Japanese, and German and Japanese car makers. Yet Auto-Latina is the biggest. It has a joint annual production capacity of 1 million vehicles, four times the average intended yearly output of 250,000 units in other automotive collaborations between competitors. And Auto-Latina has as many employees, 60,000, as VW does at its headquarters plant in Wolfsburg, West Germany.

Auto-Latina was born out of weakness; both Ford and VW had suffered many years of heavy losses in Brazil and Argentina and saw no other way to survive. Neither wanted to withdraw, because a pullout would have been costly and a reentry if the market improved would have been difficult because the governments would look askance at the companies' abandonment. "We decided to multiply our minuses in the hope that, as in mathematics, they would produce a plus," comments Kristian Ehinger, general counsel, foreign holdings, at Volkswagen. In the argot of the industry, "what's under the hood"—the chassis, engine, transmission, and so on—is identical, but the exterior and brand names of the two partners are retained. The cross-supply of parts is expected to yield economies of scale on the assembly line and in development of new models and purchasing of components. The likely result is the closure of some of their plants.

Although the venture takes the same form in Brazil and Argentina, VW and Ford decided to form separate legal entities to avoid double taxation and not injure local pride by having the operations in one country a subsidiary of those in the other. There were other potential partners VW could have chosen, most notably General Motors, which has been in Venezuela for forty years and has a 34 percent market share in motor vehicle sales there. But VW settled on Ford because GM's heavy investment and price cutting to gain market share in Brazil indicated it was not anxious to cooperate with a competitor.[1]

Together, VW and Ford have a 55 percent market share in Brazil and Argentina but that is 55 percent of a wobbly market. Although Brazil alone had production capacity of close to 2 million cars, demand over the five years preceding the formation of Auto-Latina was so slack that full output was never reached. Moreover, the fate of the venture is not entirely in its own hands but is largely under the control of the Brazilian government, which sets all prices. Shortly after the establishment of Auto-Latina, the government refused to permit the venture to raise prices commensurate with the increase in wages demanded by its unions. In an

---

1. In February 1988, GM sold 51 percent of its operations to the Mendoza Group, a diversified firm with investments in automobile assembly and distribution as well as banking and agriculture.

effort to force the government to capitulate, Auto-Latina stopped production and laid off its workers.

The match between Ford and VW, which to the discomfiture of their rivals, could very well lead to further shared efforts, brings together a relative novice to joint ventures—Ford—with a company that has made them an integral part of its international expansion. Whereas Ford was established in the nineteenth century and had plants around the globe by World War II, Volkswagen, which was 16 percent owned by the West German government until the spring of 1988 when the government sold its stake to the public, did not get fully under way until the war ended. The young company searched for untapped markets and decided on the developing nations of Nigeria, Indonesia, and Yugoslavia. Unfortunately, all three ventures fared poorly: in Nigeria, seemingly propitious circumstances turned sour; in Indonesia, the market was too small and the competition too heavy; and in Yugoslavia, there were foreign exchange problems.

In 1972, VW was jubilant when the Nigerian government allowed it in as one of two foreign car makers (Peugeot of France was the other). Nigeria appeared to be a promising place for car sales because rich deposits of oil and minerals had poured enough money into the pockets of the large population for it to afford cars. The government, in its eagerness for the development of the nation's infant auto industry, also permitted joint ventures to import "knock-down" parts for assembly at far lower customs duties than the rates on complete imported cars.

Volkswagen's glee over this concession quickly evaporated. It realized that even when at or near full production capacity, it could not compete with imports because its output was too small to justify the costs. Together with Peugeot, VW's venture could have supplied all 200,000 locally produced cars purchased yearly in Nigeria; yet there were also joint ventures involving other European car makers as well as some from the United States and Japan. If the outlook was questionable in good times, bad times would bring disaster.

Bad times came in two waves. First, the 1973 oil shock knocked car makers worldwide into a slump. Then, in 1986, a new government in Nigeria pulled the props out from under joint ventures by dropping the customs regulations that protected the industry. Sales of locally made cars plummeted to a mere ten thousand per year. British Leyland deliberately declared its joint venture bankrupt to avoid continuing losses. VW, as Ehinger puts it, is "trying to come through the winter" by paring costs to a minimum through shortened work weeks, avoiding long-term contracts, and keeping minimal inventory.

In Indonesia, however, VW elected not to weather a bad situation. It had entered a joint venture with Daimler-Benz and the Indonesian government in the early 1970s, shortly after the government reopened its doors to all foreign investment in an effort to offset massive Japanese inroads. However, Volkswagen soon saw that even though Indonesia had a population of 100 million, VW was unlikely to get much business. First, the government had not created a favorable climate of protectionist measures for joint ventures. Thus, the Japanese maintained their grip on 95 percent of the market. Second, there were insufficient pickings for the ten joint venture car makers that Indonesia had attracted. Sensing the futility of its position, VW sold out its share to Daimler-Benz.

In Yugoslavia, VW's joint venture so far is a disappointment because of foreign exchange difficulties and unrealistic expectations that Yugoslavia would provide an entry into other Eastern Bloc countries. In the venture's early years, it made use of other forex earnings by the Yugoslav partner to offset its own expenditures on imported components. But recent foreign exchange shortages in Yugoslavia have forced the venture to export as much as one-third of its production for sale by VW's distribution network.

VW's visions of exports to the Eastern Bloc were based on historically close economic and cultural ties between West Germany and Eastern Europe. During the Czarist period, Russia had invited the Germans to develop Russian industry, and German is the common language spoken by lawyers from the Eastern nations at meetings not attended by the Russians. Ostensibly, Eastern Europe is a lucrative market; East Germany, for instance, ranks among the world's top ten in terms of per capita income. However, while the potential was real, VW's hopes were grounded by the desire of each Eastern European country to develop its own car industry.

In the 1980s, as VW meteorically rose under a new chairman (the current incumbent, Carl Hahn) from Number Five to Number One in Europe, it changed the nature of its participation in joint ventures from equity to nonequity contractual arrangements. It began by supplying the nearly bankrupt Chrysler Corporation with an engine, the first time it furnished a competitor with a major component—not just a minor part, but what Kristian Ehinger vividly describes as the "beating heart of a car." Next, VW supplied Sweden's Volvo with an engine and jointly developed transmissions with France's Renault.

The international transactions paralleled a similar alteration in its domestic strategy. Basically, the engine in the Porsche 900 is that of the old VW Beetle.[2] Volkswagen's luxury, high-speed Audi 100 and 200 models and the Porsche 924 and 944 all use the Audi water-cooled engine. VW, however, does not buy components from competitors.

To outsiders, VW's decision to provide an engine to ailing Chrysler seemed an act of folly. But VW was serene. Bank guarantees made certain it would be paid. Moreover, VW cannily judged it could fulfill several other objectives through the arrangement. First, because a firm can charge outsiders more for parts than its own divisions, VW's profit margin on the sales to Chrysler was higher than its internal one. Also, with its foot in the door, it would have a better chance to acquire a U.S. plant when Chrysler put up some of its facilities for sale, and, in this, its calculation proved correct. Finally, the company viewed the transaction as a way to reassure its German employees that any connection to the United States would not cause a loss of jobs in West Germany.

Subsequently, Volkswagen, like the Big Three U.S. automakers, linked hands with its Japanese competitors, but its deal with Nissan for Nissan to assemble annually 60,000 Santanas (a taxi-type vehicle) did not work out as expected. To date, Nissan has yet to produce more than 25,000 vehicles yearly. Volkswagen believed it was also short-changed in the amount of marketing and quality control information Nissan provided as its part of the deal. Nevertheless, Volkswagen planned to renew the pact, albeit under terms more favorable to itself.

In West Germany, Volkswagen and Toyota have joined forces to produce pickup trucks. Volkswagen regards the venture as an opportunity to add a new line at less expense than if it had not shared the development costs. Also, because the trucks will be made in an under-used VW plant in Hanover, the factory can be kept open.

2. It was Ferdinand Porsche who, in 1934, first had the idea of a *Volkswagen* (people's car).

From Toyota's viewpoint, the venture is astute public relations. West Germany, the largest car market in Europe, is the only major one to grant Far East manufacturers free access. In 1986, 24 percent of Japan's automobile exports to Europe were sold in West Germany. However, with pressure rising in the European Community, to which West Germany belongs, for voluntary quotas similar to those imposed by the United States on Japan's car makers, Toyota's venture with VW is its way of saying that, in this case at least, it would rather cooperate than compete.

As part of its international strategy, Volkswagen also has a joint venture in China. Located in Shanghai, the venture assembles Santanas from components imported from West Germany and plans to construct an engine plant. About four-fifths of the engines would be exported to VW plants to earn foreign exchange. "China was the only large country that was a bare spot in our automotive map," Ehinger stated when asked why VW was the first European car maker to move into China. The ultimate target of the venture is to assemble 30,000 cars per year. In 1987, its second year, its output reached 15,000.

Like American Motors, VW found business conditions in China to be a mixture of yin (darkness) and yang (light). The yang is that VW negotiated a far tougher contract than American Motors did. While AMC's contract is extremely short, VW's runs five hundred pages. Unlike AMC, VW made no commitments about local components but only pledged its "best efforts" to develop Chinese sources. Ehinger says VW classifies its 160-million-mark investment in China as a "defensible risk" because even if "Volkswagen were to lose its entire investment, it wouldn't break down." The venture lost money at the outset but is now profitable despite several yin-type problems.

As Peter Förster, a senior lawyer in the foreign holdings department at VW points out, "China has 1 billion people but no streets." His joke underlines the problem of China's poor road system. Consequently, traffic is intracity, not intercity, depressing the need for cars. Like all joint ventures in China, the VW undertaking was hampered by the stifling bureaucracy and infrastructure and personnel problems. At one point, Martin Posth, seconded by VW as deputy manager of the venture, was so exasperated that he said if the plant were in Germany, he would lay off 80 percent of the staff. However, since replacement of workers is difficult in a country that does not have an organized labor market, Posth started a training center instead.

Just as Volkswagen used its engine to forge its web of associations, Pilkington Glass owes much of its international success to technology. Its leading position is due to its 1950s invention of the float glass process in which molten glass flows over molten tin and into a huge float tank, where it cools and hardens. This method yields higher-quality glass than the conventional sheet technique, in which the molten glass is drawn out on a bar. Float glass also is regarded as being better than plate glass, which is marred when pressed into shape by a mangle. Every year, Pilkington derives £30 million in royalty revenue from eighty-six rival plants around the world to which it has granted float glass technology transfers. Pilkington itself has eighteen float glass factories.

Because the float process yields high-quality glass at low cost, it has revolutionized the glass business. Hitherto it was a parochial industry in which each company stuck primarily to its home base. But the ease with which float glass can be made enabled glassmakers to expand globally. However, for a float glass plant to be profitable, it must produce between three and six thousand metric tonnes per week. Thus, Pilkington seeks constant demand. To ensure this, it frequently engages in joint ventures with the leading local glass producer that has an established distribution network. "This method makes it possible for Pilkington to steer clear of the problems of a hostile landing," explains company secretary David Bricknell.

In the course of time, however, a market may grow to the point where it can support more than one float plant and each partner is eager to operate its own. Pilkington recently encountered this situation in Brazil, where it has a partnership with a French firm that was there first. It resolved the potential impasse with the suggestion that each side move away from the joint manufacturing aspect of their arrangement but continue joint marketing. The side effect of this split in manufacturing is that Pilkington is in a position to install new technology without worrying about a seepage of information to other plants of the French firm, which outside of Brazil is a competitor.

Pilkington also illustrates how joint ventures by the end user can lead to the creation of joint ventures by suppliers. Twenty-five percent of Pilkington's revenue is derived from the sale of automotive glass. According to Bricknell, one out of every five cars contains Pilkington glass. None, however, is Japanese. To end this shutout, Pilkington has zeroed in on a new market— American-Japanese automotive joint ventures based in the United States.

Its task is made easier since it has a substantial U.S. presence through a big glass concern it acquired a few years ago. In the early 1980s, Pilkington purchased the 30 percent interest that Gulf & Western held in LOF, the second largest U.S. glass producer. LOF was also in hydraulics and plastics, neither of which interested Pilkington. After two years, it struck a deal with LOF in which it sold back its 30 percent in exchange for LOF's glass business.

The transaction occurred as Japanese auto imports were quickly increasing their share of car sales in the United States. The LOF glass division acquired by Pilkington supplied 65 percent of General Motors' glass. But it realized it was in potential jeopardy as the battle between Japanese and U.S. car makers intensified and moved onto U.S. soil with the establishment of Japanese plants. The problem was how to break into the closed circle of Japanese suppliers because Japanese car makers usually convince their component manufacturers to follow them into new territories.

The solution was to join Japan's second largest glassmaker, Nippon Sheet Glass, in three joint ventures: a Mexican plant that ships glass to the United States, a Korean operation that makes glass for cars intended for export, and a factory in Kentucky to supply Nissan's car plant there. Nissan is a longtime Nippon Glass customer.

Pilkington's diversification into holographic imagery for the F-16 fighter plane and into bifocal contact lenses demonstrates how unexpected, lucrative new opportunities can arise when ingenuity is used to breathe fresh life into a venture. In the 1960s, Pilkington, which already was making ophthalmic glass, determined it should move into downstream products. Lacking the expertise, it formed a joint venture with a leading American firm, Perkin-Elmer. After six years, Perkin-Elmer withdrew, but by then Pilkington had mastered the fabrication of light devices that enable night vision and the holographic techniques that led to the F-16 and the bifocal contact lens work.

Pilkington's success encouraged it to purchase in 1987 the Revlon Group's Vision Care businesses, including the Barnes-Hind line of contact lens products. Pilkington now derives 17 percent of its revenue from ophthalmic-related devices and expects the amount to reach 30 percent by the 1990s because of the graying of European and North American populations. "We are getting older, and as we get older we require more eye care," Pilkington chairman Anthony Pilkington said at the time of the acquisition.

Pilkington's company secretary David Bricknell stresses that Pilkington might never have moved into this flourishing field had it not been for the venture with Perkin-Elmer: "The joint venture lasted only a short time but what we learned has blossomed and grown enormously."

Besides its ventures in float glass in Australia, Brazil, Taiwan, and Mexico, Pilkington has one in China. Unlike most foreign firms in China, it did not chase the Chinese. The Chinese traveled to Pilkington's headquarters in St. Helens, near Liverpool, and asked if Pilkington would license its float glass process to them on a technology-transfer, royalty-fee basis.

During the talks, Pilkington officials discovered that the Chinese had approached them only after they had tried unsuccessfully to copy Pilkington's method and thereby avoid paying royalties. At that time, the Chinese were not abiding by international standards of patent protection. They had studied Pilkington's patents, read all the available literature, and toured float glass plants in the Eastern Bloc but were still unable to produce quality float glass. So they finally came to the source—Pilkington.

Pilkington entered into a series of two-week negotiating sessions under the impression that the Chinese merely wished to obtain rights to its technology. It was not until the eighth round that the Chinese declared they preferred a joint venture so as to make certain they would receive ongoing assistance in training, purchasing, and other functions in the operation of a plant. They persuaded Pilkington to provide even more—what Pilkington's chief negotiator, Solomon Kay, describes as a "complete technology package. Normally, we supply only the float bath process, but the Chinese also wanted to learn how to select the raw material from quarries and cut and melt glass." Pilkington agreed in return for a fee.

When the Chinese requested that the technology transfer be altered to a joint venture, Pilkington could have refused. After all, the nature of the agreement suddenly had shifted from one in which it was to be paid to one in which it would have to invest. The Chinese suggested that Pilkington take a 12.5 percent stake in the £60-million plant. They had neatly cornered Pilkington! Pilkington was well aware that an Eastern Bloc float glass plant, which had completed its royalty payments to Pilkington, might sell the technology to the Chinese even though such action would undoubtedly trigger a legal battle with Pilkington.

But Pilkington was a willing victim because a joint venture could provide an opportunity to make itself known in China at little risk. The Chinese agreed to bear 64 percent of the cost, including the preparation of the site and the construction of two wharves to receive and dispatch materials, a gas plant, and the building's exterior. Because all this was paid for in renminbi, the venture was able to conserve its foreign exchange. The Chinese refused, however, to give Pilkington any say regarding the plant's location. They selected Shanghai, a logical choice because Shanghai is an industrial center. Unfortunately, the land in the area is spongy clay into which everything sinks; consequently, it took a year to install sufficiently long pilings for the plant. Normally, such work takes only two months.

From his experience in negotiating the joint venture, which began operations in late 1987, four years after the deal was signed, Solomon Kay dispenses some blunt advice to foreigners starry-eyed about opportunities in China. Most important, he says, is for foreigners to be sure they are offering what the Chinese really want. "The feeling seems to be that if you're not in China, you're a poor manager," he comments. "Consequently, China is crawling with foreigners—mostly Americans—who often are offering things in which the Chinese are not interested, such as financial services, management consulting, and textbooks. The Chinese are intensely curious and are gaining information from people willing to sell their grandmother in order to gain entry into the Chinese marketplace. Moreover, their economy benefits if a lot of green-horns come and spend money on hotels and CAAC flights in a futile chase for business."

Next, he cautions that foreigners should be prepared for tough negotiations: "The Chinese grow up in a tough environment: harsh living conditions, low wages, cycling to and from work, toughness in the Party and in the Army. Thus, they can't be pushed around. They negotiate like tigers. Foreigners must be prepared to grit their teeth and do the same. Also, the Chinese are very clear-headed thinkers, and foreigners, in their anxiety to obtain a deal, should not be stampeded into agreements."

Kay practiced what he preaches. Novices to China frequently sign documents under the pressure of catching a plane home and wanting to bring back some accomplishment. Kay, however,

often refused, confident that Pilkington would be understanding
if he returned empty-handed. His adamant stand served to put the
Chinese on the defensive: as they drove him to the airport, they
bargained all the way. On those occasions, when Kay found their
revised terms acceptable, he signed by the light of the car's dome
fixture as the automobile screeched up to the terminal. He emphasizes that the Chinese have abided by the deal 100 percent:
"They have never been late in their royalty payments."

As Kay states, many foreigners have flocked to China even
though "customer pull does not equal sales push." One firm that
has elected not to rush in is Varity Corporation, formerly Massey-
Ferguson, notwithstanding its history of joint ventures in developing countries. Although Varity, whose roots date to 1847, is a
Canadian company with its world headquarters in Toronto, North
America ranks behind Asia, Africa, and Europe as a market for
its products, and its global trade is directed from London.

Varity has longstanding ties with the Chinese from its sale of
agricultural equipment to China through the World Bank. However, even though the Chinese indicated that Massey-Ferguson
tractors were their first choice for a technology transfer, Varity
rejected their overtures for a joint venture. The stumbling block
was the insistence of the Chinese that a substantial amount of
production be exported. From past experience in joint ventures,
Varity realized that the Chinese were unrealistic about the speed
with which their equipment would attain internationally accepted
standards. For example, it had taken Varity's Polish associate nine-
teen years to progress from a local assembly operation to full-scale
manufacturing of tractors.

Moreover, Varity was concerned that exports by the Chinese
would exacerbate the already grave worldwide oversupply of farm
equipment. For the past decade, the tractor industry has been
operating at half its capacity. In 1986, the market contracted by
another 10 percent, equivalent to the loss of $1 billion in business.
Varity itself suffered heavy losses in six out of eight years through
fiscal 1987. Its work force is one-third its 1979 size. Consequently,
Varity must be extremely careful as to where it makes
commitments.

For this reason, it also has refrained from licensing Russian
farm machinery producers or forming associations with them.
Lewis Hall, manager, licensee development, at Massey-Ferguson
Tractors, explains: "First, the Russians asked if Massey-Ferguson

would help upgrade their products, as we have done in Poland, but, unlike the Poles, they were unwilling to enter into a licensing agreement. They only wanted Massey-Ferguson to act as consultants and we were not in that business. Also, with the downsizing of the company, we must make the best possible use of our remaining resources.

"Next, the Russians requested a technology transfer but they were not interested in taking any product in return. Even if they had been, there is no urgency for us to be involved in a manufacturing venture in Russia because of the overall downturn in farm machinery sales."

Although the dismal outlook for farm machinery has cooled Varity's interest in China and Russia, it owes its world leadership largely to its longstanding international thrust. The company began exporting as early as the 1860s. Today, it derives 35 percent of its revenue from developing nations to which it licenses technology or in which it holds a joint venture minority interest.

Thanks to its early emphasis on international sales, Varity believes its market share in developing countries is twice that of its competitors. This dominance might not have come about had Canada's population been larger, resulting in a greater domestic demand, explains Roger Clarke, chairman of Varity World Trade. "The U.S. farm machinery producer, John Deere, operates in a large domestic market and derives a substantial portion of its sales from a two-hundred-mile radius around its Moline, Illinois, headquarters," he comments. "This is in stark contrast to the absence of grain farming in the same distance around Toronto, Varity's headquarters."

According to Clarke, Varity's participation in joint ventures went through two phases: those it initiated and those in which government rules regarding outside investment dictated a shared effort. As Clarke phrases it, the first stage was "missionary, in which Varity offered to assist in the mechanization of agriculture," and the second was "defensive, in which governments insisted on local content." Varity now has licensing arrangements in twenty-one nations, ranging from Kenya to Pakistan and Yugoslavia, and joint ventures in ten, including Saudi Arabia, India, and Peru.

Hall points out that though the licensing agreements do not involve a financial investment, they do require a substantial investment of time. "Our technology transfers are not confined to how to make products but also entail material scheduling and training in machinery operation and maintenance," he emphasizes. Varity runs a training center in England and dispatches traveling caravans to instruct users in remote locales.

While Varity's joint ventures tend to be large scale, it is exploring the potential of smaller markets that when added together, justify the attention. To test this concept, it has a 20 percent stake in a joint venture in a northern Philippine state with a group of Filipino investors and a Bermuda venture capital company. The venture rents sophisticated equipment to farmers whose plots are too small to warrant a fleet of equipment but too big to handle with water buffaloes and garden hoes. The Philippine government restricts individual farm holdings to seventeen-and-a-half acres.

Varity anticipates that this method of distributing machinery will become a potent force in agriculture because, as Clarke notes, "corporate farms are out of gear with the realities of agriculture. Tens of millions of people scratch out a living with a stick." Thus, the greening of Africa and Asia will be the chore of individual farmers. Varity believes that the total of their orders could equal a bulk sale to huge plantations. "The Philippines could support one hundred such ventures, and Africa, thousands," Clarke says. "One alone might only yield one million dollars in revenue but one thousand would be very lucrative."

While Varity is thinking small to reap big rewards, the focus of the real estate development joint venture of George Wimpey and Tishman is on projects of $30 million and up. Established in late 1987, the venture first targeted the explosive demand for new office space in London caused by deregulation of England's financial markets in October 1986. The venture functions on a project-by-project basis, leaving the partners free to accept independent assignments.

The alliance brings together well-matched companies. Best known as the United Kingdom's Number One house builder, publicly owned Wimpey is also a major contractor; an asphalt, waste management, and mining operator; and a leading commercial developer. Its office tower projects include the $800-million Hong Kong headquarters of the HongKong & Shanghai Banking Corporation, completed in 1985.

Privately owned Tishman Realty & Construction is in its third generation of family management. Of the four structures in the world that are one hundred or more stories, Tishman built three— the 100-floor John Hancock Center in Chicago and the twin 110-

story towers of the World Trade Center in New York. The fourth, the 110-floor Sears Tower in Chicago, was erected by an associated company. Tishman Realty & Construction was also in charge of developing the EPCOT Center at Disney World in Florida and of renovating Carnegie Hall in New York in 1983–1986. The firm is regarded as a specialist in "smart" office towers, buildings wired so as to control everything from air conditioning to elevators and security.

Wimpey realized that, despite its years of experience, it did not possess Tishman's particular skills. "Wimpey lacks the expertise to do high-rise, high-tech buildings that the financial services industry requires, such as raised floors for the installation of computer wiring," explains Jay Eichel, the Tishman first vice president in charge of the venture. "On the other hand, Wimpey was conversant with how to estimate and how to gather a work force in the U.K. environment."

According to John Chappel, manager of business development at Wimpey, Tishman's strength lies in its emphasis on seeing a project through from start to finish. "In the United Kingdom, the tendency is for subcontractors to deal directly with the client, whereas Tishman concerns itself with the whole package, and this approach makes sense in the changing market here," he explains. Further, he points out, Tishman's contacts with major U.S. financial houses for which it has done projects and with such well-known U.S. architects as Skidmore Owings & Merrill will come in handy now that these firms have U.K. branches.

Neither Eichel nor Chappel expresses concern about the impact on their association of the stock market crash in the fall of 1987 or a limitation on big spending by investment dealers on office towers. But, in any event, Chappel says there are ample other opportunities. A spate of mixed commercial-retail developments is expected to crop up in the suburbs now that the M25 ring road around London is completed. As major highways feed into the expressway, enough people can reach regional shopping centers to make them profitable. While such malls are a regular feature of the U.S. landscape, they have yet to come to England. Besides seeing the potential in shopping malls, Chappel emphasizes that much of London is slated for urban renewal.

While the Wimpey-Tishman joint venture will likely enrich both companies, they could prosper without it. But to International Computers (ICL), joint ventures were a lifeline in 1981, when a financial crisis cast its future into doubt. The British government had provided assistance with the proviso that management be replaced and that the new team act swiftly to restore customer confidence. The team decided that joint ventures were the speediest way to attain the latest technology, cost-effective products, and more distribution channels. It entered into many collaborations, of which only one—that with Fujitsu of Japan—proved successful.[3] ICL receives state-of-the-art Fujitsu mainframe designs for computers, which means it does not have to spend funds on research and development. The money saved is channeled into other activities.

Although ICL was in a precarious situation, Fujitsu consented to the deal because the British government guaranteed ICL's financial stability for a five-year period. Also, Fujitsu saw ICL as a gateway into the European market against IBM and the well-entrenched West German computer manufacturers, Siemens and Nixdorf. The deal is a financial windfall for ICL. Annually, in return for a $120-million payment to Fujitsu for disk drives, terminals, printed circuit boards, and so on, ICL derives $1 billion in sales from the finished products, half of its total revenue.

When the original agreement expired in 1984, it was extended until 1991. A clause in the contract calling for yearly technology meetings to examine other opportunities has prompted additional collaborations. In turn, when ICL was acquired in 1986 by Standard Telephones & Cables, STC also decided to become involved in joint ventures with Fujitsu. (In 1987, Northern Telecom of Canada purchased 28 percent of STC.)

ICL's subsequent joint ventures, each with different partners, in telephone exchange systems, personal computers, word processors, and engineering and scientific work stations were failures. The Fujitsu arrangement worked and the others did not, says Christopher Brueton, manager of collaborations strategy at ICL, because the research and development orientation of the venture with Fujitsu was better able to withstand the rapid obsolescence in information technology products. "Those ventures ICL terminated were ones in which product changes are so great that within a couple of years they no longer were useful," he says. In addition, once ICL had absorbed the necessary skills, it preferred

---

3. As described in Chapter 1, Fujitsu is also a major shareholder of the U.S. Amdahl Corporation.

to proceed on its own. "Collaborations should not be regarded as being for all time; once the maximum benefit is extracted, there is no logic in continuing," Brueton adds.

Now that ICL is confident it has a comprehensive product line and a full R&D program, its rationale for joint ventures has shifted from its initial dependence on product-oriented ones to those that emphasize distribution. Brueton states that this change is possible because ICL is again profitable and can now concentrate on growth rather than on survival. The change in direction was paralleled by a tightening of the coordination among ICL's forty product divisions to improve its rate of success in joint ventures.

In 1986, a department of collaborations was created with only one staff member, David Dace, an architect of ICL's liaison with Fujitsu. To underscore the importance of his assignment, he was appointed to ICL's board of directors. Dace oversees ICL's outside collaborations through a full- or part-time contact in each department to prevent competitive endeavors.

Brueton, originally in marketing and technical strategy at ICL, is on full-time assignment to Dace. He says the reorganization arose from ICL's recognition that "no company can afford all the R&D and marketing for every customer need. Consequently, collaborations with companies around the world are essential." While Brueton concedes that such joint ventures are particularly worthwhile for small companies, he stresses that "no firm, even IBM, can afford to do everything." IBM, which has revenue twenty-five times greater than ICL's, is engaged in more than one hundred collaborative efforts.

Brueton is convinced that the high cost of information technology development could lead to the coalescence of the many firms in this industry into a few giants in the 1990s, similar to the absorption that occurred in the 1930s in the automobile industry. To be a survivor, ICL tracks the collaborative strategy of competitors to determine what it might copy or try to join. According to Brueton, the world's top thirty information technology companies formed eight hundred collaborations during the past two-and-a-half years.

Siemens, a much larger company (1986 revenue: $26 billion) that has factories in thirty-two countries and derives half its business from outside West Germany, does not share ICL's enthusiasm for joint ventures. It is well aware of the principal incentive for such associations among information technology firms: the need to sell large quantities quickly because of the brief life span of products in this age of instant obsolescence and the attendant high costs of the R&D essential for keeping ahead.

Nonetheless, Siemens prefers to establish a subsidiary, transfer technology, or purchase a company. "It is cheaper in the long run to acquire, because R&D costs can be shared by the parent and the subsidiary and because joint ventures entail management problems that are costly in the long run," says Jörg Wehr of Siemens's contract department, which deals with technical cooperation, licensing, and joint ventures. Erwin Biermeier, of the marketing division in the telecommunications department, adds, "High-tech joint ventures raise the problem of how much technology should be shared." He points out that "it must be decided whether the venture is just for the present or also for the future, encompassing new technology."

Siemens was soured on joint ventures by a tripartite data-processing company it established in the 1970s with N. V. Philips, the Netherlands telecommunications giant, and Compagnie des Machines Bull of France. The trio believed the venture would enable them to narrow the gap quickly between Europe and the United States and Japan in computer technology by sharing their knowledge. However, as Wehr wryly comments, "If two partners in a joint venture have difficulties over management and philosophy, with three it is nearly impossible." Although the venture's name, Unidata, signified harmony, each company had its own production line and merely slapped the Unidata label on its computers. The equipment differed from firm to firm and without any common denominator and lacking profitability, Unidata fell apart.

West Germany's stringent antitrust laws also deter joint ventures. Any proposed joint venture investment of more than 25 percent cannot be undertaken unless the federal antitrust department approves. Moreover, it prohibits mergers, acquisitions, or joint ventures with foreign companies if it believes they will give a West German company excessive power in the German marketplace. Thus, when ITT offered to sell its West German subsidiary, Standard Electric Lawrence, to Siemens in 1985, Siemens was interested but was forced by the antitrust department to reject the opportunity. Instead, Standard Electric Lawrence, which had a 30 percent market share in West Germany, was purchased by Alcatel of France, to which ITT handed over its telecommunications equipment manufacturing business in 1987.

In 1973, when Siemens and Corning formed Siecor, their joint venture in fiber optics cable, both West Germany and the European Community contended the arrangement was illegal market sharing. To allay these concerns, Siemens and Corning agreed that while each would own half the venture, Corning would have management control in the United States and Siemens in Germany. In the case of Siecor, Siemens departed from its usual aversion to joint ventures because each side contributed a different technology: Siemens was expert in cable production and Corning in optical fiber. Indeed, although a West German optical fiber company simultaneously proposed a joint venture to Siemens, Siemens preferred Corning because its technology was more advanced.

In March 1988, Siemens once again overcame its usual aversion to joint ventures when it formed a series of joint ventures with another U. S. firm, Westinghouse. Their ventures will make, sell, and service factory automation equipment, industrial circuit breakers, and industrial controls.

Siemens is also in joint ventures in Japan and Korea. In Japan, it formed a cooperative marketing venture with Fuji Electric Components for the sale of its electronic parts because it had made no headway on its own in the country's cliquish marketing network. "In Japan, personal contacts are necessary to penetrate the distribution system," Wehr explains. Slowly, Siemens, which had previously lost money on this product line in Japan, moved into profitability through the venture. The process was slow partly because Fuji Electric is not big. However, it was Siemens's only resort because those Japanese companies that are as large as Siemens saw no need to cooperate in a joint venture. Siemens has ruled out extension of the venture into shared manufacturing, since its product line and that of Fuji differ substantially.

South Korea's insistence on local participation forced Siemens to enter into a joint venture there, although its preference was to establish a subsidiary. Its partner is Gold Star Tele-Electric; another Gold Star division is an AT&T associate. In India, however, Siemens refused to bow to similar pressure. India restricts the production output of subsidiaries of foreign companies but provides generous terms to joint ventures. Nonetheless, Siemens opted for a subsidiary because, as Wehr points out, "it could have its own corporate identity and management and train its own people."

A cautionary tale about the perils of even the best-intentioned joint venture is provided by that between two of Europe's leading tire makers, Dunlop Holdings of England and Pirelli of Italy. Formed in late 1970, it collapsed in 1981. Sir Campbell Fraser, chairman of Dunlop at the time of the split, says its epitaph should read: "One of the best conceived mergers in industrial history—even though it failed."

At the time of its formation, the venture, which with £343 million in combined assets became the world's third largest tire maker, was hailed as an excellent example of why England should enter the Common Market. Editorialized *The Times* of London: "In an era of intense competition, success goes to companies which retain the initiative and command the greater resources. By itself, Dunlop cannot command such resources. Nor can Pirelli. What neither can do alone the two companies hope to achieve in partnership. The industrial logic is straightforward and compelling, and writ large, it is a major plank in the overall argument for British entry into the Common Market."

In theory, the venture made sense because the companies' product lines and geographical dispersion were complementary. Dunlop was in the United Kingdom, North America, northern Europe, and the Commonwealth countries, and Pirelli was in southern Europe and South America. Also, together they could better afford the requisite R&D expenditures to duplicate the revolutionary development by Michelin of steel-reinforced radial tires, which last twice as long as conventional rubber tires made of crossed layers of rubber and textile.

When Sir Campbell refers to the joint venture as "one of the best conceived," he is alluding to the extraordinary difficulties Dunlop and Pirelli surmounted to bring about the endeavor. For Dunlop, the agreement of Britain's Chancellor of the Exchequer was crucial to avoid tax problems that would have rendered the deal worthless. Under British law, companies must own 75 percent of their subsidiaries to consolidate them fiscally for tax purposes. Such a declaration was impossible for Dunlop because of the way the venture was structured: Dunlop and Pirelli obtained 49 percent of each other's operations in Europe and 40 percent of their interests elsewhere. This obstacle was overcome when the Chancellor exempted Dunlop from the 75 percent requirement.

When similar threatening tax implications arose for Dunlop in India and the Indian government refused any concessions, the company devised an ingenious solution that removed the division from the tax department's grasp. As Sir Campbell tells the story, he and Dunlop's finance director had left Dunlop's headquarters late on a Friday night and were mulling over the problem when he casually observed their reflection in Dunlop's windows. "What if Pirelli didn't get its interest in the India operation but instead in another in Britain that is its mirror image?" he mused. The finance director pondered the idea over the weekend and told Sir Campbell on Monday that it would work.

The partners also had to iron out whether the worth of each one's businesses equaled the other's, and the management structure and the language to be employed for business—Italian or English. Sir Campbell recalls: "It's one thing to say you're going to have equal ownership in a united effort, but how do you determine the valuation of each side's operations when they are in a vast number of countries and accounting methods vary from nation to nation?" The valuation of each company's assets turned out to be unexpectedly easy and harmonious; an independent auditor balanced the two sides by removing six small Pirelli companies in Italy and a Dunlop company in Rhodesia from the deal. The venture chose English as its business language; the Italians not conversant in English took intensive language courses. Coordinating committees were established by product lines. Managers from each side traveled to their company's factories to inform workers about the deal, and the shareholders of both firms voted overwhelmingly in favor.

Why, then, did such a well-organized, warmly received venture fail? The crux of the problem had been pointed out by skeptics at the venture's outset: no separate joint venture company was established; thus, there was never a true union. The lack of fusion stemmed from the unique composition of the venture: one partner from the British side, Dunlop, and two from the other, the Milan-based Pirelli, which ran Pirelli in Europe, and the Basel-based Pirelli, which was in charge of nonEuropean activities. The autonomy of the Swiss company was evident from the exclusion of Pirelli chairman, Leopoldo Pirelli, from that position in Switzerland, where he was just one of the directors.

This diffusion of power was complicated by another difficulty: Dunlop and Pirelli had considered only one ramification of Michelin's development of radial tires—the need for competitors to catch up in technology. But they had neglected to weigh the other implication—because of their durability, radials led to a serious glut of tires on the market, since car owners no longer had to buy replacements as frequently. This problem was not perceived immediately because it was masked by other troubles: the Italian economy, which had been strong, took a nosedive and simultaneously Pirelli encountered snags with one of its product lines. Hence, in the first year of the venture, Pirelli experienced substantial losses.

For the next six years, Pirelli continued to lose money, and because it was tied to Pirelli, Dunlop was adversely affected. "Every pound made by Dunlop in the United Kingdom was offset by an equivalent loss in lira by Pirelli in Italy," Sir Campbell comments. The situation was exacerbated by the differing attitudes about heavy debt in the United Kingdom and Italy. In the United Kingdom, companies are regarded as technically bankrupt if their debt-to-equity ratio exceeds 1:1. Pirelli had a 7:1 debt-to-equity ratio; yet it was bailed out with Italian government grants because the government deemed its survival important to the Italian economy.

The tension between Dunlop and Pirelli because of the financial problems was intensified by a lack of unity in marketing. Each company's brands were well known and, Sir Campbell notes, even marketing experts disagree about whether it is best for merged operations to retain their individual labels or develop new ones. Dunlop and Pirelli elected to keep their own. Consequently, each had separate sales teams and product managers. Efforts to appoint a single coordinating manager were stalemated by each side's fear of erosion of its power.

All these problems came to a head in 1976, when the sluggish demand for tires plunged Dunlop into losses. Dunlop and Pirelli in Italy decided a merger was the solution. "With one company there still would have been problems but not conflicts of interest," Sir Campbell reflects. They proposed that the strongest member of the triad, Pirelli in Switzerland, buy them out. No deal, replied the Swiss company, independent as ever. It had no desire to take on two money-losing partners.

That compromise stymied, the venture was canceled. Although the overseas activities were profitable, the firms decided not to continue a partnership in these because they depended largely on the European operations for technical expertise. As part of the breakup, Dunlop claimed that most of the flow of dividends had been in Pirelli's favor because Pirelli had not paid them when Dunlop had. Pirelli agreed and paid £20 million in compensation. At the suggestion of British investment dealer S. G. Warburg, which supervised the breakup, the separation was gradual. Warburg stressed that in view of the bruising competition among tire makers, it would be best to phase out the sharing of technology and patents over a three-year period and to continue joint purchasing of materials during that period.

After the dissolution, both firms were buffeted by the slump in the tire industry. The Italian government continued to assist Pirelli; Dunlop, however, was dismembered. In 1985, a British conglomerate, BTR Industries (originally Birmingham Tire & Rubber Company), acquired Dunlop. BTR subsequently sold Dunlop's American operations to an affiliate of First Boston Corporation (a major U.S. investment bank), the New York Life Insurance Company, and to Prudential Insurance Company of America. In 1986, the three firms sold the U.S. Dunlop to Japan's Sumitomo Rubber Industries, of which the parent Dunlop company had once owned 40 percent.

Concluding his review of the unhappy outcome of the once widely heralded joint venture, Sir Campbell says it taught that "a merger should be a complete merger." As Siemens's Jörg Wehr said about joint ventures in general, ill-starred ones face the same fate as a pig destined to be slaughtered for ham and eggs.

# 11    *Learning from Junior*

The mission of joint ventures, in the view of many partners, is to do what they are told by their parents. But, like baby birds that grow up and fly away from the nest, joint ventures often head in their own direction. Those that are given enough leeway frequently have lessons to teach their founders. Three prominent examples are Nippon Otis, Fuji Xerox, and Yokogawa-Hewlett-Packard. These companies struggled hard to get their American parents to listen to their suggestions about cooperation and quality control. Their persistence benefited both them and their creators. Furthermore, their success vindicates the concept of joint ventures, including hands-across-the-ocean alliances from the two countries most in economic competition—the United States and Japan.

Formed in 1931, Nippon Otis has had two sets of Japanese partners. Mitsui was the Japanese participant until World War II. It was also the principal shareholder because at that time outside investors were confined to minority stakes in Japanese businesses.

Today, Otis owns 55 percent; the other 45 percent is split between Sumitomo Corporation, one of Japan's largest trading houses, and Matsushita Electric Industrial Company. Matsushita is the world's largest consumer electronics maker under the brand names Panasonic, National, Technics, and Quasar. In addition, it is the largest shareholder in Matsushita Electric Works, which makes electric wiring.

The alliance between Otis and Matsushita is to their mutual benefit. Matsushita wanted the arrangement because it made everything electrical for buildings except elevators. Since Otis is North America's foremost manufacturer of elevators for high-rise structures, its suggestion of a joint venture provided the opportunity for Matsushita to round out its product list. For its part, Otis was interested because Matsushita, through its extensive sales network, would allow Otis to achieve sales quickly in Japan, the world's second largest market for elevators after the United States.

The inclusion of Sumitomo was acceptable to Otis and Matsushita because of the longtime ties Sumitomo had as financier to both companies. Two Sumitomo branches—Sumitomo Bank and Sumitomo Mutual Life Assurance Company—own nearly 10 percent of Matsushita. Also, Sumitomo is the lead investment underwriter in Japan for Otis's parent, United Technologies Corporation. Despite its link with Nippon Otis, Sumitomo continues to act as the distributor for the joint venture's competitor, Mitsubishi Electric Company, with which it had an agreement predating its participation in Nippon Otis. Severance of that relationship was not demanded.

Management of Nippon Otis has always been in Japanese hands. "Otis was clever enough to let us handle it," says chairman Yoshinobu Ogura, formerly a senior executive in Sumitomo's international operations. President Yukio Saishoji is from Matsushita. Nippon Otis has become one of Otis's biggest stars. It has tripled its market share in Japan over the past decade to 12 percent. It is also tied with three other Otis factories, in Indiana, Spain, and West Germany, for the best productivity rate. Otis has a total of twenty-nine factories.

Despite its well-regarded track record, it took Nippon Otis fifteen years to convince Otis of the wisdom of Japan's emphasis on quality control. Ogura explains Otis's reluctance by saying it was a reflection of generally contrasting U.S. and Japanese attitudes toward how well equipment is expected to function. "In the

United States and Europe, people watch themselves because they believe machines sometimes make mistakes, whereas in Japan we are not broad-minded about such errors," he comments. "Thus, if an elevator breaks down in Japan, customers phone you and demand immediate repairs even if it is the evening and there is an overtime charge. In the United States and Europe, no action is possible until the next day, if then.

"Also, Japanese customers insist on elevators that provide a soft landing and have doors that open and close smoothly. U.S. customers tend not to care about soft landings or noise vibrations. I can tell you a personal anecdote about this cultural difference. I was stationed for three years at Sumitomo's Manhattan office on the sixty-ninth floor of the World Trade Center for which Otis supplied the elevators. The elevators shook strongly as they made their ascent and did not always open level with the floor. But instead of getting upset, the passengers warned one another to watch their step. In the United States, people are accustomed to being wary of machines."[1]

Ogura and other Nippon Otis executives hammered away at Otis's president about the benefits of the Japanese approach. Ogura says that in the past few years Otis "has paid attention," particularly to ideas about new products and factory automation. Nippon Otis also suggested how Otis could increase business in Japan and the United States: "We urged Otis to zero in on Japanese construction in the United States as well as to explore business opportunities opened up by the creation of other U.S.-Japanese ventures in Japan."

As at Nippon Otis, the management of Fuji Xerox, which was established in 1962, is Japanese. Similarly, too, the U.S. side is the more active partner. And just as Otis was unwilling at first to listen to Nippon Otis, Rank Xerox was deaf to suggestions from Fuji Xerox for years. Fuji Xerox, however, faced a more difficult challenge than had Nippon Otis: how to persuade its Western parent to allow it to blossom from being a distributor of U.S.-made Xerox copiers to being a full-fledged entity on an equal footing. To accomplish this, Fuji Xerox wanted to plan, conduct research and development, and produce rather than be a pipeline for Xerox goods.

---

1. As if to test Ogura's analysis, on the evening following my interview with him the Japanese-built elevator in my Tokyo hotel was out of order. It was fixed by the start of the next day.

Although Fuji Xerox and Rank Xerox officials got along amiably, Rank Xerox was adamant at first against Fuji Xerox's branching out. It saw no reason for the joint venture to assume more responsibilities because it was convinced that what sold well in the United States and Europe would automatically be popular in Japan. Finally, Fuji Xerox brought the issue to a head by seizing the initiative. Managing director Yoichi Ogawa recounts: "In the first two or three years, we learned a great deal from Rank Xerox, but we also realized that the Japanese market clearly differed from the American and European ones. For example, the demand in Japan for small copiers was greater than in the United States and Europe. The only information we could obtain from Xerox was industrywide data rather than proprietary information, so in 1968 we started to make our own machines. As a result, Xerox had to stop thinking of us as only a marketing company."

Subsequently, in 1971, Fuji Xerox became a full-scale manufacturer. It purchased two plants from its Japanese parent, Fuji Photo Film, acquiring the employees as part of the transaction. In addition, Fuji Xerox built a third factory. "Twenty years ago, it was a one-way relationship in which Xerox supplied information and Fuji paid royalties," Ogawa says. "Now, we trade technical information freely, although if one side uses the other's technology, it pays a fee. Throughout the year several hundred Xerox and Fuji Xerox people travel back and forth. Senior engineers meet yearly to avoid duplication in research and development."

Moreover, thanks to Fuji Xerox's persistence, Xerox was not caught unawares when Japanese copier manufacturers like Canon began to export smaller models. Nearly three-quarters of Japan's copier production is exported. Without the aid of Fuji Xerox, Xerox's position as the world's leading copier manufacturer might well have been jeopardized.

Fuji Xerox also earned respect for its productivity and quality control measures: in 1980 it received the prestigious Deming Prize for quality control. Ogawa says the award made clear to the Japanese that a hybrid joint venture could fare as well as, or better than, 100 percent Japanese firms: "Previously, the average Japanese thought that because joint ventures had foreign ownership they would do poorly compared with all-Japanese companies. Ten years ago, Japanese joint venture managers would not have been considered for positions on Japanese government committees, but today I am a member of several, including one at MITI." His appointment to the Ministry of International Trade and Industry is prestigious and influential because MITI is the principal architect of Japan's economic planning.

Xerox vice chairman William Glavin says Fuji Xerox's procedures were studied by Xerox as it formulated its "leadership through quality" program in the late 1970s. Xerox was galvanized into action by a Federal Trade Commission ruling in the mid-1970s that ordered Xerox to allow rivals such as IBM and Eastman Kodak access to its patents. Concurrently, Japanese copier manufacturers were growing fast. Xerox's reaction time, however, was slow, because, according to Glavin, "We were concentrating on a world recession at the time, whereas in reality our problem was the explosion in competition."

Having finally pinpointed the trouble, Xerox executives determined that the solution was "competitive benchmarking"—an improvement of Xerox's systems in production, inventory, billing, and other business functions based on what the company believed were better-run systems elsewhere. Household Finance Corporation and American Express served as role models for the most efficient way of processing transactions. Fuji Xerox was selected as an expert in cost efficiency because of its skill in developing internal controls and in getting the cooperation of suppliers.

"The Japanese are very good at design engineering, with the result that their products require less design time and are easily manufacturable," remarks Robert Reiser, group vice president, international, at Xerox. "For instance, their small copiers snap together, so that not even a screwdriver is required. Consequently, the assembly line process is very simple."

Xerox also profited from the way Fuji Xerox deals with suppliers. As is customary in Japan, Fuji Xerox expects its suppliers to do so much tooling that little is left for Fuji Xerox to do except put the parts together. In the days before Xerox copied Fuji Xerox, the joint venture spent two-thirds less time than its U.S. parent on assembly preliminaries. Fuji Xerox's secret was its insistence that suppliers provide top-quality components. As a result, unlike Xerox operations elsewhere, Fuji Xerox did not have to test the items on their arrival. "Now that we have trained our American and European vendors in Japanese techniques, we have cut our lead time down to Fuji Xerox's level," Glavin says.

Established in 1963, one year after the birth of Fuji Xerox, Yokogawa-Hewlett-Packard at first suffered from mismanagement and misspending. But after stern measures were imposed by nomical to manufacture even a handful of specialty tools. All this could be accomplished at little expense, HP said, by changing the production system instead of purchasing new equipment at exorbitant cost.

At first, HP's pride was hurt, because from its inception YHP had followed HP's quality assurance policy. When YHP was founded, HP's program was regarded as superior to any in Japan. But YHP came to question the methods of its American parent during the 1973 oil crisis, over which neither HP nor Yokogawa Electric Works, the Japanese partner, had control. During this period, YHP fared poorly financially, as did most Japanese companies. As YHP searched for a way to recover, it realized that in its heyday, when it had coasted along on strong sales, it had allowed the quality of its merchandise to slip, causing a loss of customers to competitors.

YHP decided to cut its dependence on HP and to anchor its recuperation in the Japanese version of W. Edwards Deming's "total quality control" teachings. Total quality control seeks to increase productivity through improving quality at each operational stage and at all levels of management. It is based on statistical analysis and can be applied to every facet of a company—production, maintenance, research and development, sales, finance, and administration—without prior knowledge of that area. "We found that total quality control, the invention of an American—Dr. Deming—taught us Japanese to base talk on facts, and hence we became able to communicate much better with people from other countries," says YHP President Kenzo Sasoaka.

YHP hired a Japanese industrial consultant, who suggested the company initiate its quality control overhaul with the dip solder process used in the manufacture of electronic printed circuit boards. Previously, YHP had retouched defects manually and did not keep records of their type and frequency. The adviser pointed out that the implementation of quality control procedures would render the correction process redundant.

He was proved right quickly. Within two years the number of defects dropped to 0.5 percent of the previous rate. Since then the proportion has been shaved even further, to 0.1 percent. As a result, overall printed circuit board assembly lead time is now one day compared to the earlier four weeks. The number of workers on the line is down from twenty-two to ten because fewer inspection points are required. To regain customer loyalty, YHP launched an annual survey of its three thousand clients, quizzing them about the quality of its sales force and sales literature. They were flattered, because surveys are rare in Japan.

Next, YHP adopted Toyota's renowned *kanban* method, which keeps production and inventory within manageable limits by placing the onus for just-in-time delivery of components on suppliers. To optimize its benefits from this system, YHP altered its production schedule. Monthly batches were split into semi-monthly lots to reduce lead times. The shorter production cycles shaved YHP's failure rate and its inventory by one-third, lowered its operational costs by half, doubled its productivity, and tripled its profit.

Thus, YHP, previously a major disappointment to HP, metamorphosed into one of its brightest performers. In 1975, YHP's productivity was half that of the average HP factory; by 1979, two years after its conversion to total quality control, YHP surpassed HP's U.S. operations by a 2:1 ratio. Subsequently, YHP chalked up more records: highest profitability, lowest field failure rate, and lowest inventory. It capped its turnaround by winning the Deming Prize.

That award crystallized YHP's progress from subordinate to prophet. "From the beginning of the joint venture, we had been a student learning everything from America; now, YHP had achieved outstanding success through its own initiative," Sasaoka comments. He embarked on a crusade throughout HP's other divisions to persuade them to adopt YHP's program. He made presentations at HP, invited managers of other operations to visit YHP, distributed documents on YHP's methodology, and sent quality control managers on tours of HP factories.

Initially, the YHP people were cold-shouldered because other managers did not see the need for switching from what worked for them. This changed when HP president John Young personally endorsed YHP's recommendations. Thereupon HP added to its corporate list of objectives the phrase "to provide products and services of the highest quality to our customers." To realize this pledge, each division was requested to set quality targets in its annual planning and to implement intensive training on the subject.

Having proved its point about quality control, YHP now seeks to expand its role further. Just like Fuji Xerox, it wants to be allowed to take the initiative in research and development.

"With the technology gap between the United States and Japan continually narrowing, HP should utilize our resources more," Muraoka comments. YHP is urging HP to establish a "high-class" laboratory on the scale of HP's in Palo Alto as a way "to absorb Japanese technology." Muraoka says it would be a Far East counterpart to HP's research and development facilities in Bristol, England. It also would propel YHP to greater status.

In this era, when corporations have made the transition from multinational to global businesses, international joint ventures are vital to their strategic planning. Given a choice, most companies would probably prefer solitary rather than shared efforts, because two partners potentially double the conflicts over management, production, and marketing. The compromises that joint venture partners must reach for their project to flourish require a shift in attitude by executives who are unaccustomed—and perhaps un-willing—to share authority.

Yet it is clear that companies can no longer be parochial. As part of their survival strategy, they must be more flexible about collaboration. Such cooperation is dictated by the sweeping eco-nomic changes of the past ten to fifteen years. Swift technological changes have shortened product life cycles and enlarged the field of competition.

High-technology companies that did not exist a decade or two ago now challenge long-established firms. The appetite for new sources of revenue has thrown giant corporations, once serene in near-monopolistic splendor, into bruising competition. For in-stance, AT&T, IBM, Xerox, Olivetti, Fujitsu, and Toshiba now overlap in the office automation market of telephones, typewriters, copiers, computers, and semiconductors.

American leadership in technological innovation is eroding under pressure from other nations. The spurt in new technology has enabled developing countries to chip away at the dominance of trade by more advanced nations. Hostility about the rapid in-crease of Japanese exports is on the rise, fueled by the reluctance of Japan to open its doors to imports. Thus, to survive, corpo-rations must react quickly; they need instant access to technology, money, and customers.

At the same time, companies do not want their excursions into fresh business opportunities to drain their existing resources.

All these concerns constitute the motivation for forming joint ventures. The ventures are regarded as an opportunity for swift product and market expansion without an infusion of capital so large that it cripples other operations of a firm. By sharing the cost, joint venture partners are able to halve their risk and double the speed of their participation in new products and markets. However, joint ventures often are formed by competitors whose partnership will be the only instance of their cooperation; otherwise, these allies of circumstance remain combatants.

Today's global economic arena dictates that international joint ventures are here to stay and are not a passing fad. On the other hand, the ventures do not presage a decline in world industrial competition. Rather, they are a reflection of that rivalry, a means to an end, an industrial version of the marriage of convenience.

# INDEX

## A

Agfa-Gevaert, 44
Alberta Natural Gas Company, 39
Albrecht, Gary, 23
Alcan Aluminium Ltd., 31, 53, 54
Alcan Pacific, 50
Alcatel, 42, 44–46, 219
Amdahl, Gene, 24
Amdahl Corporation, 23–25
American Bakery Institute, 123
American Express Co., 229
American Express Travel Related
    Services, 106
American Motors Corporation, 8, 13–
    14, 34, 92, 94–98, 150, 157, 168,
    197–198, 207
American Telephone & Telegraph
    Company (AT&T), 30, 42–44, 49,
    57–58, 60, 219, 233
American Trade Consortium, 27n
An Tai Bao Mine (China), 52, 111
APT, 43–44, 59
Arab American Vehicles, 12
Argentina: joint ventures in, 13, 203
Asahi Glass Company Ltd., 4, 47
Atlantic Richfield Co., 92
AT&T Network Systems, 23
Austin-Rover, 13–15, 161
Auto-Latina, 201–204
Automobile joint ventures:
    American-Motors-China. See Beijing
    Jeep. Austin Rover-Honda, 13–14;
    Chrysler-Arab investment group, 12;
    Chrysler-Mitsubishi. See Diamond-
    Star Motors Corporation. Ford-
    Mazda, 12–13, 173; Ford-Nissan, 12–
    13; Ford-Volkswagen. See Auto-
    Latina. General Motors-Daewoo, 11;
    General Motors-Isuzu, 10; General
    Motors-Suzuki, 10–11; General Mo-
    tors-Toyota. See New United Motor
    Manufacturing, Inc. General Motors-
    Volvo, 11; Guangzhou-Peugeot, 140;
    Toyota-Volkswagen, 13; Volkswa-
    gen-China. See Shanghai-Volkswa-
    gen Automobile Co. Ltd.
Automobile parts joint ventures.
    See Hubei Parker Seal Component
    Factory

## B

BC Development Company, 112
BCI Holdings Corporation (Beatrice
    Foods), 112, 122, 151
Bank of China, 111
Bank of China Trust & Consultancy
    Company, 52
Barnes-Hind Inc., 209
Beatrice Foods. See BCI Holdings
    Corporation
Beihai (China), 101, 104, 121, 142–143
Beijing (China), 104–105, 122, 144,
    154–155, 183
Beijing Automotive Works, 94, 198
Beijing Hotel, 142
Beijing International Trust and Invest-
    ment Corporation, 96
Beijing Jeep, 94–98, 105, 140–141, 153–
    154, 157, 197–198
Bell Canada Enterprises Inc., 53
Biehn, David, 162–163, 165
Biermeier, Erwin, 218
Black, Archie, 31, 50, 54
Bombardier Inc., 33
Bowbyes, Alan, 29, 111
Brazil: joint ventures in, 13, 54, 203,
    210
Bricknell, David, 208, 210
Bridgestone Tire Company, 25
British Aerospace PLC, 14
British Leyland, 14, 204
Brueton, Christopher, 216–217
BTR Industries, 223

## C

Cable & Wireless Company, 2
Canton. See Guangzhou
Caterpillar Inc., 16, 170
Cathay Pacific Airways Ltd., 111
Celgar Pulp Mill, 111

the U.S. parent, Hewlett-Packard, it rapidly flourished. Initially capitalized at 7.4 billion yen ($53 million at 140 yen to the U.S. dollar), the joint venture's annual revenue now tops 100 billion yen (about $715 million), a fivefold increase over 1977.

According to executive vice president Toshio Muraoka, YHP's business is 60 percent derived from imports from HP's fifty-nine worldwide sites. Referring to American complaints that Japan does not import enough, Muraoka notes that most of YHP's imports are from HP in the United States and that they have climbed by six percentage points in response to the yen's rise in value, fattening Japan's buying power. "YHP is a good citizen," Muraoka says. Another 22 percent of YHP's revenue is based on technology transferred from HP, for which YHP pays a royalty. The remaining sales come from products designed in-house by YHP.

Globally, HP manufactures six thousand types of instruments. The sheer quantity, combined with the minuscule demand for esoteric items, makes it impossible for each plant to produce all the lines. Thus, HP parcels out the manufacturing of product lines and the accompanying R&D among its operations. YHP specializes in measuring instruments that check the performance of integrated circuits and other semiconductor components.

Muraoka says that the chief lesson absorbed by HP from YHP is the principle of "total quality control." YHP instituted the quality control program in 1977, but HP paid little attention until YHP's sales and profits soared and it captured the Deming Prize in 1982. Muraoka stresses that it was vital for the rest of HP to cooperate in order for YHP's exercise to succeed: "Because HP delegates product line responsibility throughout its worldwide network, the concept of quality had to be applied to all its divisions for it to function properly."

At first, HP was skeptical about YHP's suggestions because the underlying theme contradicted accepted economic theory, which associates higher quality with higher cost and mass production with economies of scale. YHP insisted that high-quality, small-volume production of many items, even five units per lot, can yield the same low costs as the assembly line production of large lots. It noted that if larger output is poor and cannot be sold or must be recalled, the cost in lost sales can exceed the savings achieved through quantity. Furthermore, the Japanese system of just-in-time delivery by component suppliers would make it eco-

Center for Market and Trade Development (China), 105
Changhou (China), 101
Chappel, John, 215
Chappell, John, 18–19, 62
Chase Manhattan Bank, 50, 105–106, 108
Chase Manhattan Bank Egypt, 50
Chen, Pei, 191, 194
Chen, Richard, 53, 114
China:
    advertising in, 199–200; component sourcing in, 98; foreign exchange problems in, 69–70, 96–97, 132–133; government assistance to ventures, 93–94, 101, 109, 112; infrastructure in, 66, 114, 131–132, 141, 150–156; labor allowances, 67–68; land costs in, 65–66, 93; lawyers, use of in, 128; living and working conditions, 130–131, 139–157; management of joint ventures, 113–135, 142, 181–200, 207, 210–212; merchandising in, 150, 199; national holidays in, 194; quality control, 196–198; special economic zones in, 100–101, 107; staff recruitment for joint ventures, 183–185, 187, 191, 193; tax breaks for joint ventures, 99; wages and incentives at joint ventures, 67–68, 94, 130–131, 182, 191, 193
China Advertisement and Information, 199
China Automotive Industry Corporation, 94
China Design Bureau, 123
China Electronics Import and Export Corporation (CEIEC), 116
China Hewlett-Packard, 115–116, 131, 150, 155, 182, 184–185, 188, 195
China International Engineering Consulting Corporation, 107, 110
China International Trust and Investment Corporation (CITIC), 110–112, 116–117
China Investment and Finance Ltd., 111
China Machinery Import-Export Corporation (MACHIMPEX), 114, 117–118
China Merchants Steam Navigation Company, 123–125
China National Coal Development Corporation, 52
China National Technical Import Corporation, 187
China Phone Book, 114, 116
China Schindler Elevator Company, 34

China State Economic Commission, 92
China Tianjin Otis Elevator Company, 35, 110–111, 120–121, 131, 135, 140, 146, 181, 184–85, 188, 196
Chinon Industries, 21
Chips. See Semiconductor joint ventures
Chong, Josephine, 142
Chongquing (China), 185
Chrysler Corporation, 8, 10–12, 14, 64, 89, 98, 168, 174, 205–206
Chrysler Nuova-Automobili F. Lamborghini, 13n
Cie Générale d'Electricité (CGE), 42, 46
CITIC. See China International Trust and Investment Corporation
Civil Aviation Administration of China (CAAC), 150
Clare, Tod, 34, 92, 95, 98, 105, 150
Clarke, Roger, 213–214
Clough, Roger, 129–130, 132
Coca-Cola Company, 152
Compagnie des Machines Bull, 218
Compagnie Générale de Constructions Teléphoniques (CGCT), 44
Control Data Corporation, 41
Coopers & Lybrand, 34
Copiers. See Photocopier joint ventures
Corning Glass Works, 30, 219
Cotter, Joseph, 144
Cox, Patricia, 16
Crossett, George, 47, 124, 130
Crystal Palace Hotel, 121
Cultural Palace of Nationalities (China), 117
Cultural Revolution (China), 183, 192, 199
Cycles Peugeot, 15

D
Dace, David, 217
Daewoo Motor Company, 11
Daihatsu Motor Company, 14, 33
Dalian (China), 101–102
Dataquest Inc., 4, 16, 26
Decker, Hans, 45
Deere & Company, 17, 213
De Martino, Carl, 31–32, 39
Deming, W. Edwards, 80, 231
Deming Prize, 80, 228, 232
Deng, Chairman Xiaoping, 192, 199
Diamond-Star Motors Corporation, 11–12, 64, 174
Dieu, Eng Seng, 132, 141, 182
Diodosio, Charles, 122

Doi, Sosuke, 177, 179
Doolittle, William, 114
Dulude, Richard, 30
Dunlop Holdings Ltd., 125, 220–223
Dunlop-Pirelli joint venture, 220–222
Du Pont, E.I. de Nemours & Company, 3, 5, 31–32, 39–43

E
Eastman Kodak Company, 20–22, 151–152, 164–165, 229. *See also* Kodak Japan K.K.; Kodak Nagase K.K.
Ehinger, Kristian, 2, 203, 205–207
Eichel, Jay, 215
Electronics joint ventures:
    Hitachi. *See* Fujian Hitachi Television Company Ltd.;
    Siemens-Fuji Electric Components, 219;
    Toshiba-Westinghouse. *See* Toshiba Westinghouse Electronics Corporation;
    Yokogawa Electric Works-Hewlett Packard. *See* Yokogawa-Hewlett-Packard
Elevator joint ventures. *See* China Schindler Elevator Company; China Tianjin Otis Elevator Company
*Endaka* (rise of the yen, Japan), 6–7
Energy joint ventures. *See* An Tao Bao Mine
Ericsson, L.M., 43
European Economic Interest Groups, 26
European Strategic Program in Information Technologies ("Esprit"), 26
Expatriates, posting of, 68, 139–142, 145–146

F
Federal Trade Commission (United States), 63–64, 174, 229
Felix, Samuel, 27
Fiat, S.p.A., 14, 17
Fiber optics. *See* Optical fiber joint ventures
Financial joint ventures. *See* BC Development Company; China Investment and Finance Ltd.
Firestone Tire & Rubber Company, 25, 125
First Boston Corporation, 223
First Machinery Bureau of Tianjin, 110, 131
First National Bank of Chicago, 111, 125n

Food Products joint ventures (China):
    Guangmei Foods Company, 112, 122, 151;
    Heinz-General Corporation of Agriculture, Industry and Commerce and United Food (Guangzhou), 37, 122. *See also* Yili-Nabisco Biscuit and Food Company
Ford Motor Company, 8, 11–13, 27, 170, 173, 201–204
Förster, Peter, 207
Fox Meyer Corporation, 175
Fraser, Sir Campbell, 220–223
Fricke, Philip, 11
Fuji Electric Components, 219
Fuji Photo Film Co. Ltd., 4, 20, 152, 161, 228
Fuji Xerox Co. Ltd., 4, 146–147, 160–161, 225, 227–229, 232
Fujian Electronic Import & Export Corporation, 188
Fujian Hitachi Television Company Ltd., 188
Fujisawa Pharmaceutical Company, 18, 166
Fujitsu Limited, 23–25, 201, 216, 233
Fujiwara, Yoshiaki, 98–99, 133, 187
Fukuyama Works, 178
Fuzhou (China), 101, 103

G
Gandhi, Indira, 148
Garnet Hotel Systems, 113, 116
General Electric Company (United Kingdom), 44–45
General Electric Company (United States), 24, 33, 79–80
General Foods Corporation, 17–18, 22, 31, 36, 37n, 57, 61, 105, 122, 149,174
General Motors Corporation, 8–13, 63–64, 168–173, 203, 209
GenRad Corporation, 84
Gerwitz, Gerry, 107
Gilchrist, Ronald, 11
Gillette Company, 5, 32–33, 36, 61, 105, 113, 117–119, 123, 132–135, 140–141, 145, 148–149, 152–153, 182, 188, 191, 193
Glass joint ventures. *See* Pilkington Brothers PLC; PPG Industries, Inc.
Glavin, William, 5, 147, 160–161, 229
GM-Group Lotus, 13n
Goldman, Sachs & Co., 11
Gold Star Semiconductor Limited, 42–43, 60
Gold Star Tele-Electric Company, 219

Goodyear Tire & Rubber Company, The, 22, 25, 125
Gorbachev, Mikhail, 27
Great Wall Sheraton Hotel, 143–144
Greeta Musical Instrument Ltd., 17
Guangdong Province (China), 125
Guangmei Foods Company, 112, 122, 151
Guangzhou (China), 100–101, 103–104, 122
Guangzhou Peugeot Automobile Company, 111, 140
*Guanxi* (connections, China), 114–115, 125

H
Hahn, Carl, 205
Hainan Island (China), 101–102
Hall, Lewis, 212–213
Hammer, Armand, 114
Hammes, Michael, 12
Hanazuka, Kazuya, 58
Hansen, Larry, 33, 86
Hartnagel, Michael, 40
Heinz, H.J. Company, 36–37, 122
Hewlett, William, 115n
Hewlett-Packard Company, 2, 80–83, 114–117, 123, 131, 167n, 188, 195, 230–233
Hitachi Ltd. 16, 58
Holiday Corporation, 143
Honda Motor Co. Ltd., 13–15, 161, 169–70
Hotel joint ventures. *See* Garnet Hotel Systems; Great Wall Sheraton Hotel
House of Malhotra. *See* Malhotra, House of
House of Poddar Enterprises. *See* Poddar Enterprises, House of
Household Finance Corporation, 229
Hua Ting Sheraton Hotel, 144
Hubei Auto Industry Company, 186
Hubei Parker Seal Component Factory, 185
Hughes Aircraft International Services, 75
Hughes Communications Inc., 15–16, 57, 75–77, 115, 159, 163
Hules Mexicanos S.A. (Humex), 55–57
Humex. *See* Hules Mexicanos S.A.
Hutchison, Whampoa, 2
Hyatt Tianjin Hotel, 12
Hyundai Corporation, 12

I
IBM. *See* International Business Machines Corporation

ICL Ltd., 201, 215–217
Ikeda, Yoshio, 24
Ikemi, Kiyoshi, 161–162
India: joint ventures in, 139, 148–150
Indian Shaving Products Ltd., 148–149
Individual Validity License (United States), 133
Industrial Bank of Japan, 111
Industrial Technology Research Institute (ITRI) (Taiwan), 26
International Business Machines Corporation (IBM), 117, 216, 229, 233
International Computers Ltd. *See* ICL Ltd.
International Leasing Company, 187
International Music Company (IMC), 17
International Telegraph & Telephone (ITT), 42, 45–46, 218–219
Island Creek Corporation. *See* Occidental Petroleum Corporation
Isuzu Motors Ltd., 10–11
Italtel, 44
Itoh, C. & Co. Ltd., 57, 75–77, 159
Iwai, Rinzo, 25

J
Japan:
    component sourcing in, 58, 172; land costs in, 65; lawyers, use of in, 76; living and working conditions in, 139–157; management of joint ventures, 74–75, 159–180, 225–233; merchandising in, 146–147; national holidays in, 194n; quality control, 172, 227–228, 230–232; staff recruitment for joint ventures, 164–168
Japan Communications Satellite Company (JCSat), 15–16, 57, 75–77, 159, 163, 166
Joint ventures:
    compared with agents, 2; compared with distributors, 2; contractual terms of, 63–70; component sourcing, 17, 57–58, 151; definition of, 1; government assistance to, 26–27, 54, 93–94, 99, 101, 109, 112; vs. licensing, 3, 40; marketing problems and techniques, 146–147, 149–150, 152–154, 199–200; merits of, 2–6, 8–9, 16–23, 40–42, 53, 202, 217, 233–234; negotiations for, 33, 48–50, 76–78, 128–130; ownership split, 29, 50–51, 57, 76, 80; relationship to parent companies, 34–39, 65, 160–161, 165, 167, 178, 190, 217, 225–233; selection of partner for, 30–33, 55–56, 77, 79,

114; site costs, 65–66, 93; technology transfer to, 57, 59–60, 69; termination of, 32–33, 50, 56–57, 64, 70, 87–88, 216–218, 220–223; trademark protection, 60–62, 69; unions' role in, 77–78, 169–174, 176
Judge, Fred, 77, 163, 166

K
Kadono, Kinichi, 79–80
*Kaizen* (productivity improvement, Japan), 172
*Kanban* (inventory control, Japan), 172–173, 232
Kano, Samuel, 87–88
Ka Wah Bank Ltd., 111
Kay, Solomon, 210–212
Kazanowski, L.M., 13
Keidanren (Japan Federation of Economic Organizations), 7
Kentucky Fried Chicken, 156n
Kia Motor Corporation, 13
Kiewit, Peter Sons' Inc., 52
Klipstine, Thomas, 11, 173–174
Kobayashi, Taiyu, 24
Kodak. *See* Eastman Kodak Company
Kodak Japan K.K., 21, 78, 165
Kodak Nagase K.K., 78, 162–163, 165, 168
Koehler, John, 16, 75, 77
Korea, South: joint ventures in, 11, 19, 36, 42–43, 60, 116, 124, 219
Kubo, Thomas, 84–85, 88
Kusuda Business Machines Ltd., 21, 78

L
Lam, David, 87
LAM Research Corporation, 84, 87–88
Latvala, Eino, 49
Leasing joint ventures. *See* International Leasing Company
Lewis, John, 23, 25
Li, C.I., 193
Li, Ruihan, 102
Lianyungang (China), 101, 103
Lipton, Thomas Company, 149
LTV Corporation, 175

M
McDonald's Corporation, 3, 74
McInerney, Francis, 43, 45–46
McLouth Steel Products Corporation, 175
MACHIMPEX. *See* China Machinery Import-Export Corporation
Mahindra Ltd., 149–150
Malhotra, House of, 148–149

Mallett, William, 35, 111, 131, 134, 183–184, 188, 190, 196
Management Center for Economic Cadres (China), 183
Manfredi, John, 18, 31
Mao, Zedong, 183
Massey-Ferguson. *See* Varity Corporation
Massey-Ferguson Tractors Ltd., 212–213
Matsushita Electric Corporation, 22, 226
Matsushita Electric Works, 226
Mazda Motor Corporation, 12–13, 173
Merner, Edwin, 73–74
Mexico: joint ventures in, 13, 55–57, 210
Michelin Tires, 25, 125, 220–221
Miki, Kazuya, 89–90
Mills, Rodney, 5, 32–33, 36, 119, 135, 148
Ministry of Foreign Economic Relations and Trade (MOFERT, China), 105, 107, 109, 117
Ministry of International Trade and Industry (MITI, Japan), 228–229
Ministry of Light Industry (China), 119
Mitsubishi Chemical Industries Ltd., 21
Mitsubishi Corporation, 79–80, 89–90, 121, 174
Mitsubishi Electric Company, 226
Mitsubishi Heavy Industries Ltd., 17
Mitsubishi Motors Corporation, 10–12, 64, 89
Mitsui & Co. Ltd., 57, 75–77, 98, 133, 159, 187, 225
Mizukami, Akira, 76–77
Monsanto Company, 27
Morton, Dean, 115
Motorola Corporation, 16–17
Muraoka, Toshio, 168, 230, 233

N
Nabisco Brands Inc., 37, 48, 61–63, 105, 112, 122–123, 134
Nagase & Co. Ltd., 20–21, 164–165
Nakamura, Yoshio, 7
Nantong (China), 101, 103
National Aeronautics and Space Administration, 24
National Bank of Egypt, 50
National Council for United States-China Trade, 92–93, 105, 122, 182
National Intergroup, Inc., 6, 168, 175, 177–180
National Steel Corporation, 6, 168, 174–180

NEC. See Nippon Electric Co. Ltd.
New United Motor Manufacturing, Inc. (NUMMI), 10–12, 63–64, 168–174, 176
New York Insurance Company, 223
Ng, K.K., 187
Ningbo (China), 101, 103
Nippon Electric Co. Ltd. (NEC), 77, 85
Nippon Kokan K.K., 6, 168, 175–179
Nippon Otis Elevator Company, 33, 35, 225–227
Nippon Sheet Glass, 209
Nippon Telegraph & Telephone (NTT), 15–16
Nissan Motor Co. Ltd., 9–10, 13, 169–170, 206, 209
Nisshin Steel Company, 51–52
Nissho Iwai Corporation, 84
Nixdorf AG, 216
Nixon, Richard, 115
Noble, Reginald, 142
Nomura Securities Company, 165
North American Philips, 79n
Northern Business Information, 43
Northern Telecom Ltd., 53–54, 216
NUMMI. See New United Motor Manufacturing, Inc.

O
Occidental Petroleum Corporation, 27, 52–53, 92, 111, 114, 116, 151
Ogawa, Yoichi, 146, 228
Ogura, Yoshinobu, 226–227
Olin Corporation, 4
Olivetti Corporation, 233
Open coastal areas (China), 101–102
Optical disk joint ventures. See Philips-Du Pont Magnetics Company
Optical fiber joint ventures: Alcan-Sumitomo, 3; See also Siecor Corporation
Optical Storage International, 41
Organization for Economic Cooperation and Development (OECD), 23
Oshima, Shoji, 7
Otis Elevator Company, 34–35, 49, 63, 107, 109–110, 119–121, 134–135, 140, 183–184, 190, 226–227

P
Pabst Brewing Company, 122
Packard, David, 115
P'an, Albert, 106
P'an, Virginia, 106, 134
Parker Hannifin Company, 185–187

People's Bank of China, 122
Pemex. See Petroleos Mexicanos
PepsiCo. Inc., 27
Perkin-Elmer, 209–210
Petroleos Mexicanos (Pemex), 55–56
Peugeot SA, 14–15, 204
Philips, N.V., 5, 40–42, 44–45, 49–50, 60, 79n, 218
Philips-Du Pont Magnetics Company, 41
Phillippi, Joseph, 9
Photocopier joint ventures. See Fuji Xerox Co. Ltd.; Rank Xerox
Pilkington, Anthony, 210
Pilkington Brothers PLC, 125, 201, 208–211
Pinyin, 37n
Pirelli, Leopoldo, 221
Pirelli, S.p.A., 25, 125, 220–223
Pizza Hut, 27
Poddar Enterprises, House of, 148–149
Polysar Ltd., 37–38, 53–57
Porsche, Ferdinand, 206n
Portman Properties Ltd., 92
Posth, Martin, 207–208
Poticny, David, 49–50, 60
PPG Industries Inc., 47, 113, 123–125, 129–130, 132, 140
Price, Waterhouse & Company, 75, 90
Prudential Insurance Company of America, 223
Ptok, Peter, 117
Pursell, William, 38, 55

Q
Qingdao (China) 101–102
Qintuangdo (China), 101
Quality control. See under China and Japan
Quanzhou (China), 101

R
Rank Organization, 4, 51, 161
Rank Xerox, 4, 51, 161, 227–228
RCA Corporation, 33
Regehr, Ernest, 157, 197–198
Régie Nationale des Usines Renault, 14, 96, 206
Reiser, Robert, 51, 229
Revlon Group Inc., 209
Riley, James, 4
Rockefeller, David, 105
Rodriguez, Gerardo, 113, 122–123, 135
Roessel, Paul, 3, 32, 39
Royal Bank of Canada, 29, 111

## S

St. Pierre, Donald, 97–98, 141, 153
Saishoji, Yukio, 35–36, 226
Sakama, Taiichi, 14
Sasaoka, Kenza, 231–232
Satellites. *See* Japan Communications
  Satellite Company
Schindler Management, 119–121, 131.
  *See also* China Schindler Elevator
  Company
Schroders Investment Management
  (Japan), 73
Seidler, William, 48–49, 61–63, 134
Semiconductor joint ventures, 16, 33,
  84–87
Shanghai (China), 101, 103–104, 107,
  118, 120–122, 125, 144, 211
Shanghai-Volkswagen Automobile Co.
  Ltd., 140, 207
Shantou (China), 100
Shapiro, James, 48, 59, 122, 129
Sharp Corporation, 33
Shekou (China), 125, 129–130, 141
Shenmei Daily Use Products Company
  Ltd., 118–119, 132–133, 135, 145,
  152–153, 183, 188, 191, 193–195
Shenyang (China), 119
Shenyang Municipal Daily Use Com-
  pany, 119
Shenzhen (China), 100
Sheraton Hotels, 46, 144
Sherkin, Charles, 127–128
Shimokawa, Koichi, 9–10
Siecor Corporation, 30, 219
Sieg, Albert, 21, 78
Siemens, AG, 3, 30, 45, 117, 202, 216–
  219, 223
Siemens Capital Corporation, 45
Singer Corporation, 27
Skidmore Owings & Merrill, 215
Skow, Richard, 151–152
Smith, Richard, 6, 177–179
SmithKline Beckman Corporation, 18,
  22, 62, 147, 157, 166
Southland Corporation, 74
Soviet Union: joint ventures in, 27–28,
  212–213
Spanninger, Philip, 22
Spaulding, R. Barry, 108
Special Economic Zones (SEZs,
  China), 100–101, 107
Standard Electric Lawrence, 218
Standard Telephones & Cables, 216
State Council (China), 110
State Economic Commission (China),
  183

Steel joint ventures. *See* National Steel
  Corporation; Wheeling-Nisshin
Stevens, George, 186
Sumitomo Bank, 226
Sumitomo Corporation, 31, 226–227
Sumitomo Mutual Life Assurance
  Company, 226
Sumitomo Rubber Industries Ltd., 223
Suntory Company Ltd., 147
Suzhou (China), 135
Suzuki Motor Co. Ltd., 10–11
Switzer, G.H., 23, 57

## T

Taiwan: joint ventures in, 36, 41–42,
  116, 124, 210
Tam, Kelvin, 119, 152–153, 183, 193,
  195
Technology transfer. *See* Joint ventures
Telecommunications joint ventures,
  42–46, 53–54, 218
Terasawa, Yoshio, 74, 165
Texas Instruments Inc., 16
Thermco Systems Ltd., 84
Tianjin (China), 101–102, 107, 120–122,
  140
Tianjin Elevator Company, 110, 184
Tianjin International Trust and Invest-
  ment Company, 127
Tianjin Rubber Industrial Company,
  127
Tianjin Tire Company, 127
Ting, Lee, 2, 115
Tire joint ventures: Goodyear-Toyo,
  22; United Tire-China, 125–129. *See
  also* Dunlop-Pirelli joint venture
Tishman Realty & Construction Com-
  pany, 202, 214–215
Tokyo Electron Ltd., 84–88
Toshiba Corporation, 3, 16, 79–80, 233
Toshiba Westinghouse Electronics Cor-
  poration, 80
Toyo Tire & Rubber Company, 22
Toyoda, Tatsuro, 170
Toyota Motor Corporation, 8–14, 64,
  168–170, 172, 174, 206–207, 232
Trademark protection. *See* Joint
  ventures
TransCapital International Inc., 106,
  134
Trinity Development Company, 126
Turkish Post, Telephone & Telegraph
  (PTT), 53–54

## U

Unidata, 218

Unions, role in joint ventures. *See* Joint
  ventures
United Auto Workers, 168–171, 173–
  174
United Steelworkers of America, 175–
  176
United Technologies Inc., 35, 226
United Tire & Rubber Company, 125–
  127

**V**
Varian Associates, Inc., 33, 84–87
Varity Corporation, 201, 212–214
Varity World Trade, 213
Vickers da Costa Ltd., 7
Volkswagen AG, 2, 13–14, 201–208
Volvo AB, 11, 206
Volvo White, 11

**W**
Wang, James, 191–192
Wang, Jeffrey, 153, 193
Wang, Yun Qi, 35, 190
Warburg, S.G. Ltd., 223
Waters, George, 106
Wehr, Jörg, 202, 218–220, 223
Wella AG, 184
Wenzhou (China), 101, 103
Westinghouse Electric Corporation, 23,
  80, 219
Wheeling-Nisshin, 51
Wheeling-Pittsburgh Steel Corporation,
  51–52, 175

Whirlpool Corporation, 44
Wilkinson Sword PLC, 148
Wimpey, George PLC, 201, 214–215
Wright, John E. III, 52
Wu, Zhi Peng, 191, 195
Wuhan (China), 185

**X**
Xerox Corporation, 4–5, 48, 51, 58–59,
  122–123, 129, 147, 160–161, 228–229,
  233
Xiamen (China), 100–101, 151
Xi'an (China), 144

**Y**
Yamakawa, Thomas, 75, 90
Yantai (China), 101–102
Yili Food Factory Company, 113, 123
Yili-Nabisco Biscuit and Food Com-
  pany, 37, 155–156, 187
Yishang Trading Company Ltd., 184
Yokogawa Electric Works (YEW), 80–
  83, 167–168, 231
Yokogawa-Hewlett-Packard, 81–84,
  167–168, 225, 229–233
Young, John, 115, 232
Yu, Yan, 111

**Z**
Zhangzhou (China), 104
Zhanjiang (China), 101, 104
Zhuhai (China), 100
Zimmerman, Andrew, 33–34